The Writings of John Calvin

The Writings of John Calvin

An Introductory Guide

Wulfert de Greef

Translated by Lyle D. Bierma

Baker Books
A Division of Baker Book House Co
Grand Rapids, Michigan 49516

APOLLOS

Originally published as *Johannes Calvijn: Zijn werk en geschriften*
© 1989 Uitgeverij De Groot Goudriaan—Kampen
  Uitgeversmaatschappij J. H. Kok B.V.

English translation © 1993 Baker Book House Co.

Published by Baker Books,
a division of Baker Book House Company
P.O. Box 6287, Grand Rapids, Michigan 49516–6287

and

APOLLOS (an imprint of Inter-Varsity Press)
38 De Montfort Street, Leicester LE1 7GP, UK

Printed in the United States of America

Library of Congress Cataloging-in-Publication Data

Greef, W. de (Wulfert), 1939–
  [Johannes Calvijn. English]
  The writings of John Calvin : an introductory guide / Wulfert de Greef : translated
    by Lyle D. Bierma.
      p.   cm.
  Includes bibliographical references and indexes.
  ISBN 0-8010-3021-8
  1. Calvin, Jean, 1509–1564. I. Title.
BX9418.G74   1994
230'.42'092—dc20   93-42701

British Library Cataloging-in-Publication Data

A catalogue record for this book is available from the British Library.
ISBN 0-85111-435-0

Contents

Contents

Foreword

A guide to the study of John Calvin is not a mere luxury. The Reformer of Geneva wrote more in a space of thirty years than one person can adequately study and digest in an entire lifetime. Moreover, the time in which he lived is so far removed from ours, and life in our century is so totally different from his, that it is not easy to bridge the gulf between them. Calvin's use of so many literary genres is yet another reason why an overall picture of the factors that motivated his writing and speaking is most welcome.

The *Institutes*, of course, is well known. Because Calvin worked so carefully on its form and content, it may be regarded as a prime source, easily accessible to anyone, even though it is too little used and known by those who like to appeal to Calvin. A helping hand in reading it is not superfluous.

Calvin's commentaries do not show us a different theologian from the one in the *Institutes*, but the light they shed on him is rather surprising. This particular angle on Calvin is indispensable, lest we harbor the illusion that what we meet in the *Institutes* is the whole Calvin.

In the many writings found in the *Corpus Reformatorum*, we get to know Calvin the polemicist, the apologist, and the defender of the Reformation in a way that still speaks to us today—though not nearly enough, because life today makes so many demands on us. But whoever becomes acquainted with the Reformation in this way can be substantially enriched.

And then there are the sermons. It is said that the Calvin we meet here is different from the Calvin we encounter in the *Institutes*, in the many treatises, and even in his commentaries. And yet it is in the sermons that Calvin must have been most himself: in this direct, eye-to-eye contact with a congregation consisting mostly of refugees and looking for a word of encouragement. Here he is pastoral, moved with a subdued passion.

Are we left, then, with four Calvins—the dogmatician, the exegete, the polemicist, and the pastor? That is what we might conclude if careful study did not show that what we are always dealing with here is simply one man who was converted to *docilitas,* to teachableness, when in a *subita conversio* God enlisted him in service. Calvin—what else is he than the human face of a life that in unity of heart and mind, in unity also of knowledge and trust, desired to serve God according to his Word?

To see this unity, one must understand the time in which Calvin lived and view his works against that background. His theology did not simply come out of the blue, but was closely related to that of the preceding centuries. That is precisely why his influence could extend so far, right up to the present. Something that we today must often learn was clear to him: renewal does not have to represent a break with the past, and real reformation does not have to lead to revolution.

Wulfert de Greef modestly offers his study as a guidebook to the vast quantity of secondary literature on Calvin and also as an orientation to the many writings that flowed from Calvin's own pen. This is the kind of book that is among the materials given to a traveler about to embark on a fascinating journey. It contains descriptions of the route, calls attention to points of interest, and here and there offers us views which even today take us by surprise. A guide to the study of Calvin—who would not gratefully welcome such a book? With it one can become acquainted with the Reformer. With it one can gain sufficient experience to be able later on to proceed alone—when, that is, one has discovered that Calvin himself is a reliable guide to a time in need of the reminder that in all situations human beings stand *coram Deo,* before the face of God. Thus the study—genuine study—of Calvin can serve to promote *pietas* ("devoutness"). In that respect this book renders a real service.

Willem van 't Spijker

Author's Preface to the English Edition

In 1989 my book *Johannes Calvijn: Zijn werk en geschriften* was published by De Groot Goudriaan in Kampen, the Netherlands. I am very grateful to Baker Book House for undertaking the publication of an English edition. The study of the Reformation, and of Calvin's contributions in particular, extends far beyond the small Dutch-speaking world, and this English edition will now make my work available to a much wider audience. I hope through this translation to be of help to students, pastors, theologians, church historians, and other interested persons who wish to engage in the study of Calvin and his writings.

I also wish to thank Baker Book House for the opportunity they gave me to make some minor corrections in and additions to the original edition. They will certainly enhance the value of the English translation.

I first met Lyle Bierma in 1990 at the International Congress on Calvin Research in Grand Rapids, and I was pleasantly surprised when I learned recently that he was translating my book. My thanks to him for the careful way in which he has carried out that task.

Author's Preface to First Edition

John Calvin is a man of distinguished reputation, one of the great figures of church history. But who exactly was he, and what did he write? To answer that, one can consult a variety of books. However, when I personally set out to gain a better understanding of Calvin and wanted especially to work with his writings, I could not find an introductory guide to help me. The book before you is an attempt to fill that gap.

I begin this book with an outline of Calvin's life. Before delving into someone's works, one likes to know, of course, something about the author. It was not my intention to write a full-length biography. Therefore in chapter 1 I first limit myself to an overview of Calvin's life up to his return to Geneva. Then I select a number of events from the years 1541–64 that I consider important for understanding him. In this way I hope to have given a responsible sketch of his life.

In the succeeding chapters I seek to provide an overview of Calvin's writings. The best way to do this, it seemed to me, was to organize them by topic. In addition, the sequence of the topics more or less follows the course of Calvin's life. Thus, after treating Calvin's first publications in chapter 2, I discuss "Calvin and the Bible" in chapter 3 because in 1535 he was involved in the translation of the Bible into French. In this chapter I also deal with his commentaries, lectures, sermons, and weekly Bible discussions.

It is not only the course of Calvin's life that has guided me, however; I have also followed a more or less logical sequence of topics. After discussing the "First Publications" (chapter 2) and "Calvin and the Bible" (chapter 3), I turn in chapter 4 to the building up of the church and related matters, and in chapter 5 to publications in the category of "Debating with Roman Catholics." In chapter 6 I treat debates with other movements and individuals, and in chapter 7 Calvin's quest for unity and the debates it produced. I turn to the *Institutes* in chapter 8, and in chapter 9 to a number of miscellaneous publications that have not yet been discussed. In chapter 10 I take a look at Calvin's letters and try to demonstrate their importance by examining a sampling of his correspondence. The last chapter contains bibliographical data that are important for further study.

Those who wish to consult this book on a particular topic are best advised to start with the table of contents and the indexes, for the way that I have chosen to organize the material means that a given topic is not always treated in the place that one might expect. Predestination, for example, is discussed only briefly in the section "Debating about Doctrinal Issues" (pp. 171–81), since I had to deal with it already in connection with the *congrégation* (weekly Bible study) on election (pp. 118–19). I also wanted to cover the debate with Albertus Pighius and the work *De aeterna Dei praedestinatione* in the chapter on Calvin's debates with Roman Catholics, and thus had to treat predestination there as well (pp. 158–59). I hope that in addition to the table of contents the indexes will lend a helping hand to those trying to find their way through the book.

This book is intended as an introduction and orientation both for those wishing to begin a study of Calvin and for those already engaged in it. Every section could be developed more fully. My references to the *Corpus Reformatorum*, translations, and secondary literature will, I hope, be of further assistance. As far as secondary sources are concerned, it was impossible to mention everything, since such an enormous amount has been written about Calvin. I have tried, therefore, to include the most recent literature, and there one can find references to older sources.

If this book can serve as a resource for anyone about to engage in the study of Calvin, my goal in writing it will have been attained.

Translator's Acknowledgments

To the following I owe a special debt of gratitude for their assistance with this project: Henry Baron, professor of English at Calvin College; Paul Fields, curator of the H. H. Meeter Center for Calvin Studies; Diane Zandbergen, librarian at Reformed Bible College; Ray Wiersma, editor at Baker Book House; and especially Harry Boonstra, theological librarian at Calvin Seminary, who generously gave of his time and translation skill to answer my many questions. Final responsibility for the translation, however, remains mine alone.

Lyle D. Bierma

Abbreviations

AESC	*Annales: Economies, sociétés, civilisations*
ARG	*Archiv für Reformationsgeschichte*
ARG.B	*Archiv für Reformationsgeschichte, Beiheft*
BHR	*Bibliothèque d'humanisme et renaissance*
BSHAG	*Bulletin de la société d'histoire et d'archéologie de Genève*
BSHPF	*Bulletin de la société de l'histoire du protestantisme français*
BSRK	*Bekenntnisschriften der reformierten Kirche*
CO	*Ioannis Calvini opera quae supersunt omnia* (*Corpus Reformatorum*, vols. 29–87)
CR	*Corpus Reformatorum*
CRHPhR	*Cahiers de la Revue d'histoire et de philosophie religieuses*
CTJ	*Calvin Theological Journal*
EvQ	*Evangelical Quarterly*
FZPhTh	*Freiburger Zeitschrift für Philosophie und Theologie*
JPH	*Journal of Presbyterian History*
JR	*Journal of Religion*
JSG	*Jahrbuch für schweizerische Geschichte*
LCC	*Library of Christian Classics*
Menn.QR	*Mennonite Quarterly Review*
MGKK	*Monatsschrift für Gottesdienst und kirchliche Kunst*
NAK	*Nederlands archief voor kerkgeschiedenis*
NTT	*Nederlands theologisch tijdschrift*
OS	*Johannis Calvini Opera Selecta,* ed. Peter Barth, Wilhelm Niesel, and Dora Scheuner
RGG	*Religion in Geschichte und Gegenwart,* 3d ed.
RHPhR	*Revue d'histoire et de philosophie religieuses*
RKZ	*Reformierte Kirchenzeitung*
RThPh	*Revue de théologie et de philosophie*
SC	*Supplementa Calviniana*
SCJ	*Sixteenth Century Journal*
SJTh	*Scottish Journal of Theology*
SVRG	*Schriften des Vereins für Reformationsgeschichte*
ThBl	*Theologische Blätter*
ThR	*Theologia Reformata*
ThStKr	*Theologische Studien und Kritiken*
TRE	*Theologische Realenzyklopädie*
WA	*Martin Luthers Werke,* Weimar edition
WAB	*Martin Luthers Werke, Briefwechsel,* Weimar edition
WThJ	*Westminster Theological Journal*
ZKG	*Zeitschrift für Kirchengeschichte*

Calvin at 53

I

Overview of Calvin's Life

Youth and Education up to Arrival in Geneva

Jean Cauvin (Calvin's original name) was born on July 10, 1509, in Noyon, a little town in Picardy in the north of France. His father, Gérard Cauvin, hailed from nearby Pont-l'Evèque, but in 1479 had settled in Noyon, where he was employed by Bishop Charles de Hangest and the cathedral chapter to perform a variety of administrative functions. In 1497 he married Jeanne Lefranc, a pious woman who died while Calvin was still young. Calvin recalls in his *Treatise concerning Relics* (1543) that during his childhood he and his mother once visited an abbey in Orcamps where, according to tradition, the skull of Saint Anne was enshrined (*CO* 6:442).

After the death of his wife, Calvin's father remarried. Charles, Calvin's older brother, became a priest, but was later accused of heresy and died excommunicate in 1537. Calvin had two younger brothers: Antoine (another brother Antoine had died young), who later accompanied him to Geneva and did a lot of clerical work for him;[1] and François, who died at a young age. He also had two sisters, of whom Marie is the better known; she like his brother Antoine later accompanied him to Geneva. The first school that Calvin attended was the Collège des Capettes, a boys' school run by the cathedral chapter in Noyon.

Charles de Hangest, bishop in Noyon until 1525, was of noble origin. Calvin had a great deal of contact with the family of Charles's brother Louis de Hangest, who was lord of Montmor. Calvin took part, for example, in the education that the children of this family received at home, and there he also learned aristocratic manners. When he was eleven years old, his father succeeded in obtaining a benefice for him, which he was awarded on May 19, 1521. The benefice entailed a fourth of the income from a chaplaincy established to attend to the altar of Gésine in the cathedral of Noyon. His father wanted him to become a priest.

In August of 1523 Calvin and some of the boys of the Montmor family moved to Paris for further study.[2] There Jean Vallière was executed on August 8 for his Lutheran ideas. Since the beginning of 1519, the intellectual elite had been reading the works of Luther that were printed in Basel, and on April 15, 1521, the theological faculty of the Sorbonne in Paris had followed the lead of Pope Leo X in condemning Luther's teachings. Four months later the Parlement of Paris banned all of Luther's writings.

A number of new ideas were emerging in France around 1523. Especially noteworthy was the influence of Jacques Lefèvre d'Etaples (Latin name: Jacobus Faber Stapulensis),[3] who had been called to Paris around 1508 by Guil-

---

1. In 1548 Antoine's wife Anne was charged before the Council with having committed adultery, but was not prosecuted because of a lack of evidence. She did, however, have to appear with her husband before the Consistory, which tried to reconcile them to each other. That proved successful, but the marriage ended in divorce in 1557 following Anne's adultery with a servant who worked in Calvin's house. Anne was banished from Geneva.

2. This is the generally accepted date. However, T. H. L. Parker, Appendix 1, "Arguments for Re-dating," in *John Calvin* (Philadelphia, 1975), 156–61, thinks that Calvin began his studies in Paris earlier (1520–21).

3. See *TRE*, s.v. "Faber Stapulensis"; Hermann Dörries, "Calvin und Lefèvre," *ZKG* 44 (1925): 544–81; and Richard Stauffer, "Lefèvre d'Etaples, artisan ou spectateur de la Réforme?" *BSHPF* 113 (1967): 405–23 (this article is also found in *Positions luthériennes* 15 [1967]: 247–62; and in Richard Stauffer, *Interprètes de la Bible: Etudes sur les réformateurs du XVIe siècle* [Paris, 1980], 11–29).

laume Briçonnet, head of the abbey of Saint-Germain-des-Prés.[4] Lefèvre could work undisturbed at the abbey on his study of the Bible and the church fathers and on his writing of commentaries. He gathered around himself a circle of younger men who were interested in the Bible, spiritual life, and the renewal of the church. Suspected by the Sorbonne of Lutheran sympathies, he had to leave Paris in 1521 and retreated with his disciples to Meaux, where Briçonnet had become bishop on December 31, 1515. Lefèvre's circle included Briçonnet, Guillaume Farel, Gérard Roussel, Pierre Caroli, and François Vatable. Some of these men worked in Briçonnet's diocese, where the bishop devoted a lot of attention to the building up of the congregations. The circle was supported and protected by Marguerite of Angoulême, who was both the sister of King Francis I and the duchess of Alençon.

In 1523, however, the Sorbonne took action against the circle in Meaux. Bishop Briçonnet was accused of heresy and was forced to take measures against those inclined toward reform, whether toward Lutheranism or simply toward moderate change within the Catholic church. Luther's teachings were condemned and his books became forbidden reading. Farel had to leave the Meaux circle in 1523 because Briçonnet limited the freedoms of the preachers. When Francis I was in prison in Madrid, having been defeated at Pavia in 1525 by the Holy Roman Emperor Charles V (who had captured Milan from France in 1522), Briçonnet had to appear before the Parlement on more than one occasion, and the Meaux circle completely disintegrated. Lefèvre, Roussel, and Caroli fled to Strasbourg in 1525.

When Calvin first arrived in Paris, he stayed at the house of his uncle Richard, but after a couple of months he settled in at the Collège de La Marche. The humanistic education provided there was preparatory to university study. In the course of instruction one first focused on grammar, rhetoric, and logic (the so-called trivium) and thereafter on arithmetic, geometry, astronomy, and music (the so-called quadrivium). The study of these seven subjects concluded with a master's exam. Whoever passed received a master of arts degree and could now go on to study theology, law, or medicine at the university.

At the Collège de La Marche, Mathurin Cordier taught Latin grammar.[5] Cordier was known for his modern method of teaching; in his view children were to be taught first of all to love Christ. Although Calvin attended this school for only a few months, Cordier must have made a deep impression on him, for in 1562 Cordier at Calvin's behest moved to Geneva to teach.

---

4. See *TRE*, s.v. "Briçonnet, Guillaume."
5. See J. Lecoultre, *Maturin Cordier et les origines de la pédagogie protestante* (Neuchâtel, 1926).

While in Paris Calvin changed his name to its Latin form, Ioannis Calvinus, which in French then became Jean Calvin. Towards the end of 1523 he entered the more renowned Collège Montaigu, where Erasmus and Rabelais had also studied. The Montmor boys' tutor, who also had charge of Calvin, had a hand in this change of schools. From 1514 to 1528 the head of the Collège Montaigu was Pierre Tempête, successor to the conservative scholastic Noel Bédier (Beda), who, though still closely associated with the college, was even more heavily involved in theological duties at the Sorbonne. The strict spirit that prevailed at the college can be seen in, among other things, the nickname given to Tempête—*horrida tempestas.* It was at this school that Calvin learned the art of disputation, which had an important place in the curriculum. The *devotio moderna* movement, which included the Brethren of the Common Life (Gerhard Groote, Thomas a Kempis and his work *De imitatione Christi*) was also influential there, but to what degree is difficult to say.[6] Both the philosophy and theology were influenced by nominalism.

Among the faculty (since 1525) was the Scottish scholar John Major, a nominalist who was probably influenced by Duns Scotus. Major brought Calvin into contact with the thought world of Peter Lombard and Augustine, but he dismissed Martin Luther out of hand, comparing him to John Wycliffe and John Hus.[7] Another faculty member at the Collège Montaigu was the Spanish philosopher Antonio Coronel, who taught the philosophy of Aristotle, the Stoics, Epicurus, and Plato.[8]

During this time Calvin developed friendships with several members of the Cop family. Guillaume Cop was the court physician to King Francis I and thus had contact with various humanistic and reform-minded circles. His four sons were schoolmates of Calvin. Since Calvin often came to the Cop family home, he too was exposed to those contacts. It is likely that during this time he also became acquainted with Pierre Robert Olivétan (Olivetanus), a cousin who was also studying in Paris. According to Theodore Beza (*CO* 21:121),

6. See J. F. G. Goeters, "Thomas von Kempen und Johannes Calvin," in *Thomas von Kempen: Beiträge zum 500. Todesjahr 1471–1971* (Kampen, 1971), 87–92.

7. For the relationship between Major and Calvin see A. N. S. Lane, "Calvin's Use of the Fathers and the Medievals," *CTJ* 16 (1981): 149–205. In Appendix 1 Lane gives a "Bibliography of Modern Works on Calvin and the Fathers/Medievals." See also Alister E. McGrath, "John Calvin and Late Mediaeval Thought: A Study in Late Mediaeval Influences upon Calvin's Theological Development," *ARG* 77 (1986): 58–78; and idem, *A Life of John Calvin* (Oxford, 1990), 36–39.

8. For the relationship between Calvin and philosophy see Charles B. Partee, *Calvin and Classical Philosophy* (Leiden, 1977); Gerd Babelotzky, *Platonische Bilder und Gedankengänge in Calvins Lehre vom Menschen* (Wiesbaden, 1977); and N. T. van der Merwe, "Calvin, Augustine and Platonism: A Few Aspects of Calvin's Philosophical Background," in *Calvinus Reformator: His Contribution to Theology, Church and Society* (Potchefstroom, 1982), 69–84.

Marguerite of Angoulême

Olivetanus must have been the one who instructed Calvin in the true religion, which led to his reading of the Bible and conversion from Roman superstition. Whether while at the Collège Montaigu Calvin encountered Ignatius of Loyola, who began studying in Paris in 1528, is not certain.

On September 27, 1527, Calvin received a second study benefice, income from the pastorate of Saint-Martin-de-Martheville, a little village not far from Noyon. In 1527, however, his father became involved in a conflict with the cathedral chapter of Noyon over a business matter and advised him to pursue the study of law rather than theology. The reasons for this advice must have been both fear that his son might now have to study without benefices and expectation that the young Calvin's possibilities for the future would be broadened if he studied law (see the foreword in the commentary on the Psalms—*CO* 31:32).

Because Calvin could study only canon (not civil) law in Paris, he moved at the end of 1527 or the beginning of 1528 to Orléans, where the famous jurist Pierre de L'Estoile was lecturing. De L'Estoile's erudition impressed Calvin greatly. In Orléans he also came into contact with Melchior Wolmar, who had been influenced by Luther and taught Greek in Orléans.[9] Following Calvin's decision to study law, Wolmar encouraged him to learn Greek. Among Calvin's other friends during this time were François Daniel, François de Connan, and Nicolas Duchemin.

9. See D.-J. de Groot, "Melchior Volmar, ses rapports avec les réformateurs français et suisses," *BSHPF* 83 (1934): 416–39.

In the summer of 1529 Calvin changed universities. Instead of continuing with the lectures of the more orthodox and traditional de L'Estoile in Orléans, he and his friends François Daniel and Nicolas Duchemin went to Bourges because the famous Italian jurist and humanist Andrea Alciati, founder of the historical school of thought, was lecturing there. Alciati had been brought there by Marguerite of Angoulême, who through her second marriage in 1527 had become queen of Navarre and who as the duchess of Berry was patroness of the university in Bourges. In 1529 Wolmar also came to Bourges at the invitation of Marguerite, and along with him came the still very youthful Beza. Calvin must certainly have become acquainted with Beza at Wolmar's home.

A significant event at this time was the publication in Paris on April 30, 1530, of a *Determinatio facultatis* by the Sorbonne. In this document the faculty of the Collège Royal, founded by Francis I in that very year, were attacked for their support of scholarly exegesis of the biblical text. The rector of this college was Guillaume Budé, the king's librarian and a great humanist scholar.[10] It was he who had urged the king to establish the college. Other faculty members included Pierre Danès (Greek) and François Vatable (Hebrew). The Sorbonne suspected the faculty of Lutheranism.

When Calvin returned to Paris in March 1531, he took along a work by Nicolas Duchemin, *Antapologia*, to have it printed. On March 6, 1531, Calvin wrote a foreword to this book, his first publication (see p. 84). While he was in Paris, he heard that his father was very ill, so he proceeded immediately to Noyon. His father died on May 26, 1531. Calvin's brother Charles led the negotiations with the cathedral chapter for a church burial for their father, who two years earlier had been excommunicated by the church.

Calvin headed back to Paris by way of Orléans, this time for further preparation in languages at the newly founded (1530) Collège Royal (later called the Collège de France), where there was an attempt to combine humanist learning with biblical faith. It was at this time that Calvin probably began to study Hebrew. In Paris he had the opportunity to renew his acquaintance with the Cop family and also visited regularly at the home of Etienne de La Forge, a wealthy merchant sympathetic to reform. Because of ongoing persecution, individuals of like mind often met secretly at this house under the leadership

10. François Wendel, *Calvin: The Origins and Development of His Religious Thought*, trans. Philip Mairet (New York, 1963; Durham, N.C., 1987), 130: "Calvin's work has retained many important traces of Budé, which have been pointed out, with meticulous care, by Bohatec." See Josef Bohatec, *Budé und Calvin: Studien zur Gedankenwelt des französischen Frühhumanismus* (Graz, 1950); on Budé see also *TRE*, s.v. "Budé, Guillaume." For Calvin's relation to humanism see François Wendel, *Calvin et l'humanisme* (Paris, 1976).

of the preacher Gérard Roussel. After staying with several families in Paris, Calvin finally took up lodgings in the Collège Fortet.

On April 4, 1532, Calvin published his first scholarly work, a commentary on *De clementia,* which was a work by the Roman philosopher Seneca (see pp. 84–86). In May 1532 he returned to Orléans, where he spent at least a year finishing his law studies. It appears from Calvin's oldest extant personal letter, written in Paris to François Daniel on October 27, 1533 (*CO* 10b:25–26), that a couple of important events had taken place during the previous month. On October 1 students from the Collège de Navarre had presented a stage play in which Marguerite of Angoulême and court preacher Roussel were ridiculed. In addition, the theological faculty of the Sorbonne placed Marguerite's *Miroir de l'âme pécheresse* on the index of forbidden books. She complained to her brother Francis about the censure, and he ordered an investigation of the matter. Nicolas Cop, son of Guillaume Cop and rector of the university since October 10, 1533, persuaded the university to rescind the censure. It is noteworthy that in Calvin's account of these events, he always takes the side of Marguerite, Roussel, and Cop.

On November 1, 1533 (All Saints' Day), at the official opening of the new academic year and in the presence of professors and ecclesiastical dignitaries, Nicolas Cop delivered a sharply worded address in which he spoke about Christian philosophy and about the relationship between law and gospel (see pp. 86–87). A complaint was lodged against Cop with the Parlement of Paris, but before he could be called to account, he fled the city. King Francis I decided to persecute the "cursed Lutheran sect." Leaving behind his books and letters, Calvin also secretly fled the city before the authorities could have him arrested. He stayed somewhere in the vicinity of Paris, returned to the city once again, and then in late 1533 or early 1534 set out for the province of Saintonge in the south of France. Using the pseudonym Charles d'Espeville, he spent considerable time at the home of Louis Du Tillet, a pastor in Claix and canon of the cathedral in Angoulême. There Calvin had peace and quiet to study in Du Tillet's extraordinarily large library and to work on the first edition of his *Institutes.*

It is possible that in 1533 Calvin experienced the sudden and unexpected conversion that he writes about in the foreword to his commentary on the Psalms, but that is not at all certain.[11] Calvin says in the foreword that he was

11. Parker places Calvin's conversion before 1530; see Appendix 2, "Calvin's Conversion," in *John Calvin,* 162–65. A lot has been written about Calvin's conversion. We mention here only the following secondary sources: Paul Sprenger, *Das Rätsel um die Bekehrung Calvins* (Neukirchen, 1960); Willem Nijenhuis, "Calvijns 'subita conversio': Notities bij een hypothese," *NTT* 26 (1972): 248–69; and Ernst Koch, "Erwägungen zum Bekehrungsbericht Calvins," *NAK* 61 (1981): 185–97. The Latin *subitus* can mean both "suddenly" and "unexpectedly," the latter of which is underscored by

very strongly devoted to the superstitions of the papacy. By an unexpected conversion God drove him to "teachableness" (*docilitas*), a word that has to do with readiness to listen to Scripture. "One will never be a good teacher [*doctor*] if one does not show oneself to be teachable [*docilis*] and always ready to learn" (commentary on 1 Corinthians 14:31).

In April 1534 Calvin went to Nérac to visit the eighty-year-old Lefèvre. Lefèvre was spending his last days (he died in 1536) in a castle in Nérac that belonged to Marguerite of Angoulême. Calvin also paid a visit to Gérard Roussel, the court preacher, who lived in the abbey at Clairac.

In May 1534 Calvin brought an end to the income he had been receiving from several ecclesiastical benefices, since it was customary that at age twenty-five one either officially entered the service of the church or surrendered his benefices. Calvin risked staying in the vicinity of Paris and visited the circle of Etienne de La Forge in the city. There he probably met the Flemish preacher Quintin Thieffry, a prominent Anabaptist. An appointment he had made with Michael Servetus, who was studying medicine in Paris and wanted to meet with Calvin, never took place because Servetus did not show up (according to Nicolas Colladon—*CO* 21:57; see also 8:481).

Calvin went with Du Tillet via Claix to supporters in Poitiers and preached outside the city in a cave at Saint-Benoît. They also celebrated a new form of the Lord's Supper in the little village of Crotelles. In a letter dated February 20, 1555, Calvin reminds the congregation in Poitiers of the teaching "which you received in part from us, because it pleased God to make use of our effort for your salvation" (*CO* 15:437). Leaving Poitiers, Calvin traveled with Du Tillet to Orléans, where he wrote his *Psychopannychia* (see pp. 165–67).

During the night of October 17–18, 1534, placards containing opprobrious articles against the Eucharist were posted all over Paris (even on the door of the king's bedroom) and elsewhere throughout the country (*affaire de placards*).[12] The drafter of these articles was Antoine Marcourt, who after his forced departure from Lyons, became a minister in Neuchâtel.[13] The king, urged on in part

---

Nijenhuis in *TRE*, s.v. "Calvin, Johannes" (7:570): "not considered before, with no point of contact with previous human thought or experience, but exclusively a work of the Holy Spirit. With the phrase *subita conversio*, Calvin wished to follow the analogy of Paul's Damascus Road experience and trace his ministry back to a special calling by God."

12. See Appendix 1, "The Placards of 1534" (translated from the text established by Robert Hari, "Les Placards de 1534," in *Aspects de la propagande religieuse* [Geneva, 1957], 114–19), in John Calvin, *Institutes of the Christian Religion* (1536 edition), ed. Ford Lewis Battles, rev. ed. (Grand Rapids, 1986), 339–42.

13. Gabrielle Berthoud, *Antoine Marcourt, réformateur et pamphlétaire du "Livre des Marchans" aux placards de 1534* (Geneva, 1973).

Renée of France (pencil drawing)

by the humanist Guillaume Budé, took certain measures, and the situation in France became increasingly more dangerous. In November several hundred men were arrested, and during the following months a number were executed (among them, Etienne de La Forge). Calvin and Du Tillet went via Strasbourg to Basel.[14]

Calvin lived in Basel under the pseudonym Martianus Lucianus. His most important friends were Oswald Myconius, who had succeeded Johannes Oecolampadius, the Reformer of Basel, in 1531, and Wolfgang Capito, a minister in Strasbourg. He also became acquainted with Simon Grynaeus, who taught Greek in Basel; Sebastian Münster, whose lectures he attended (according to Beza—*CO* 10b:124); and the lawyer Bonifacius Amerbach.

During this Basel period Calvin once again made contact with Nicolas Cop, who had arrived there a year before. He also came to know Pierre Viret, his future colleague in Geneva, and in February 1536 made the acquaintance of Heinrich Bullinger, Zwingli's successor in Zurich, who was taking part in a meeting of delegates from various Protestant cities. It is not known whether Calvin also encountered Erasmus, who had settled in Basel in June 1535 and died on July 12, 1536.

14. Paul Wernle, *Calvin und Basel bis zum Tode des Myconius, 1535–1552* (Tübingen, 1909); Eugénie Droz, *Chemins de l'hérésie: Textes et documents*, 4 vols. (Geneva, 1970–76), 1:89–129.

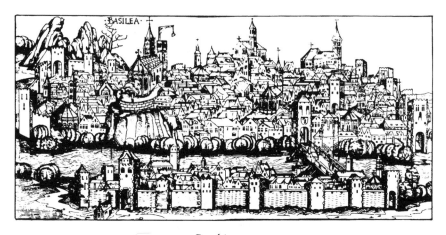

Basel in 1493

On June 4, 1535, the French translation of the Bible by Olivetanus was published. The Latin foreword was from Calvin's hand, and a second foreword preceding the New Testament has been attributed to Calvin since 1545. He also collaborated in the revision of this translation (see pp. 90–93).

During this time Calvin also wrote the foreword to an edition of sermons by Chrysostom (see p. 90) and worked some more on the first edition of his *Institutes*, which he completed in 1535. The foreword to the *Institutes* is dated August 23 and is addressed to King Francis I. The first (Latin) edition of the *Christianae religionis institutio* appeared in Basel in March of 1536 and quickly sold out (for more on the *Institutes* see pp. 195–202).

In February 1536, right before the publication of the *Institutes*, Calvin, using his earlier pseudonym Charles d'Espeville, traveled to Italy with Louis Du Tillet. He stayed for a few weeks in Ferrara among kindred spirits at the court of the reform-minded Duchess Renata (Renée of France), daughter of King Louis XII of France and sister-in-law of King Francis I. In 1527 she had married Hercule d'Este, duke of Ferrara.[15] In Ferrara, Calvin met Protestant refugees from France, including the French poet Clément Marot. He also wrote letters to his friends in France, two of which were published in Basel in 1537. The first of these letters was written to Duchemin, who had obtained an ecclesiastical position in the diocese of Le Mans, and the second was addressed to Gérard Roussel, who had accepted an appointment as bishop in the diocese of Oléron (see p. 150). While Calvin was still in Ferrara, the Roman Catholic

---

15. H. Lecoultre, "Le Séjour de Calvin en Italie d'après des documents inédits," *RThPh* 19 (1886): 168–92; C. A. Cornelius, *Der Besuch Calvins bei der Herzogin Renata von Ferrara im Jahr 1536* (1893).

Geneva in 1575 (engraving by Sebastian Münster)

Duke Hercule d'Este was forced by Charles V, at the urging of the pope, to ask the guests to leave the court.

Calvin and Du Tillet returned to Basel by way of Aosta, but Calvin immediately set out once again for France, where a temporary amnesty had been declared (refugees were allowed to return and had six months to renounce their heresy). In Paris he looked up his friends and put his affairs in order in anticipation of leaving France for good. His brother Antoine and sister Marie accompanied him. The plan was to go to Strasbourg to study in complete peace, but war had broken out between Francis I and Charles V, so Calvin had to make a detour around troop movements that were blocking the road. He intended to stay overnight in Geneva.

First Stay in Geneva (1536–38)

Geneva in 1536 was a city of approximately ten thousand inhabitants.[16] It had won its independence from the duchy of Savoy in 1526 and had allied itself with the cantons of Bern and Fribourg in a so-called *combourgeoisie*, which meant that whenever one of them was in trouble, the others would offer assistance.[17] The bishop of Geneva, Pierre de La Baume, was largely dependent on

16. Amédée Roget, *Histoire du peuple de Genève depuis la Réforme jusqu'à l'Escalade*, 7 vols. (Geneva, 1870–83); Michel Roset, *Les Chroniques de Genève* (Geneva, 1894—republished by Henri Fazy); Jean-Antoine Gautier, *Histoire de Genève des origines à l'année 1691*, 9 vols. (Geneva, 1896–1914); and E. William Monter, *Calvin's Geneva* (New York, 1967).

17. Emile Dunant, *Les Relations politiques de Genève avec Berne et les Suisses de 1536 à 1564* (Geneva, 1894); Eugène-Louis Dumont, "Histoire des traités," in *Genève 26–27 mai 1976, commémoration des traités de combourgeoisie avec Fribourg, Berne 1526 et Zürich 1584* (Geneva, 1976), 49–59.

Guillaume Farel

the support of Savoy and therefore strove to restore the power of the duke of Savoy in Geneva. On the other hand, at the initiative of Bern, which had been Protestant since 1528, Guillaume Farel and his assistants had been trying since October 1532 to introduce the Reformation into Geneva as well. With Bern's support Geneva succeeded during those years in breaking away completely from the duke of Savoy and the bishop. The bishop-supported alliance with Roman Catholic Fribourg broke apart. Geneva also succeeded in maintaining its independence over against Bern, although it had to promise in a treaty with Bern on August 7, 1536, that it would always remain an open city and not form any other alliances without Bern's permission. Shortly before, on May 21, 1536, the entire population of Geneva, under Farel's leadership, had taken an oath to accept the Reformation.[18]

As Calvin was passing through Geneva, he was noticed by Du Tillet. Farel, who had officially become minister there in 1534, also heard about Calvin's presence and adjured him to remain in Geneva and assist in the further reformation of the city. Calvin gave in. He later wrote about this episode in the foreword to his commentary on the Psalms: "Guillaume Farel detained me in Geneva, not so much by counsel and exhortation as by a dreadful curse, as if

18. J. M. Lange van Ravenswaay, "Calvin und Farel—Aspekte ihres Verhältnisses," in *Actes du colloque Guillaume Farel*, ed. Pierre Barthel et al., 2 vols. (Lausanne, 1983), 1:63–72; Charles B. Partee, "Farel's Influence on Calvin: A 'Prolusion,'" in *Actes du colloque Guillaume Farel*, 1:173–86.

God had from heaven laid his hand upon me to arrest me."[19] Calvin went to Basel to put some matters in order, and then sometime before September 5, 1536, began his duties as a lecturer (*sacrarum literarum doctor*) at Saint Pierre in Geneva by expounding on the epistles of Paul. We know also that before 1537 he was active as a minister in Geneva.

In October Farel and Pierre Viret took Calvin along to Lausanne to participate in a public religious disputation, in which Calvin made quite an impression with his knowledge of the church fathers (see pp. 150–51). Before returning to Geneva, he also sat through another synodical meeting in Bern, where nearly three hundred Swiss ministers deliberated about the Wittenberg Concord and the First Helvetic Confession (i.e., the Second Confession of Basel), a confession that was drafted in Basel in 1536 and that reflects the influence of Zwingli and Oecolampadius. Martin Bucer and Wolfgang Capito, who were strongly committed to unity, explained the Wittenberg agreement. What Calvin's contribution to the synod was is not clear. Both Bucer (*CO* 10b:67–68) and Capito (*CO* 10b:75) did write him letters on December 1 in which it appears that they expected much from him. Bucer was particularly interested in holding a conference that would unite the Germans and the Swiss in their conception of the Lord's Supper.

On January 16, 1537, the ministers of Geneva presented to the Council of the city a series of articles in which they stated the most important steps that still needed to be taken in the reformation of the Genevan church (see p. 122). As a result of the acceptance of these articles, all the inhabitants of the city had to make their relation to the church clear. A confession of faith—the *Instruction et confession de foy* (see p. 124)—was placed before the residents of the city, but subscription to it did not proceed smoothly. An additional problem was posed by Anabaptists in the city who were stirring up unrest. When in January 1538 the ministers wanted to begin excluding from the celebration of the Lord's Supper those who had not yet subscribed to the confession of faith, they were forbidden by the Council to do so. Tensions mounted when the Council, at the request of Bern, wanted to introduce some of Bern's ecclesiastical practices into Geneva (see p. 57). Because the ministers would not willingly adapt to these changes, they were forced to leave the city on April 25, 1538. Calvin and Farel traveled through Bern and Zurich to Basel.

19. Henri Heyer, *L'Eglise de Genève, 1535–1909* (Geneva, 1909); Henri Naef, *Les Origines de la Réforme à Genève*, 2 vols. (Geneva, 1936; reprint, 1968); and Robert M. Kingdon, "Calvin and the Government of Geneva," in *Calvinus ecclesiae Genevensis custos*, ed. Wilhelm H. Neuser (Frankfurt am Main, 1984), 49–67.

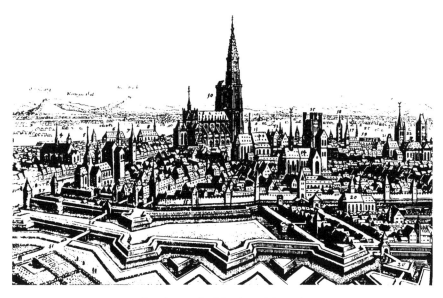

Strasbourg (by Matthäus Merian)

Stay in Strasbourg (1538–41)

After a few weeks' stay in Basel, Farel moved on to Neuchâtel, where he became a minister. Calvin chose to stay in Basel to devote himself entirely to his studies and prepare a second Latin edition of the *Institutes*. But in early September 1538 Martin Bucer and Wolfgang Capito repeatedly urged him to come to Strasbourg.[20] Calvin finally gave in, especially at the insistence of Bucer (see the preface to the commentary on the Psalms—*CO* 31:26–27), and became the pastor of a newly formed congregation of four to five hundred French refugees. In this position Calvin had to devote a lot of thought to the liturgical structure of the worship service (see pp. 127–28). In 1539 he also took up duties at the local gymnasium, where he taught New Testament interpretation.

During his stay in Strasbourg, Calvin produced several important works. In 1539 he published the second Latin edition of the *Institutes*, which was

20. Alfred Erichson, *L'Eglise française de Strasbourg au XVIe siècle* (Strasbourg, 1886); François Wendel, *L'Eglise de Strasbourg, sa constitution et son organisation* (Paris, 1942). On Calvin's stay in Strasbourg, see Emile Doumergue, *Jean Calvin: Les Hommes et les choses de son temps*, 7 vols. (Lausanne, 1899–1927), 2:293–98, 376–524; Jacques Pannier, *Calvin à Strasbourg* (Strasbourg, 1925); Jean-Daniel Benoit et al., *Calvin à Strasbourg, 1538–1541* (Strasbourg, 1938); Wendel, *Calvin: The Origins*, 57–68; Richard Stauffer, "L'Apport de Strasbourg à la Réforme française par l'intermédiaire de Calvin," in Stauffer, *Interprètes*, 153–65.

MARTINVS BVCCER

BVCCER· HAT · VIEL· GVTEN· VÑ· GLERT
ENGELANT· HAT· ER· AVCH· BEKERT
DAR· IST· BEGRABE· NACH· SEIM· ENDT
AVCH· WIDR· AVSGRABEN· VÑ· VERBRENT
ABER· DIE· KÖNGIN· LOBESAN·
HAT· DIE· ASCH· EHRLICH· BSTATTEN· LAN

Martin Bucer (woodcut by Balthasar Jenichen)

three times as large as the 1536 edition (see pp. 198–200). In 1540 his commentary on the Epistle to the Romans appeared (see pp. 94–95), the first of his many commentaries. During this time he also responded to requests that he write for lay people an explanation of the meaning of the Lord's Supper. This *Short Treatise on the Lord's Supper* was published in Geneva in 1541 (see pp. 134–35).

Almost immediately after his arrival in Strasbourg, Calvin had to cope with several tragedies in the circle of men with whom he had long been in contact. In early October 1538 he heard about the death of Elie Coraud, who after his banishment from Geneva had become a minister in Orbe. He also learned that his cousin Olivetanus had died in Italy and had left him a number of books. Finally, he was grieved to learn that Louis Du Tillet, who had left Geneva already in 1537, had now returned to the Roman Catholic Church in France (for the correspondence with Du Tillet, see p. 151).

In addition to his other responsibilities, Calvin became involved in September and October 1539 with the effort by Pierre Caroli to become a minister in Strasbourg (see p. 173). During the Strasbourg period Calvin also had a number of other contacts that we mention because of their special character. According to Theodore Beza (*CO* 21:62), Calvin had a great role in the return of Paul Volz, who after a long dispute had been dismissed from the office of minister on January 13, 1537. Volz had refused to sign the Wittenberg Concord, which was required by the Council. In July 1539 he publicly renounced his errors (aberrant views of the Lord's Supper—influenced by Kaspar Schwenckfeld—and of infant baptism) and was reinstated to his office.[21]

Jean Stordeur was an Anabaptist who under Calvin's influence joined the congregation in Strasbourg along with his wife and their two children, a boy and a girl. In the spring of 1540 he died of the plague, and on August 6, 1540, Calvin married his widow, Idelette de Bure. Already on May 19, 1539, Calvin had written in a letter to Farel that he was thinking about marriage, and a couple of times it had almost worked out. But for one reason or another these earlier possibilities had come to nothing. Calvin and Idelette's marriage was officially contracted in Strasbourg and almost certainly confirmed by Farel in a church service.

On July 28, 1542, Calvin and Idelette welcomed the birth of a son, whom they named Jacques. Born prematurely, however, the little boy soon died (see Calvin's letter of August 19 to Pierre Viret—*CO* 13:430). Idelette herself died on March 29, 1549. Calvin wrote to Viret on April 7 (*CO* 13:230–31) about his wife: "As long as she lived, she was a faithful helper in the fulfilment of my office. She never placed even the slightest obstacle in my way." He also talked about her death in a letter to Farel (dated April 2—*CO* 13:228–29). Because on her deathbed she did not say anything about her children (from her first marriage), Calvin told her in the presence of others that he would care for them as if they were his own. She replied that she had already committed them to the Lord. When Calvin said that that would not prevent him from doing what he could for them, she answered, "I know that if they are loved by the Lord, then they are also commended to you." In 1557 Calvin was deeply ashamed when his stepdaughter Judith was found guilty of adultery.

While in Strasbourg Calvin also came into contact in 1539 with the Bohemian Brethren when one of them, Mattias Cervenka, stayed for some time in Bucer's home. There Calvin came to know him and gained information about the Bohemian Brethren through conversations. He learned then that the Brethren were acquainted with some of his writings. In Strasbourg Calvin also met a certain Guillaume de Fürstenberg, a count from South Germany, for whom he drafted a couple of apologetic works (see pp. 203–4).

The contacts that Calvin was able to establish outside of Strasbourg were also of great significance for him. In February 1539 he went on his own initiative

---

21. See Robert Stupperich, "Calvin und die Konfession des Paul Volz," *RHPhR* 44 (1964): 279–89.

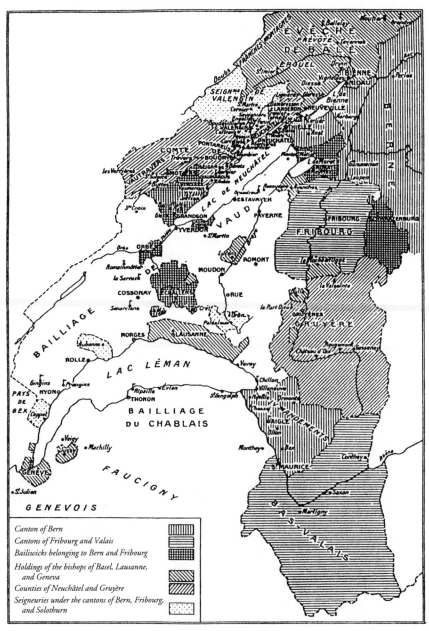

Map of Switzerland

with Jean Sturm to Frankfurt, where Charles V was trying through negotiations to win the support of the German Protestant princes in his struggle against the threatening Turks. The emperor also wanted to prevent the Protestant princes from forming a coalition with Francis I. During discussions about military support, the princes succeeded in getting the emperor to consider their theological and ecclesiastical demands. Charles V announced that he would convene a religious colloquy whose results would be placed before the imperial diet in order to bring about reformation of the church in Germany.[22]

While in Frankfurt, Calvin sought support for the persecuted Protestants in France. He also wanted to speak with Philipp Melanchthon about religious and ecclesiastical matters, and in their conversation the twelve articles that Calvin had drafted concerning the Lord's Supper and had sent along with Bucer when he went to Wittenberg in October 1538 (the relevant letter has been lost) came up for discussion. Melanchthon agreed with the articles, but he pointed out that there were Lutherans who thought "more crudely" about the presence of Christ in the Lord's Supper and that therefore the articles were not suitable for an attempt to unify Wittenberg and Zurich. Calvin also spoke with Melanchthon about the necessity of ecclesiastical discipline, the many Lutheran ceremonies, and images in the church.

The religious colloquy that Charles V had discussed and promised in Frankfurt began in June of 1540 in Haguenau. Calvin was present on that occasion and also took part in the subsequent colloquies in Worms and Regensburg. (For developments at the colloquies and what Calvin published in connection with them, see pp. 153–56.)

Finally, we shall describe the contacts that Calvin had with Geneva during his period in Strasbourg. He definitely did not forget about Geneva during this time. On October 1, 1538, he wrote a letter (*CO* 10b:251–55) to his "dear brothers in the Lord who are left after the dispersion of the church in Geneva." In the letter he reminds them of their duty in the difficult situation in which they live. Whatever suffering they experience at the hands of people comes from Satan, who uses people as his instruments. They must not repay evil with evil but humble themselves before God. They should find comfort in the fact that chastisement assists their salvation, and they should always put their trust in God.

In a letter to Farel on October 24, 1538 (*CO* 10b:273–76), Calvin discussed the situation in Geneva, where confusion now reigned. Supporters of Farel and Calvin were calling themselves *Guillermins* after Farel's first name. They

---

22. For the text of the *Frankfurter Bestand*, see *Die Vorbereitung der Religionsgespräche von Worms und Regensburg 1540/41*, ed. Wilhelm H. Neuser (Neukirchen, 1974), 75–85.

included, among others, Ami Perrin (a member of the Council), Antoine Saunier (rector of the Collège de La Rive, founded in May 1536), and Mathurin Cordier (associated with the same college since 1537). They refused to recognize the new ministers (in addition to Henri de La Mare, who had never left, these ministers were Jacques Bernard, Jean Morand, and Antoine Marcourt) and wanted to know whether they should participate in the Lord's Supper.

Calvin responds that Christians should have such a great aversion to schism that they constantly keep themselves as far away from it as possible. The ministry of the Word and the sacraments are so sacred in nature and worthy of respect that a church exists wherever they both are found. Accordingly, his supporters ought not to withdraw from the fellowship of the Lord's Supper, even if there were something reproachable about the way the new ministers had acquired their positions. The fact that the preaching is not altogether pure must not stand in the way of participation either. There is hardly a church, he says, that bears no traces of earlier ignorance.

Because the Lord's Supper was celebrated in Geneva at Christmas in accordance with the practice in Bern, Saunier and his followers refused to participate. As a result, Saunier, Cordier, and a number of others were banished from the city. But then on December 31, 1538, the ministers in Geneva, being unable to handle the disorder that they themselves had created with their ideas about the relationship of church and such matters as civil government and discipline, asked the Council for their release.

Several ministers in Bern became concerned about the sad state of the church in Geneva and organized a conference in Morges on March 12, 1539, in which Farel, the Genevan ministers, and delegates from surrounding churches took part. Reconciliation was achieved after the Genevan ministers agreed that they should have consulted with the banished ministers before accepting their offices in Geneva. They also promised to give attention to a number of matters that had been neglected.[23] A report of the conference was sent to Calvin in Strasbourg. He was delighted that the illness of the discord was coming to an end, although he had hoped that there would be even more unity in the Lord. But at least the recovery had begun.

The Roman Catholics, meanwhile, were trying to profit from the difficult situation in Geneva after the banishment of Calvin and Farel. Cardinal Sadoleto, bishop of Carpentras, wrote a letter to Geneva, which was ultimately answered by Calvin (see pp. 152–53).

---

23. For the text of the agreement see A.-L. Herminjard, *Correspondance des réformateurs dans les pays de langue française,* 9 vols. (Geneva, 1866–97), 5:243.

The relationship with Bern also presented some problems, which worked to the advantage of the followers of Farel and Calvin. In June 1539 the Council of Geneva received from the Council of Bern a letter containing a copy of an agreement that the latter had reached with representatives from Geneva. They wanted the Council of Geneva to ratify this agreement. That presented problems for Geneva, however, because the twenty-one articles of agreement placed her at a great disadvantage. At stake in this matter was a further adjustment of the claims that Bern could make on territories that had formerly come under the chapter of Geneva. No such stipulation had been part of the agreement between Bern and Geneva in 1536, and the Council of Geneva proceeded to accuse the negotiators of treason. Those in the Council who had had a hand in the banishment of Calvin and his colleagues and who now agreed with the negotiators were called *Articulants* or *Artichauds,* which was tantamount to "traitors to one's country." The influence of the other party, the Guillermins, increased.

On June 25 Calvin wrote a letter to his supporters in Geneva (*CO* 10b:351–55) in which he addressed the situation there. He wished to lead the city back to the path of unity between ministers and congregation. He dealt with the responsibility of both congregational members and office-bearers. He would not deprive the members of their right to criticize the ministers; the true shepherds must be distinguished from the voracious wolves. The congregation must see to it that ministers also obey their calling. But as far as Geneva is concerned, Calvin calls upon his supporters to recognize the authority of the ministers working there because they faithfully preach the most important articles of the Christian faith (those concerning what is necessary for salvation) and administer the sacraments.[24]

On March 29, 1540, Calvin indicated in a letter to Farel (*CO* 11:30–31) that he had long been expecting to hear from him because a lot had been happening in Geneva. In February the Articulants and Guillermins had settled their differences. And Calvin had also learned from Geneva that others were possibly working for his return. He, however, would rather die a hundred times in some other way than on that cross (of being in Geneva) on which he had died a thousand times per day. In passing he also appealed to Farel to oppose those who wanted to try to call him back to Geneva.

Calvin wrote to Farel in May 1540 (*CO* 11:37–42) to express his delight that the disunity and strife in Geneva had come to an end, although he suspected that the two sides were still not completely one in Christ, relying more on

24. See D. Nauta, "Calvijns afkeer van een schisma," in *Ex auditu verbi: Theologische opstellen aangeboden aan Prof. Dr. G. C. Berkouwer* (Kampen, 1965), 131–56.

mutual reconciliation than on peace with God. But fortunately there were signs of healing. He indicated further that he was not at all keen on returning to Geneva. He saw more and more clearly what kind of maelstrom God had rescued him from when he was banished from the city. He anticipated Farel's arrival in Strasbourg shortly. Then they would discuss further the situation in Geneva (where on June 17 the Council decided to try to turn back to God and restore the situation to what it had been four to five years earlier). Calvin and Farel met each other at the end of June and traveled together to Haguenau.

On September 21, 1540, Ami Perrin, an ardent Guillermin, was instructed by the Council of Geneva to devise a way to get Calvin to return to Geneva. That same year, in July and September, respectively, the ministers Morand and Marcourt had left Geneva. Henri de La Mare and Jacques Bernard remained and had recently been joined by Aimé Champereau.

During October and November of 1540, Calvin was being pressured from many sides to return to Geneva. At the beginning of October Farel came to Strasbourg with various letters, including one from Marcourt, and Cordier and Viret also urged him to return. Calvin wrote to Farel in confidence on October 21 (*CO* 11:90–93) that deep in his heart he was shuddering as the discussion about his return continued; he remembered what he had gone through the whole time he was in Geneva. He also still felt bound to the task that God had given him in Strasbourg. Besides, it would be foolish to head back into the very danger from which God had rescued him. Indeed, how could he be of any use to Geneva? His conscience was torn. Would the people in Bern who had hurt him and Farel in the past perhaps now be ready to help? And what about their colleagues in Geneva? Moreover, said Calvin, I no longer know how to lead. Why not call Farel back instead? Calvin did not wish to neglect his calling, but he was greatly torn. Though not inclined to go voluntarily, he was ready to listen to the advice of others. But first he would go to Worms, where a follow-up to the colloquy at Haguenau was to be held.

The Council of Geneva decided on October 13 to send Calvin a letter with the request that he return. (A brief official letter followed on October 22—*CO* 11:94–95.) It upset him for two days. He responded in a letter on October 23 (*CO* 11:95–97) in which he expressed his affection for the church in Geneva. But he was in a real dilemma. On the one hand, he was faced with the call to return to Geneva, which with God's help he indeed wanted to obey. On the other hand, he could not simply give up a task to which he had been called by God. Had he not always taught that a minister must remain in the position to which he has been called, and that he may not leave it without an inner certainty and the consent of the believers?

PETRVS VIRETVS
VIRETA SECTANS TVA,
QVO DISSIDENT GENTIIIVM
RITVS SACRIS SCRVTANS MODO,
VIRETE VERBORVM POTENS·
EXOSVS HINC MAGNIS SOPIIIS,
ARCANA QVI DETEXERIS·

Pierre Viret

The following day, October 24, Calvin wrote to Farel (*CO* 11:99–100) that if it were up to him, he would not do what Farel wanted (that is, return to Geneva), "but because I know that I am not my own master, I offer my heart as a true sacrifice to the Lord." These words, which became Calvin's motto, are depicted in his emblem, which included both the figure of a hand holding out a heart and the inscription *prompte et sincere* ("promptly and sincerely").

In the midst of this inner confusion and uncertainty, Calvin placed the letter from Geneva before the other ministers in Strasbourg, who had the welfare and upbuilding of the church in Geneva at heart and therefore wanted to help her in every possible way. According to Calvin's letter of October 23 to the Council of Geneva, the Strasbourg ministers suggested that Viret be called to Geneva during Calvin's trip to Worms. And indeed he was. In January 1541 Viret was relinquished by Lausanne to Geneva, with Bern's consent, for half a year, and in May 1541 the term was extended another six months (*CO* 11:228–29). After mentioning the possibility of calling Viret, Calvin went on to say in his letter that God would determine the outcome. At the same time he promised that he would do his best to serve Geneva insofar as God and the people would allow him.

On October 24 Calvin and Jean Sturm left Strasbourg for Worms. Even in Worms, however, the matter of his return to Geneva kept him occupied. On October 27 he received a visit from a Genevan delegation carrying the official letter of October 22 (*CO* 11:94–95). This group had traveled first to Strasbourg; not finding Calvin there, they had gone on to Worms. The Strasbourg Council did not want to promise the delegation anything since Calvin himself was not there, but they did write a letter to the Council of Geneva (*CO* 11:102). They also quickly sent a messenger to the Strasbourg contingent in Worms to make sure that Calvin made no promises to the Genevan delegation.

After a conversation with the delegation, Calvin wrote a letter to the Genevan Council on November 12 (*CO* 11:104–6) in which it appears that he was ready to return to Geneva but could not do so right at the moment; Strasbourg also had to give its consent.

Calvin wrote to Farel on November 13 (*CO* 11:113–14) about what was keeping him so busy. He could not make a definite decision. Deliberation by the Strasbourgers in Worms had led them to promise not to stand in the way of his return if Bern also agreed. Capito was not in favor of it, but Bucer would plead that Calvin not be detained in Strasbourg. On November 13 the ministers from Strasbourg and Basel who were in Worms wrote a letter to Geneva (*CO* 11:106–13). The Genevan delegation took the letters from Calvin and the ministers back to Geneva, where their contents were well received.

Farel arrived in Worms on December 22 and remained there for a couple of days. On December 24 Calvin sent along with him a letter intended for the ministers in Neuchâtel (see *CO* 11:133–35). Not much has been happening, writes Calvin; no real colloquy has yet begun. He promised to plead the cause of the persecuted brethren in France.

Returning to Strasbourg on January 23, 1541, Calvin continued to be pressed from various sides to return to Geneva. He received, among others, a letter from Jacques Bernard, who had zealously opposed him in 1538 but now insisted on his return (*CO* 11:147–48). The letter, however, did not make a favorable impression on him (see Calvin's answer in *CO* 11:165–66). He responded to a messenger from Geneva by writing to the Genevan Council (February 19, 1541—*CO* 11:158–59) that he, also on behalf of Geneva, had to go to the religious colloquy in Regensburg. Moreover, he was pleased by the fact that Viret had gone to Geneva in January to serve as minister there. He himself hoped to be able to come in due course.

In a letter to Farel (March 1, 1541—*CO* 11:169–70) Calvin seemed frightened by a letter in which Farel had clearly intimated that Calvin ought to hasten his return to Geneva. "The thunderbolts which you so strangely hurl at me—for what reasons I do not know—have frightened and thoroughly upset me," responded Calvin, realizing that he was beaten.

On April 29, 1541, Calvin wrote Farel (*CO* 11:174–80) that at the end of the imperial diet he planned to go with Bucer from Regensburg to Strasbourg by way of Geneva. On May 1 the Council of Geneva revoked the ban against Calvin and unanimously decided to recall him. Calvin, Farel, Saunier, and others were held up as men of God.

Before the imperial diet had finished discussing the "result" of the religious colloquy, Calvin chose, against the wishes of Bucer and Melanchthon, to return to Strasbourg. The stay in Regensburg had lasted too long for him; he felt he had to be in Strasbourg again. He arrived there on June 25.

On June 20, before Calvin's return to Geneva and after the Council had tried in vain at the beginning of June to get Cordier to come to Geneva from Neuchâtel, it nominated Sebastian Castellio and one other person to be rector of the school.[25] In May 1540 Castellio, who did not have an easy time financially, had stayed for a few days with Calvin. After Castellio had worked in Geneva for three months, he resigned his position because he had not yet received any pay. After a second unsuccessful attempt to call Cordier to Geneva, a new agreement was reached with Castellio: he would also lead church services in the little village of Vandoeuvre, although he was not officially a minister.[26] During his Genevan period Castellio wrote a textbook for religious instruction in which Bible stories were told in dialogue form in both Latin and French (*Dialogi sacri*).

On July 25, 1541, Marguerite of Angoulême, queen of Navarre, wrote Calvin a letter of thanks in the name of her brother Francis I because during the religious colloquy in Worms he, together with Melanchthon and Bucer, had urged Philip of Hesse (alas, in vain) to forge an alliance between the German Protestant princes and the king of France against Charles V. Such an alliance would have brought an end to the persecution of the French Protestants.

Calvin finally left for Geneva at the beginning of September 1541. He himself gave the impression that various circumstances had held him up. On August 13 he had written in a letter to Viret (*CO* 11:261–63) that he regretted a hundred times not going to Geneva immediately after his return from Regensburg. This would have given him more peace, but on the other hand he was not able to

---

25. Ferdinand Buisson, *Sébastien Castellion, sa vie et son oeuvre*, 2 vols. (Paris, 1892; reprint, Nieuwkoop, 1964); Etienne Giran, *Sébastien Castellion et la Réforme calviniste* (Paris, 1914); Hans Martin Stückelberger, "Calvin und Castellio," *Zwingliana* 7 (1939): 91–128; and *TRE*, s.v. "Castellio, Sebastian."

26. Calvin wrote to Viret in March 1544 that this had been arranged without his knowledge, and that it was incorrect to suppose that Castellio now occupied the office of minister (*CO* 11:688).

go. Meanwhile, he had stopped lecturing but was delaying his departure in the hope that Bucer would accompany him. A powerful letter from Farel, dated August 25 (*CO* 11:265–66), must have finally compelled Calvin to go.

Again in Geneva

When Calvin finally got under way to Geneva, he traveled by way of Neu-châtel because he had heard that Farel was in a difficult situation: Farel's rather forceful preaching against moral abuses was creating problems for him. On September 7, 1541, Calvin wrote from Neuchâtel to the Council in Geneva that he was in Neuchâtel at the moment to see whether he could lend Farel a hand. Furthermore, it was his intention to travel to Geneva via Bern the following day with the man whom the Genevan Council had sent to accompany him. Calvin arrived in Geneva on September 13 with various letters of recommendation, among them one from the Council of Strasbourg (*CO* 11:267–68). Immediately upon his arrival, he made his way to the Council, which was in session, and handed over the letters from the Strasbourg Council, the ministers from Strasbourg, and the Council of Basel. The Strasbourg ministers had written: If Calvin finds it necessary in the interests of the churches in Strasbourg to return to the city, you must send him back at once!

Originally, Calvin intended to stay in Geneva only temporarily, but after the Council immediately granted his request to compose a written draft of a church order, he promised the Council that, as far as he was concerned, he would always be the servant of Geneva. A committee consisting of six members of the Council, Calvin, and the four other ministers of Geneva, went to work on the new church order and presented a draft to the Council on September 26. During this time arrangements were also made for the coming of Calvin's wife and for the moving of their belongings. In addition, Calvin took up his responsibilities as minister once again. When he led his first church service since coming back—he wrote in a letter to an unidentified friend (*CO* 11:365–66)—everyone waited in great suspense to see what he would say. He did not refer to what had happened, however, but merely said something about the task of an office-bearer and then began to preach at the very place in Scripture where he had left off in 1538. He wanted to show thereby that what had happened had been merely an interruption in the carrying out of his office.

On November 20, 1541, the church order, *Les Ordonnances ecclésiastiques*, was approved in the General Council, although not everything that Calvin had in mind was included in it (see pp. 144–46). The church order was supplemented in 1547, and a number of modifications were made in 1561 (see pp. 146–47).

Calvin's Involvement in Civil Legislation

On November 21, 1541, the day after the *Ordonnances* were approved by the General Council, a small committee of three persons was appointed by the Council to revamp the civil legislation. Calvin was a member of this committee.[27] Towards the end of 1542 he was even relieved of his preaching responsibilities on every day but Sunday because of his work on this legislation. On January 28, 1543, the General Council of Geneva adopted the civil legislation, with the exception of the portion dealing with the administration of justice, which was adopted at the beginning of 1544.

This legislation was not entirely new. The duties of both the four syndics and the councils were the same as they had been in the past. The influence of the people was somewhat diminished, however, because the form of government had become more aristocratic. The four syndics met daily. They formed a part of the Little Council, which was made up of twenty-five people and as a rule met three times per week. (It is usually this Little Council that we have in mind when we refer to the Council.) There was also the Council of Sixty, a carryover from the fifteenth century with only minimal significance. The Council of Two Hundred, along with the retiring and new syndics, elected all the members of the Little Council except for the four syndics. The syndics were elected annually by the General Council from a slate of eight nominees drawn up by the retiring syndics. The General Council, which was made up of all the citizens, met two times per year. The inhabitants of the city consisted of *citoyens*, *bourgeois*, and *habitants*. The *citoyens* had been born and baptized in Geneva; their parents were also *citoyens*. The *bourgeois* were longtime residents who had to purchase their civic rights and could not be elected to the Little Council (although their children could). The *habitants* were registered aliens in Geneva. Calvin belonged to the third group. In 1559 he was offered civic rights at no cost, and on December 25 of that year he accepted. He thanked the Council for the rights conferred on him and noted at the same time that he had never asked for them, lest he be suspected of having political ambitions in mind.

---

27. Marc-Edouard Chenevière, *La Pensée politique de Calvin* (Geneva, 1937; reprint, 1970), 197–221 (Chapter 4, "Calvin et la constitution politique de Genève"); Robert M. Kingdon and Robert D. Linder, eds., *Calvin and Calvinism: Sources of Democracy?* (Lexington, Mass., 1970); Andrew J. L. Waskey, Jr., "John Calvin's Theory of Political Obligation: An Examination of the Doctrine of Civil Obedience and Its Limits from the *New Testament Commentaries*," Ph.D. diss., University of Southern Mississippi, 1978; and Harro Höpfl, *The Christian Polity of John Calvin* (Cambridge, 1982; reprint, 1985).

Conflicts in Geneva

Although Calvin's return led to a real effort to conduct the city's affairs properly through the drafting of a church order and the revamping of the civil legislation, problems still arose. These had to do, on the one hand, with the need to precisely define the roles of the Council and the church and, on the other hand, with persons who opposed the stricter way of life that had been introduced into the city. These people gradually united with the *enfants de Genève*, the old Genevan population, to form a party that more and more resisted the way things were going in the city. Centuries later this party came to be described as the Libertines, but this name creates misunderstanding since Calvin directed one of his writings against the sect of the Libertines (see pp. 169–71). A connection between the Libertine party in Geneva and the Libertine sect, however, has never been demonstrated.

Struggle over the Right of Excommunication

We begin our examination of the conflicts in Geneva with an overview of a struggle between the Council and the church. The regulations concerning discipline and excommunication in the church order of 1541 turned out in practice to create problems because it was not stated clearly whether the church or the civil authorities had the right to excommunicate. Thus on March 19, 1543, the question came up in the Council of Sixty whether the Consistory had the authority to forbid someone to participate in the Lord's Supper. The answer was negative. The Consistory could indeed pass judgment, but the punishment was to be imposed by the Council. Upon being communicated to the Consistory, however, this decision elicited a vehement reaction from Calvin: he would so totally oppose the decision that the Council could enforce it only by killing or banishing him. At the request of Calvin and several others, an extra session of the Council was held; Calvin explained his position and without any difficulty achieved what he asked for (as he wrote to Pierre Viret—*CO* 11:521).

A serious difference of opinion between the church and the civil authorities about the right of excommunication arose again in 1553 during the prosecution of Michael Servetus. On September 1, 1553, Philibert Berthelier, who a year and a half earlier had been denied access to the Lord's Supper by the Consistory because of drunkenness, asked permission of the Council to be reinstated to the sacrament.[28] Although Calvin was consulted and said that the right to

---

28. On the significance of the conflict between Berthelier and the Consistory, see Walther Köhler, *Das Ehe- und Sittengericht in den Süddeutschen Reichsstädten, den Herzogtum Württemberg und in Genf*, vol. 2, *Zürcher Ehegericht und Genfer Konsistorium* (Leipzig, 1942), 605–14.

allow or deny admission to the Lord's Supper belongs to the Consistory, the Council decided to grant Berthelier permission to participate. The following day (September 2) the Council met at Calvin's request; he protested the Council's decision with an appeal to the church order, but without success. When he led the church service on September 3, a service at which communion was scheduled to be celebrated, he made very clear in his sermon that he stood by his position. Berthelier, who had been warned by the Council to stay away from the Lord's Supper this time, did not partake. In the afternoon service Calvin sounded very much as if he were preaching his farewell sermon.[29]

On September 7 the ministers sharply protested to the Council about the way matters were going and declared that they would rather die, be banished, or submit to some other punishment than depart from the regulation adopted in 1541. The Council asked the ministers to demonstrate the correctness of their position from the *Ordonnances*, and Calvin on behalf of the ministers gave an explanation in the Council the following day. According to the ministers, the Consistory was to determine whether someone should be denied admission to the Lord's Supper. The Council ruled on September 18 that they would continue with what had been decided in the past (but had been interpreted differently!).

When at the beginning of November Berthelier again asked permission to be reinstated to the Lord's Supper, the struggle began anew. On November 7 the Council declared that the Consistory could not refuse to admit someone to the Lord's Supper without the Council's knowledge, and this was upheld by the Council of Two Hundred. Calvin announced on behalf of the ministers that they could not accept this decision. Because the situation had reached an impasse, the Little and Great Councils decided to seek the advice of Bern, Zurich, Basel, and Schaffhausen. In a letter (*CO* 14:675–78) Calvin wrote on November 26 to the ministers in Zurich (the letter was delivered by Jean Budé), Calvin gives an account of the state of affairs in Geneva because surely before long they will be asked for advice by the Council of their own city. He writes that there are different ideas about excommunication. Some people are of the opinion that it is not necessary under a Christian government. But excommunication is in agreement with the instruction of Christ. In places where it has not been implemented, says Calvin, the situation is different from ours. He asks the ministers in Zurich whether it is clear to them that in the order of discipline followed in Geneva up to now there is nothing that conflicts with the teaching of Christ; if so, they should make every effort

29. On the conflict involving Berthelier see Calvin's letter to Viret on September 4 (*CO* 14:605–6).

to ensure that the Council of Zurich relates that information to the Council of Geneva.

On December 31 Calvin wrote to Guillaume Farel (*CO* 14:723–24) that Zurich had advised against any change,[30] and that Basel had sent a copy of the order being used there without any comment on the matter.[31] Schaffhausen had proved to be the most courageous, and Bern's reaction was derisively cool, which he had expected. On January 1, 1554, the responses from these cities were reviewed in the Council, but no decision was made. Berthelier, meanwhile, did not gain admission to the Lord's Supper, and his opposition continued.

The Council appointed a committee on October 24, 1554, to investigate the right of excommunication once again and to come up with a proposal for a definitive settlement of the matter. On January 24, 1555, the Council of Sixty and the Council of Two Hundred decided to adhere to the *Ordonnances*, which meant that they would agree with the judgments of the Consistory. Calvin wrote to Heinrich Bullinger on February 24, 1555: "Recently, it was finally decided after a long struggle that the right of excommunication belongs to us" (*CO* 15:449).

Conflicts Stemming from the Strict Way of Life

Resistance to the stricter way of life that had been introduced into the city can be clearly seen in several cases. In January 1545 the wife of Pierre Ameaux, a former manufacturer of playing cards, member of the Little Council, and captain of the artillery, had been condemned for life because of immoral behavior. The marriage was dissolved and Ameaux received permission to remarry. On January 26, 1546, Ameaux, who was convinced that Calvin had worked against him in his recent divorce suit, strongly criticized Calvin's doctrine and life. Ameaux was arrested. The Little Council could not decide between a mild and severe form of punishment and laid the matter before the Council of Two Hundred, which decided to impose a mild punishment: Ameaux had to kneel at the door of the Council hall and ask Calvin for his forgiveness. Calvin had initially supported a mild punishment also and had wanted to visit Ameaux in prison, but was prohibited by the Council. Later he (and the Consistory) did not concur with the sentence of the Council, because Ameaux had publicly offended God with the assertion that Calvin had been preaching heresy for seven years without the church's intervention.

---

30. See also Calvin's letter to Heinrich Bullinger that is dated the same day (*CO* 14:722–23). For the Council of Zurich's reply to Geneva, see *CO* 14:699–703.

31. The question stirred up quite a bit of controversy in Basel. See Uwe Plath, *Calvin und Basel in den Jahren 1552–1556* (Zurich, 1974), 98–111. For an extensive quotation from the reply from the Council of Schaffhausen, see the letter from Jacobus Truger to Bullinger (*CO* 14:710).

Now Calvin favored a more severe punishment, namely, that Ameaux in penitential dress, bareheaded, and with a burning torch in his hand, be led from prison to the town hall. Kneeling there between the two doors, he was to beseech God and the tribunal for mercy. Ameaux was sentenced to this public penance on April 8.

Also in 1546 problems arose concerning a violation of the prohibition on dancing, which had been in place long before Calvin's arrival in Geneva. Among those involved were Amblard Corne (syndic) and Ami Perrin (head of the artillery). In a meeting of the Consistory, Perrin's wife vehemently lashed out against its members because she believed that they had something against her family (the Favres). They had, after all, also taken measures against her father for adultery. By contrast Corne, strongly condemning his own behavior and that of the others, confessed his guilt. He and Calvin planned to talk with Perrin after a church service, but Perrin never showed up. So Calvin wrote Perrin a letter (*CO* 12:338–39) stating that in the church, too, one may not operate with a double standard. He was seeking the good of both the church and Perrin. He was not at all concerned about the threat from the Perrin family to see to it that he soon leave Geneva. He had not come to Geneva for leisure or personal gain, and he would not regret having to leave again. He intended only to do his duty and called upon Perrin to obey God and to maintain community discipline.

Also in 1546 the actor Roux Monet requested permission from the Council for his company to present a stage play with a good moral. The Council granted permission after consulting with the ministers about the matter. The performance took place on Sunday, May 2; the time of the church service was changed to accommodate it. On May 24 the actors asked to be allowed to present the play *The Acts of the Apostles*, which had been performed in Bourges in 1536. The performance required two weeks' time and a cast of nearly 550 people. Abel Poupin (who shortened the extremely long play) and Calvin were at first entirely opposed to it, but the other ministers did not support them. Calvin wrote to Farel (*CO* 12:347–48): "We declared that this performance did not at all have our approval, although we did not want to go too far in opposing it because of the danger that the esteem we enjoyed would be weakened if we opposed it strongly and still lost. I realize that one cannot deny people every one of their amusements."

Even before the performance, Michel Cop railed against the actors in a sermon, an action that Calvin did not criticize, and problems developed. The actors were furious and enlisted the help of the Council, which had given its approval for the performance. Calvin and his colleague Poupin succeeded in calming them down, but not without difficulty (see Calvin's letter to Farel of July 4—*CO* 12:355–57).

In August 1546 there were more problems with the Perrin-Favre family. When Poupin officiated at the marriage of a brother-in-law of Ami Perrin, the groom did not hear a question being put to him, and when he was asked to respond by saying yes, he shook his head. Ami Perrin stood nearby laughing. Both were punished by the Council. In addition an uncle of Perrin's wife was in prison. And the day before the aforementioned marriage ceremony, Perrin's mother caused trouble by beating up a family member during a quarrel. She was supposed to appear before the Consistory but ran away. What am I supposed to do? wrote Calvin to Viret on August 11 (*CO* 12:368–70). Win the favor of one man (Perrin) by keeping silent and be considered a traitor by the whole church? Calvin realizes that he will have to exert a lot of effort to ensure that Perrin never has an excuse to become angry. In addition, Perrin's wife must be constrained to keep herself under control, for she seizes upon and defends every wicked thing.

Farel appealed to Perrin in a letter to reconcile with Calvin. Calvin had read the letter beforehand rather superficially, and when it turned out that Perrin was furious about the sharp tone of the letter, Calvin was sorry that he had not paid closer attention to its contents, for he had not intended that Perrin be treated so harshly (see the letter to Farel that is dated October 12—*CO* 12:395–96).

On June 27, 1547, a libelous letter was found attached to the pulpit at Saint Pierre. Calvin and his supporters were vehemently attacked and threatened with death. Suspecting that a plot against both the church and the state was behind it, the Council appointed a commission to investigate. A search of the house of Jacques Gruet, a suspect in the case, uncovered documents attacking both the Council and Calvin. Gruet admitted that he had written the letter and fastened it to the pulpit. On July 26 he was beheaded.[32]

A few years later, in 1550, there was found in Gruet's house a book he had written which denied the existence of God, ascribed false doctrine to Scripture, and called the Virgin Mary a whore, Jesus Christ a liar (and much more), the prophets fools, and the apostles scoundrels. When the Council asked Calvin for his opinion, he insisted that appropriate measures be taken (*CO* 13:568–70). Upon the Council's decision the book was publicly burned on May 25, 1550.

32. For several documents from the case—a letter written by Gruet, the prosecutor's requisitory, and the sentence—see *CO* 12:563–68. See also Henri Fazy, "Procès de Jacques Gruet, 1547," *Mémoires de l'Institut national genevois* 16 (1886); and M. François Berriot, "Un Procès d'athéisme à Genève: L'Affaire Gruet (1547–1550)," *BSHPF* 125 (1979): 577–92.

In a Council meeting on September 20, 1547, Ami Perrin sharply attacked the Council in connection with the imprisonment of his wife and father-in-law. Perrin was also arrested, and on October 9 the Council relieved him of his duties as captain general. During the proceedings against him, the accusation was made that in May he had served as Bern's representative at the coronation of Henry II in Paris, and there had agreed to an offer by Cardinal Du Bellay that would give Perrin command of several hundred horsemen in the region of Bern and Geneva against a possible attack by Charles V. Bern backed up Perrin and revealed that Laurent Maigret, who had brought the charge against Perrin, had also tried to obtain assistance from the French court at the same time that Perrin was in Paris. Maigret was also arrested. The debate raged in the Council, and on November 29 Perrin was released for lack of evidence. Maigret remained in prison. On December 12 Calvin pointed out to the Council the disorder in the city, which threatened to ruin not just the city but the church as well. He wrote to Viret on December 17 (*CO* 12:632) that the situation in the city gave him little hope that the church could remain at all orderly: "Believe me, I am a broken man if God does not extend his hand to me." Because of threatening anarchy in the city, the Council made an effort to bridge the differences by appointing a commission with Calvin at its head.

The difficult situation in Geneva brought Farel and Viret to the city at the beginning of January 1548 in order to give Calvin support and to appeal to the parties for reconciliation. Both ministers were received before the Council of Two Hundred on January 10. Five days later Perrin was again accepted as a member of the Council when he showed a conciliatory spirit. Maigret was released from prison the following day and cleared of all charges.

In the summer of 1548 Calvin got into difficulty over a letter he had written to Viret on February 12, 1545 (*CO* 12:32–33). In the letter he had discussed the Council elections and written that people sought to govern under the guise of Christianity but without Christ. The letter in question was stolen by a member of the Perrin family and used as a weapon against Calvin. Jean Trolliet translated it into French and brought it up on several public occasions. On September 14 Calvin turned to the Council; Trolliet was required to come as well. Calvin acknowledged writing the letter and offered his apologies. Both men were admonished to live in peace.

For Calvin, however, the unfavorable effects of the letter would not go away. He called upon Viret (whose letter it was, after all) and Farel to help. Both of them appeared in turn before the Council on more than one occasion at the end of September and during the first half of October. On October 18 the Council finally considered the matter settled, but in the future Calvin would have to perform his duties more responsibly.

The autumn of 1548 proved to be another difficult period for Calvin. In Lausanne the rumor was spreading that Calvin, who was being called Cain, would soon be driven out of Geneva (see Calvin's letter of October 28 to Viret—*CO* 13:92–93). Then in the November elections his opponents were victorious. They now held the important posts related to the administration of justice. Calvin feared that the upcoming election of syndics would produce a total revolution in the government. Meanwhile, Trolliet was working against the printing of Calvin's books and sermons (see Calvin's letter to Farel that is dated November 27—*CO* 13:109–10). Calvin wrote to Farel on December 12 that the future looked bleak (*CO* 13:125–26). On December 14 he brought up in the Council, among other items, that various people, Perrin among them, were not participating in the Lord's Supper; and he appealed to the Council to help. On December 18 the Council called Perrin to account, and after doing everything in their power to bridge the differences, they arranged a meal for the Council members and ministers in order to promote mutual harmony.

On January 18, 1549, the Council issued a proclamation calling on the entire city to abide by the regulations concerning religion, which involved reformation in accordance with the gospel (*CO* 13:158–60). Everyone was exhorted to lead a Christian life and to faithfully attend church services. Those charged with seeing that the regulations were observed were to carry out their task responsibly. Those in positions of leadership were expected to set a good example. The ministers were to discharge their office with care. The proclamation was to be made public before the next church services.

As Calvin feared, in February 1549 Ami Perrin was chosen as the first syndic. But the elections in February 1555 brought about a complete victory for Calvin's followers. All four syndics supported him, and the followers of Perrin (the *enfants de Genève*) lost their influence on all fronts.

In the months that followed, a number of French refugees (around fifty) acquired their rights as Genevan citizens. The old Genevan families, including Perrin's, found it increasingly difficult to accept the fact that so many French refugees were settling in the city. On May 6, 1555, the Council rejected Perrin's proposal that French refugees who had obtained their civic rights not be permitted to vote or to carry weapons for ten years. To support such demands, a group of no fewer than five hundred citizens held a protest demonstration in Geneva on May 16. When it was over, a number of them were treated to a meal put on by leaders of the *enfants de Genève*. During the night a tumult broke out on the street, and as syndic Aubert was about to arrest someone, Perrin snatched away his staff of office. An investigation was conducted the following day, and on May 23 several of the ringleaders were imprisoned. The next day both the Little Council and the Great Council took up the case of Perrin, who had fled the city with three others before they could be arrested. Twelve of those involved were condemned to death. Three of them were executed; the rest fled into exile. The Council of Bern came to their aid and requested safe-conduct for those who had been condemned in absentia. One of them, François-Daniel Berthelier, returned to Geneva, was taken prisoner, and was beheaded on September 11. These events spelled the end of the party of Perrin.

What happened in Geneva stirred up feelings in other places. Bullinger, who had received a letter dated June 5 in which Calvin described the events in Geneva (*CO* 15:640–42), asked Calvin for more information. Calvin sent him a more detailed report (dated June 15—*CO* 15:676–85) with the intention that others, for example, the Council of Zurich, his colleagues in Schaffhausen, and the Council of Schaffhausen, be accurately informed. Bern continued to work in behalf of Perrin and his followers, demanding that they be allowed to return to Geneva.

The defeat of the Perrinists in May 1555 had far-reaching results. From then on Calvin rarely mentioned the circumstances in Geneva in his letters. The strife in the city was over, and there were time and space now for the continuation of the Reformation. Calvin also became more and more involved in the affairs of churches in neighboring countries.

Theological Conflicts

Conflict regarding the Song of Solomon and Christ's descent into hell. Debate over theological issues arose a number of times in Geneva. One such instance occurred in December 1543, when Sebastian Castellio, rector of the Latin school, expressed his desire to become a minister. The Council wanted to oblige him, but problems developed in the course of the colloquium between him and the ministers that was stipulated by the church order. Castellio indicated that he had a different view of the Song of Solomon. He considered it to be a love song by Solomon, which could better have been left out of the canon. Furthermore, he could not agree with the statement in the Genevan Catechism that Christ's descent into hell refers to his suffering on the cross.

On the latter point, the ministers asked Castellio to express his agreement at least with the summary of the faith given in the catechism, for they felt that the congregation would be thrown into confusion if matters of the faith that have to do with the edification of the congregation were understood in various ways. The principal point of discussion, however, was Castellio's conception of the Song of Solomon. No agreement was reached, so the ministers were not able to admit Castellio to the office of minister.[33]

Castellio resigned as rector of the school in February 1544 and tried to find work in Lausanne. He was supported by a letter of recommendation that Calvin had written on behalf of the ministers (*CO* 11:674–76). The letter states why Castellio has not been admitted to the ministry. His merits as rector are praised. There is nothing reproachable in his conduct. And when it comes to the essential matters of the faith, he has not taught anything wicked.[34]

Castellio did not succeed in finding work in Lausanne and returned to Geneva, where on Friday, May 30, 1544, he disrupted the ministers' *congréga-tion* (Bible study) on the text 2 Corinthians 6:4 ("as servants of God we commend ourselves in every way"). Castellio drew a sharp distinction between Paul and the ministers of Geneva. Calvin held his tongue at the time because he did not wish to create an even greater commotion in the presence of so many strangers. Afterwards he lodged a complaint against Castellio with the Council, and Castellio had to leave Geneva. He found work in Basel as a proofreader for the printer Oporin. His Latin translation of the Bible was published in 1551 and his French translation in 1555. In 1553 he became a professor of Greek at the University of Basel.

Conflict regarding predestination. In 1551 a case was brought against Jérôme Bolsec, who had caused serious problems by disputing the doctrine of predestination during a Bible study. Bolsec was banished from Geneva in December 1551 (for more on Bolsec see pp. 118–19), but that was not the end of the matter.

On June 13, 1552, Calvin complained in the Council about Jean Trolliet, whose attempt in 1545 to become a minister in Geneva had not been successful because of the opposition of the other ministers. Trolliet later became the Council censor. Calvin's complaint to the Council had to do with the fact that during a meal on a public occasion Trolliet had accused him of a variety of things (see *CO* 14:334–35). Trolliet was called to defend himself before the Council (for the content of his defense see *CO* 14:335–37). On September 1, after several debates, a dispute between Trolliet and Calvin arose on the floor of the Council over predestination.

Trolliet presented his arguments in writing on October 3 (see *CO* 14:371–77). He began with several excerpts from Calvin's *Institutes* (1550) and, with an

33. See also the two letters from Calvin to Viret (*CO* 11:686–88, 690–91), from which it is evident that Calvin does not favor Castellio's becoming a minister. He does wish to help Castellio find work, however.

34. See also Calvin's letter to Farel on May 31 (*CO* 11:719–22).

appeal to Philipp Melanchthon, accused Calvin of locating the origin of sin in God himself.

Calvin gave his written response to the Council on October 6 (see *CO* 14:378–83). He states that it is blasphemy to identify God as the author of sin and that he is offended by what Trolliet has said. What Trolliet has adduced from the *Institutes* has been ripped out of context. He confuses what Calvin himself says with what is claimed by those whom Calvin is disputing.

In his written response Calvin does talk about a necessary sinning, but whoever sins cannot use the excuse of being coerced to sin (necessity is something different from coercion). Calvin says that there are two causes for being lost: the one lies hidden in the eternal decree of God, and the other, which is fully manifest, lies in the sin of the individual. The heart of the issue, according to Calvin, is that all who are going to be lost will be convinced in their own consciences that they are guilty and that therefore their condemnation is just. They are wrong to bypass this entirely clear truth and to attribute their lostness instead to the "Little Council" of God, which is inaccessible to us. The Scriptures clearly show that God has destined us for the goal that he chooses us to reach. But why and how that happens we cannot know because it is not explained to us.

Calvin admits that there is a difference in the way Melanchthon and he teach this doctrine. Melanchthon has been too willing to accommodate to human understanding, concerned as he is not to give the curious any opportunity to probe the secrets of God too deeply. Thus he has spoken on this issue more as a philosopher (he even mentions Plato) than as a theologian.[35] Calvin makes clear, however, that whoever sets Melanchthon and him against each other does both them and the entire church a great injustice. Finally, he says that he is convinced that what he teaches does not come out of his own head; he has received it from God and must cling to it for the sake of the truth.

Farel and Viret came to Geneva on November 7 to stand up for Calvin in the meeting of the Council, and the Council indicated their support for Calvin on November 9. The *Institutes* is a good book, they said, and Calvin is a good and true servant of the city. In the future no one must dare to allege anything against the *Institutes* or the doctrine of predestination. Trolliet had to recant his positions but was not prosecuted any further.

An important theological debate took place in 1553 in connection with the case against Servetus (see pp. 173–76). Then in June 1554 the Council of Geneva received an anonymous letter in which not only Calvin but also the

---

35. Cf. Calvin's letter to Melanchthon of November 27, 1552 (*CO* 14:415–18).

councils and ministers of Neuchâtel and Zurich were attacked because of their stance against Servetus, Bolsec, and others. It is not clear who wrote the letter, though Calvin thought it was Castellio.[36] Calvin went to the Council about the matter, believing that he could no longer serve the church if he was not cleared of these charges.

The Council supported Calvin but was not able to do anything. In Basel, however, measures were taken against Celio Curione and Castellio, both of whom in 1554 had challenged Calvin's ideas about predestination. Curione had attacked Calvin indirectly in the revision of a treatise he had written in 1552, *De amplitudine beati regni Dei,* which, however, could not be printed because Basel refused to give its assent. Similarly, a marginal note in a new edition of Castellio's Latin translation of the Bible challenged Calvin's interpretation of Romans 9:13, but the printer was required to remove the note.[37]

The Academy of Geneva

Geneva was keeping an eye on the threat posed by the duke of Savoy, who after the Peace of Cateau-Cambrésis was able again to assert his claims on Geneva and other territories. While the city was busy fortifying itself, the opening of the Academy of Geneva took place in a convocation at Saint Pierre on June 5, 1559, with Calvin presiding.[38] Already in 1541, after his return from Strasbourg, he had conceived the plan to establish an academy, but for various reasons nothing came of it until the political situation in Geneva changed in 1555. En route to Frankfurt in 1556, Calvin paid a visit to Strasbourg to get advice from Jean Sturm, who was head of the academy there. Except for the lingering matter of a new treaty with Bern, the establishment of an academy received full attention. First, a new building was needed. A suitable site was found in early 1558 near the Bourg-de-Four Hospital. Because no government money was available for the construction, Calvin oversaw the collection of a considerable sum of money.

Calvin and the other ministers worked out a plan of instruction and submitted it to the Council for approval. In the new academy the already existing school, the Collège de La Rive, was to become the *schola privata,* with seven classes. In the first two classes the children learned to read and write the French and Latin languages. Next they concentrated on the Latin and Greek authors.

36. See his letter of August 7 to Simon Sulzer (*CO* 15:209).
37. Plath, *Calvin und Basel,* 164–72.
38. Charles Borgeaud, *Histoire de l'Université de Genève,* vol. 1, *L'Académie de Calvin, 1559–1798* (Geneva, 1900).

Special stress was placed on reading comprehension and on clear verbal articulation of one's thoughts. There were no classes on Wednesdays. In the mornings students went to church, and in the afternoons there was time for relaxation. On Saturdays the students spent time reviewing what had been taught and studying the catechism material for the following Sunday. Each instructional day began with the prayer that was included in the catechism especially for school. Praying and psalm singing had a fixed place in the teaching schedule. The students also learned to recite the Lord's Prayer, the Apostles' Creed, and the Ten Commandments. The teachers were nominated by the ministers and professors and presented to the Council for their approval.

The students who had attended the *schola privata* could go on to study at the *schola publica,* a considerably less common type of institution. A student enrolled, signed the confession of faith, and took twenty-seven lecture courses from five professors, who were appointed in the same way as were the teachers. The professor of Hebrew taught the students Hebrew, exegeting a book of the Old Testament with the use of Hebrew commentaries. The professor of Greek read Greek philosophers (ethics received special attention) and poets with the students. The professor responsible for the "arts" instructed the students in natural science, mathematics, and public speaking, the last with a view to the preparation of ministers and lawyers. On Saturday afternoons attention was given to training in practical theology; under the guidance of a few ministers, students presented a sermon and were then evaluated. In addition to those already mentioned, there were two professors of biblical interpretation. Calvin and Theodore Beza filled those posts in the early days of the academy. The professors also took part in the Friday meetings (*congrégations*) of the ministers. During the grape harvest there was a three-week vacation.

The Council gave Calvin the responsibility of finding professors for the academy, something at which he was not so successful. An effort to secure the services of Mathurin Cordier as a teacher in the *schola privata* failed because Calvin was not able to obtain Cordier's release from Lausanne. On February 16, 1562, however, he was finally appointed to the school—at the age of eighty-two! Calvin was also unsuccessful in his approach to Jean Mercier, who taught Hebrew at the Collège Royal in Paris (letter dated March 16, 1558—*CO* 17:94–95). In 1563 Calvin tried again to woo Mercier to Geneva (see Calvin's letters of May 3 and October 17—*CO* 20:4–5, 170–71). Immanuel Tremellius, who was of Jewish origin and had taught Hebrew in Cambridge before taking his current post in Heidelberg (his Hebrew translation of Calvin's catechism was published in Geneva in 1554), also declined Calvin's invitation to come to Geneva (see Calvin's letter of August 29, 1558—*CO* 17:310). A more fortunate

Theodore Beza

development in Calvin's search for professors was a serious conflict that arose between Bern and a number of professors in Lausanne, which lay in Bern's territory. The Council of Bern had wanted to exert its influence in ecclesiastical issues like the right of excommunication. In October 1558 the conflict led to Beza's leaving Lausanne, where he had taught Greek at the academy since 1549. Others, including Pierre Viret, later followed him. Beza headed to Geneva and at Calvin's suggestion was installed in November as a professor of Greek. His wish to become a minister was fulfilled in March 1559. Professorial chairs were also given to others from Lausanne, such as Antoine-Raoul Chevallier (Hebrew), François Béraud (Greek), and Jean Tagaut (philosophy).

On June 5, 1559, Beza, whom the ministers had proposed to the Council as rector of the academy, gave the opening address at Saint Pierre (see *CO* 17:542–47), after Michel Roset, the secretary of the city, had read aloud the academic statutes[39] and the teachers had taken an oath of subscription to the statutes and

---

39. *Leges academiae Genevensis* (for the Latin and French texts see *CO* 10a:65–90).

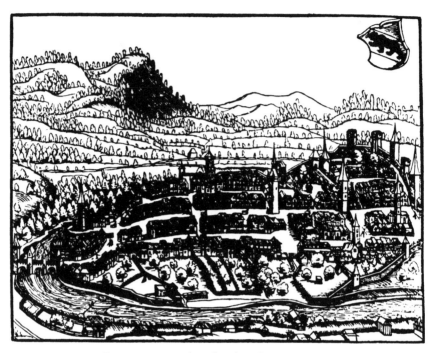

Bern in 1547–48 (woodcut by Johannes Stumpf)

the confession of faith. The building in which the academy was housed was not completely finished until 1564. At that time there were approximately fifteen hundred students, the majority of them from abroad. They could study either theology or law.

Calvin's Relations with Others

Calvin and the Relationship of Geneva with Bern

In the relationship between Geneva and Bern tensions would occasionally run high. When Calvin returned in 1541, Bern was still asserting its claims on territories in the immediate environs of Geneva. Basel had been called upon to mediate and made its position known in January 1542, after eighteen months of deliberation. Calvin took part in the advisory committee appointed by the Council of Geneva. The matter dragged on until 1544, when on February 19 the citizens of Geneva ratified the agreement that brought Geneva and Bern together. Tensions between the two cities continued, however. These had to do not only with political matters, such as Bern's fear in 1546 that

Geneva would break away from Bern and join the side of the French king, but also with religious matters.

We have already mentioned that problems arose in Geneva in 1538 when, at the request of the Council of Bern, the Genevan Council sought to introduce several of Bern's ecclesiastical practices. One of these involved the celebration of the four great feast days that did not fall on a Sunday: Christmas, circumcision, the annunciation, and ascension. These feast days had been abolished in Geneva in 1536 but were restored after the banishment of Calvin and Farel. When Calvin returned in 1541, he adjusted to the existing situation. In 1544 the Council introduced a unique change in the celebration of the feast days: in the future, church services would be held and workplaces closed only on feast-day mornings; in the afternoons everyone would go back to work. But because some continued to protest against this measure, and quarreling and dissension broke out over whether workplaces should be open on feast-day afternoons, Calvin asked the Council in November 1550 to do something to ease the dissension. He said nothing about abolishing the four feast days, however; as far as he was concerned, it was all right simply to conform to Bern. Thus it was a complete surprise to him when on November 16, 1550, the Council decided to abolish the four feast days. Had he been asked for his opinion, he would not have supported that decision (see Calvin's letter to John Haller on January 2, 1551, and his letter to Heinrich Bullinger on April 23, 1551—*CO* 14:4–6, 104–5).

That tensions could run high over such matters can be seen, for example, in what happened in 1551. In Bern and her dependent territory it was customary to celebrate the Lord's Supper on Christmas Day, whereas in Geneva it was celebrated on the Sunday closest to December 25. On December 27, 1551, Jean de Saint-André, minister in Jussy (under Geneva's jurisdiction), preached a sermon in nearby Fontenay (under Bern's jurisdiction) in which he criticized the fact that the congregation had celebrated the Lord's Supper on December 25 according to the custom of Bern. On February 7, 1552, when he again had to be in Bernese territory, he was taken prisoner. Calvin went to Bern with the endorsement of the Council of Geneva on February 17, 1552, in order to assist Saint-André. After speaking with the Council in Bern, Calvin on February 26 reported to the Council of Geneva, which on March 7 received a letter from the Bernese Council with the news that Saint-André had been banished from Bern's territory because of the judgments he had expressed. In April he became a minister in Geneva, and at the insistence of the Council of Geneva, Bern lifted the sentence against him in November.

A major factor in the interaction between Geneva and Bern was the different relationship between church and civil government in the two cities. In Geneva the church was more independent from the government than in Bern.[40] The Council of Bern, for example, abolished the *congrégations* (ministers' Bible studies) in 1549. After the Bolsec case in Geneva, the Bernese Council prohibited the ministers in their territory from addressing the subject of predestination in their preaching. A few ministers from the area of Thonon who did not heed the prohibition were dismissed and banished. Moreover, Bern forbade members of the congregations in its territory to participate in the celebration of communion in territory under Geneva's control.

Geneva did not simply ignore the many anti-Calvin actions that people like Bolsec and André Zébédée, a minister in Nyon, were taking in Bern and its territory. However, protest letters from the Genevan ministers and even from the ministers of Lausanne had no effect.[41]

In March 1555 Calvin and syndic Raymond Chauvet went as representatives from Geneva to Bern to discuss a variety of issues. Conversations with the Council, however, got them nowhere. The Council of Bern, for example, wanted the Genevan Council to ban all publications about predestination. Calvin and Chauvet reported back to the Council of Geneva on April 11.

In the ensuing months the correspondence with Bern continued. Calvin twice wrote to the Council of Bern, the first time immediately following their talks there (*CO* 15:550–51). In that letter he deals with, among other things, Bern's effort to prevent the publication of books on predestination and the Bernese proposal to burn books that run counter to what Bern understands by reformation. In the second letter (May 4—*CO* 15:600–604) he goes into even more detail on Bern's rejection of what the Genevan ministers had written in 1552 about predestination and on Bern's effort to prevent publications about the subject. He believes that such a great and elusive mystery ought to be writ-

40. See Kurt Guggisberg, "Calvin und Bern," in *Festgabe Leonhard von Muralt* (Zurich, 1970), 266–85.

41. The Genevan ministers wrote a letter to the Council of Bern on October 4, 1554 (*CO* 15:250–52). Another letter followed on October 6 (*CO* 15:256–58), which they had Christophe Fabri personally deliver to Bern. Bern responded on November 17 in letters to the ministers in its territory and to the Council of Geneva (*CO* 15:311–14). The ministers of Geneva, who were not wholly satisfied with what Bern had written, replied on November 27 in a letter composed in consultation with the Council (*CO* 15:319–20). Still another letter was dispatched to Bern on December 29 (*CO* 15:363–64). The complaints in these letters have to do primarily with Bolsec. See also the reactions of the Council of Bern in a letter to the Council of Geneva (*CO* 15:400–404), in which various charges are made against the ministers of Geneva, and the letter to the ministers in the Vaud territory (*CO* 15:405), calling upon them to abide by the established practices. In February 1555 the ministers of both Geneva and Lausanne complained to the Council of Bern about the various slanders (*CO* 15:430–33).

ten about with sobriety and humility, as he himself has done. His intent is to overcome human recklessness and to teach people to worship the majesty of God without giving free reign to curiosity. To deny the doctrine of predestination, writes Calvin, is impossible because it is spoken of in Scripture. He also refers to the slander that he has experienced at the hands of, among others, Jean Lange and Zébédée. Because his intent has always been to serve the church and to see her evangelical doctrine flourish, he hopes that the Council will make sure that the faith is not mocked under his name. The ministers of Lausanne and the Council of Geneva also wrote to Bern (May 2 and May 6— *CO* 15:585–91, 608–13). In early June the correspondence on these matters came to a halt.

The negative influence of these issues became clear with the approach of February 8, 1556, the date that the agreement between Bern and Geneva on the rights of citizens (the so-called *bourgeoisie*) was due to expire. The Council of Geneva had indicated in 1555 that it was in favor of continuing the agreement. Bern, however, did not respond, and after much urging finally let it be known that it wanted to make changes in the stipulations. These changes included a promise by Geneva not to make alliances with any cities except Bern (this had been agreed upon by the two cities in 1536, but had not been included in the treaty on civic rights). Geneva, however, wanted the freedom to make, with Bern's consent, agreements with other Swiss cities, which would strengthen Geneva's position over against France. The rumor began to spread in Zurich and elsewhere (see Bullinger's letter of September 28, 1555—*CO* 15:797–801) that Calvin was the instigator of these Genevan ideas, so he defended himself in a letter to Bullinger in October (*CO* 15:829–36). When February 8, 1556, arrived and a new agreement had still not been reached, Geneva appealed to Zurich, Basel, and Schaffhausen for help. Negotiations resumed but with no results. Perrin and his cronies, who had left Geneva in May 1555, also continued to work against Geneva.

In the fall of 1557 the prospects for a new agreement between Bern and Geneva finally improved as a result of pressure from the outside. The Swiss cities had gradually shifted to the side of Geneva and supported the inclusion of Geneva in a Swiss alliance. What settled the matter, however, was the fact that Duke Emmanuel Philibert of Savoy, who in August 1557 had succeeded in getting France to recognize his claims upon the territories his father had lost (including Geneva and territories under Bern's jurisdiction), intended to retake those areas with his army. Bern and Geneva now found themselves facing a common threat to their freedom. On January 9, 1558, they formed an *alliance perpétuelle*, in which Geneva for the first time stood on an equal footing with Bern. The two cities pledged to protect each other. Bern took a positive stance vis-à-vis the inclusion of Geneva in a Swiss alliance. In Geneva the people held a feast to celebrate the fact that they were now a free and independent city.

Calvin was constantly involved in the affairs between Geneva and Bern because the Council would ask him for advice on such matters as the stipulations of the agreement. On February 21, 1556, he wrote to Nikolaus Zurkinden, Bern's city clerk, about his personal involvement in politics. He would prefer to keep his distance, he says, but sometimes circumstances force him to become involved. He feels that it is better to do all that he can to restore peace than to be an idle spectator, even if such involvement is accompanied by all sorts of trouble (*CO* 16:43–45).

We see in other letters also how strongly Calvin felt about the relationship between Bern and Geneva. In a letter to Bullinger on March 1, 1556, for example, he expresses the hope that the Genevans will not become embittered by the disgraceful treatment they have received at the hands of Bern. He calls for prayer and generosity (*CO* 16:52). When he stopped in Basel in August 1556 en route to Frankfurt, he wrote a letter from there to the Council of Geneva to inform them of the experiences of the Genevan delegation in Basel: in Basel, Zurich, and Schaffhausen, the delegation had had to refute charges brought against Geneva by the banished Perrin and his henchmen (*CO* 16:270–71). And when a new alliance with Bern was finally formed on January 9, 1558, Calvin wrote the following day to François Hotman in Strasbourg that after much discussion a permanent alliance with Bern had at last been achieved. He did not think that it would bring an end to all disputes, but he did consider the agreement to be a good thing because impartial arbiters would now settle cases of discord (*CO* 17:15).

Calvin's Relations with Neuchâtel and Frankfurt

There were a few places with which Calvin had a great deal of contact. We shall take a closer look at Neuchâtel and Frankfurt in particular to give somewhat of an idea of his involvement in events in other places.

Neuchâtel was not very far from Geneva. Moreover, Farel had become a minister there in 1538 following his banishment from Geneva. Calvin and Farel regularly met, stood by each other in a variety of situations, and corresponded frequently. We shall describe just a few of the contacts that Calvin had with Neuchâtel. It is clear from these contacts that he did not work in isolation in Geneva, but several times was to some extent forced to become involved in events in Neuchâtel.

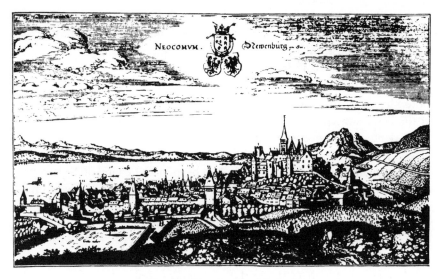

Neuchâtel in 1642 (by Merian)

In May 1543 Calvin was invited by the classis of Neuchâtel to come and defend himself against a charge by Jean Courtois that he held unorthodox views of the Trinity and of Christ. Courtois, who had been a minister in Neuchâtel since 1542, was encouraged in this action by his brother-in-law Jean Chaponneau, who had become a minister in Neuchâtel in 1537–38 and had made things difficult for Farel on more than one occasion. Calvin had known Chaponneau from his student days in Bourges. The invitation reached him too late, however, so he defended himself in writing (see his letter of May 28 to the ministers in Neuchâtel—*CO* 11:559–62).

In November 1543 Calvin reported in a letter to the ministers in Neuchâtel a conversation in Geneva with Courtois about the Trinity and the person of Christ (*CO* 11:652–54). Courtois stated that he had not come to Geneva to argue but to learn, and he indicated that he was ready to agree on what Calvin discussed with him. Courtois also took to heart what Calvin said about the danger of stirring up discord in the church and about true knowledge and instruction. He promised to do his duty, and Calvin commended him to his fellow office-bearers.

Calvin wrote a letter to the ministers of Neuchâtel on behalf of the Genevan ministers on November 8, 1544 (*CO* 11:762–66), in which he dealt with the difference of opinion that had arisen there about mutual censure between ministers. The ministers in Neuchâtel had drawn up a regulation for mutual censure, but the aforementioned Chaponneau considered the practice to be unnecessary among ministers on the basis of Matthew 18:15–17. He presented six thesis statements on the subject, and the whole matter was passed on to Geneva for discussion.

According to Calvin's letter, the Genevan ministers felt that the regulation was worthwhile. Censure served to promote common deliberation and admonition by the entire group of one's peers. It was good, however, to emphasize at the beginning of the discussions how careful one must be not to turn the salutary medicine of censure into a poison.

Chaponneau was called upon to agree with the others, but he turned against Calvin instead. When Calvin had been in Neuchâtel on September 17 on the way back to Geneva from Bern, Chaponneau had presented him with a list of passages from the *Institutes* that he wanted explained. Calvin had answered him by letter (now lost). Chaponneau now wrote Calvin a long critical letter in early December (*CO* 11:781–802) in which he challenged Calvin's view of the divinity of Christ and accused Calvin of heresy. The Genevan ministers reacted with a letter to the ministers of Neuchâtel (*CO* 11:805–9). In his own letter to the ministers of Neuchâtel, which was dated January 21, 1545 (*CO* 12:13–20), Calvin responded to the attack by Chaponneau, who in large part abandoned his earlier positions during 1545 (he died on October 22, 1545).[42]

In August 1545 efforts were made to call Farel to Geneva as minister after Moreau had been dismissed, Aimé Champereau transferred to Draillans, and Matthieu de Geneston had died of the plague. The efforts proved fruitless, however, because Neuchâtel could not find a worthy successor to Farel (Pierre Toussaint, who had left Montbéliard, had been nominated—see *CO* 12:124–25). On September 24 Michel Cop became a minister in Geneva, soon followed by Nicolas Des Gallars.

On March 4, 1551, Calvin was present at a synodical gathering in Neuchâtel. The Council of Neuchâtel had permitted the ministers of the city to hold a meeting at which a variety of ecclesiastical regulations would be discussed, provided that ministers from the outside would also be invited. One of the accounts, located in the Bibliothèque des Pasteurs in Neuchâtel, is from the hand of Calvin.[43]

Calvin paid a visit to Farel in Neuchâtel in March 1553 when the latter was seriously ill. In the presence of Calvin and a few others, Farel drew up a last will and testament. Calvin left thinking that Farel would die in a matter of days, but he recovered; and in a letter written on March 27 (*CO* 14:509),

---

42. For more detailed information see *Guillaume Farel, 1489–1565* (Neuchâtel, 1930), 540–50.
43. Ibid., 605–10.

Calvin heartily wished him the best and expressed the hope that Farel would outlive him.

On September 26, 1558, Calvin wrote a letter to the ministers in Neuchâtel (*CO* 17:351–53), who were greatly shocked and indignant that the sixty-nine-year-old Farel was about to marry the still youthful Marie Torel, a fugitive (with her mother and brother) from France. Both mother and daughter lived in Farel's home. Farel had personally informed Calvin of his plans, probably in July. Calvin was shocked at the great difference in age, and he had advised Farel to make his wedding plans public so as to prevent all sorts of talk in the community. Farel did not comply at once (see Calvin's letter of September 12 [*CO* 17:335–36] in which he writes that he neither can nor wishes to be present at the upcoming marriage to which Farel has invited him). To the ministers in Neuchâtel, who were contemplating disciplinary measures, Calvin wrote that he understood how offended they were by Farel's action, because he had said nothing about it earlier. He, too, regarded what Farel was doing as foolish, but called upon them to keep in mind what Farel had done for the church over the past thirty-six years. That was not to say that they had to approve of what he was doing, but only that they should keep from responding too harshly. Calvin hoped that God would give them enough wisdom that their offense at Farel's actions would diminish as much as possible and poor brother Farel would not die of sorrow.

Unlike Neuchâtel, Frankfurt was a long way from Geneva, so it would not be immediately obvious that Calvin had a lot of contact with that city. In fact, however, he did; one can go as far as to say that he was very intimately involved with what took place in the ecclesiastical life of the city.[44] We outline his contacts with Frankfurt in order to demonstrate the extent of his involvement in troublesome situations elsewhere.

Calvin's contacts with Frankfurt began in early 1555. A congregation made up of people who had fled from England after Mary became queen had formed in Frankfurt. Problems arose in the congregation over the liturgy. Some wished to use the Book of Common Prayer; others preferred a Reformed liturgy. Included in the latter group were John Knox and William Whittingham, who on December 11, 1554, wrote Calvin a letter asking him for advice (*CO* 15:337–44). They had attached a summary of the English liturgy and their own critical notes, and were hoping that Calvin would condemn the ridiculous Roman Catholic elements still in the liturgy.

---

44. Karl Bauer, *Die Beziehungen Calvins zu Frankfurt a. M.*, SVRG 38 (Leipzig, 1920).

In his reply dated January 18, 1555 (*CO* 15:393–94), Calvin first expresses how terrible he finds it that disunity exists among brothers who have been banished for the same faith. It is obvious to him that the refugees must adapt to the church to which they are bound by language and religious persuasion. In his judgment, arguing about forms of prayer and other ceremonies is inappropriate when a congregation is being formed; he condemns the stubbornness that can stand in the way of this process. He is willing to be indulgent when it comes to indifferent matters like the structure of the worship service, but he also does not want simply to go along with those who choose to hold on to customs in foolish obstinacy. As far as the English liturgy is concerned, he says that there appear to be many absurdities to endure. By that he means that there is quite a lot to find fault with in the English liturgy, but at the same time it does not endanger piety to the point that one cannot temporarily bear with it until improvements can be made. He also says that the forming of a new congregation is a propitious time to revise the liturgy. He warns, however, not to be extraordinarily strict in revising if some people talk of weakness (that is, of not being able to go through with the revision). He also admonishes the latter group not to be so foolish as to let their obstinacy impede the building of a new congregation. All parties involved must make sure that they are not carried away by foolish envy. Furthermore, they must not be afraid of the calumny coming out of England that those who were driven out for their faith have now fallen away from it. Rather, a sincere confession by the refugees should compel those believers who remain behind to consider the depth of the abyss in which they find themselves.

The English congregation in Frankfurt was able to reach a compromise between the parties. But problems arose once again with the arrival of new refugees under the leadership of Richard Coxe, who wished to hold firmly to their own liturgy and church organization. Knox, who had attacked the emperor in a little piece he had written, was charged by his opponents and banished by the authorities. Calvin's mediation was again requested by Whittingham in a letter dated March 25, 1555 (*CO* 15:523–24). Coxe and a number of others informed Calvin at the beginning of April about the current situation and some concessions that they had made (*CO* 15:552–54). Calvin wrote to Coxe on May 31 (*CO* 15:628–29) that he was happy about the reconciliation, but that he disapproved of the way in which Knox had been treated. In connection with the possible coming of a number of Coxe's group to Geneva, Calvin expressed the hope that that would not happen at the cost of mutual harmony.

In the second half of September 1556 Calvin was in Frankfurt for two weeks in connection with a number of disagreements that had arisen.[45] They concerned, in the first place, the French refugee congregation, where the discord had arisen from the fact that the members of the congregation had come from different areas, England and Wesel. Even the minister, Valérand Poullain, contributed to the friction. Calvin had tried to bring about peace by means of letters.[46]

During Calvin's sojourn in Frankfurt, he presided over a seven-person commission which cleared Poullain but forced him to resign. He also held a two-day discussion in Frankfurt with Justus Wels, who disagreed with predestination and defended the freedom of the will. In addition Calvin requested a meeting with the English refugee congregation. He did not succeed in making contact with the Lutheran ministers, however. (In a letter to Wolfgang Musculus that is dated October 26 [*CO* 16:319–21], Calvin reports on his experiences in Frankfurt, calling the dispute in the French refugee congregation "an unpleasant affair.")

In a communication on February 23, 1559 (see *CO* 17:440–42), Calvin addressed the French congregation in Frankfurt, where discord reigned once again. The most serious problem was that two ministers, Guillaume Houbracque, who had replaced Valérand Poullain, and François Perrucel, were quarreling. If strife between lay members of the congregation is a blight upon the church, writes Calvin, what then if the messengers of peace are fighting with each other? Therefore, he is in a hurry to help and eager to put an end to the strife that is destroying the bond of peace. He also warns about contacts with Sebastian Castellio, who had produced a French translation of the mystical work *Theologia Germanica,* which was being circulated throughout the congregation along with other treatises.

Calvin wrote a letter at the same time to Augustin Legrand (see *CO* 17:442–43), a member of the congregation in Frankfurt whom he had come to know in the past as a very vehement man. Calvin earnestly entreats Legrand not to disturb the peace in the congregation through talk that is full of deadly venom. Let him return in peace to the congregation and prove that it is not his fault if there is no harmony there.

---

45. Ibid., 47–51.

46. See, for example, the letters that Calvin wrote to Poullain on June 24 (*CO* 16:201–3); to Johann von Glauburg, a member of the Council in Frankfurt whom Calvin knew from the colloquy in Regensburg and whom he now asked to mediate in the French congregation (*CO* 16:203–7); to the elders and deacons of the congregation (*CO* 16:207–10); and to the entire congregation (*CO* 16:210–13).

Calvin's Relations with France

It is not our intention to give a complete survey of Calvin's relations with France. In this section we shall focus only on his concerns for the Protestants in France when they became enmeshed in difficult circumstances. Around 1545 the Waldenses found themselves facing dire persecution. That year in the vicinity of Rouen a terrible bloodbath occurred in which several thousand people sacrificed their lives. Calvin was greatly shocked by what a couple of Waldenses reported to him. On May 4, 1545, he wrote Guillaume Farel about what had happened and about the decision of the Council to send him around to the Swiss churches to see what could be done for the Waldenses (*CO* 12:75–76). Perhaps Farel could accompany him from Bern on.

After visiting various cities, including Strasbourg, Calvin went to Aarau, where at Zurich's initiative a conference of a large number of Protestant cities was being held to deal with the plight of the Waldenses. It was decided to address a written plea to Francis I in behalf of those being persecuted, and if the king responded, to send a legation. The cities agreed to keep in contact about the matter. That was as much as Calvin was able to do (see the letter written to Pierre Viret on May 28—*CO* 12:82–83).

Calvin remained interested in the persecuted Waldenses, however, who were being cast in a bad light by their opponents. He wrote to Heinrich Bullinger on July 24 (*CO* 12:110–12) that he considered Count Aymar de Grignan, governor of Provence, and Cardinal de Tournon the instigators of the persecution. Bern and Basel must be urged to do something for the Waldenses. He also encouraged Bullinger himself, along with his colleagues, to appeal to their political authorities and insist that some measures be taken. That same day (July 24) Calvin also wrote to the ministers of Schaffhausen, Oswald Myconius in Basel, and Vadianus (Joachim von Watt) in Saint Gall (see *CO* 12:112–18). The result was that a Swiss legation and a deputation from the German evangelical princes approached Francis I. The Waldenses who were still in prison were set free, and many made their way to Switzerland.

In January 1548 the Council of Geneva received a letter from Henry II, who had succeeded Francis I as king of France in 1547 and would reign until 1559. He was persecuting the Protestants with an even greater intensity than his father had done. To begin with, on October 8, 1547, he established the *chambre ardente* for the persecution of heretics. A number of notable people took refuge in Geneva: Laurent de Normandie in August 1548; Theodore Beza on May 3, 1549 (in November he became a professor of Greek in Lausanne); Guillaume Budé's widow and several of her children on June 17, 1549 (he had died in 1540); and the printer Robert Estienne on November 13, 1550. In the letter mentioned above, Henry II called the city to unity and to vigilance with respect to Charles V, and he promised not to leave the city in the lurch (see Calvin's letter of January 15 to Viret—*CO* 12:651).

The Edict of Châteaubriant was officially published in France on September 2, 1551. Calvin refers to it in a letter to Bullinger on October 15 (*CO* 14:186–88): Christians have been deprived of that which poisoners, counterfeiters, and highwaymen have always been allowed and still enjoy, namely, the right of appeal to the highest court of justice. The order has gone out that ordinary judges can drag them to the stake at once without any appeal. Calvin thinks that the utmost must be done to help the poor brothers. He deeply regrets that no aid can be expected from Bern, with whom Geneva had extended the alliance on March 8. While swords are being sharpened to murder us, he writes, we as brothers neglect to consult with each other.

On February 29, 1552, Calvin discussed with the Council his plans to go to Germany to plead the cause of persecuted fellow believers in France. He thought he would be able to do something for them because on October 3, 1551, the Protestant prince Maurice of Saxony had formed an alliance with King Henry II of France against Emperor Charles V; and in the Treaty of Chambord on January 15, 1552, Maurice had recognized Henry's claims on the cities of Metz, Toul, and Verdun. These agreements were beneficial to the Germans living in France. Because the French king desperately needed the support of the Swiss cities in his struggle against the emperor, Calvin hoped to be able to accomplish something in behalf of his fellow believers in France, for whom the king's Edict of Châteaubriant had created serious problems. The articles of the edict prescribed, among other things, mandatory attendance at mass on feast days and state seizure of fugitives' property.

Calvin began his journey on March 6, 1552, and stopped with Farel in Bern to seek support from the Council for their fellow believers in France. He reported on this to Bullinger in a letter dated March 13, 1552 (*CO* 14:302–5). In the meantime, he and Farel had arrived in Basel, where they hoped to get the Council to go along with a plan for four Swiss cities to send a legation to the French king. In Bern Calvin and Farel had heard that this was not the best time to send such a legation: in some correspondence between the four cities and the king, Henry indicated that he had been angered recently by the fact that he was not viewed as a gentle, Christian prince. In connection with this, Calvin and Farel had been dissuaded in Bern from going to Zurich. The Bernese wanted to wait for a further letter from the king in which he would perhaps have changed his mind.

On March 21 Calvin was back in Geneva, where he reported to the Council on his experiences. Accompanying him from Basel was Caelso Martinengo, an Italian who had fled from Brescia for religious reasons and who became pastor of the Italian congregation in Geneva.

In Lyons five French students from Lausanne, who had just completed their studies and were on their way home, were arrested on April 30 and condemned to death on May 13. This produced a flurry of activity in their behalf in Protestant Switzerland. Calvin, too, became involved by writing letters to them and to other prisoners (*CO* 14:331–34, 491–92, 561–64) and by sending Nicolas Colladon and Laurent de Normandie to cities in Switzerland to raise support for a joint protest to the French king. The students were ultimately burned in Lyons in 1553.

In Paris on September 4, 1557, students disturbed an evening meeting of the Protestant congregation in the rue St. Jacques. Nearly two hundred members were arrested, including many older people and women.

Calvin sent Jean Budé (see *CO* 16:747) to Germany and appealed to Bern to allow Beza to travel there as well to participate in a meeting of evangelical princes and theologians. Calvin wanted Budé and Farel to try to get the evangelical princes to act in behalf of the Protestants in France.

Meanwhile, Nicolas Des Gallars had been sent to serve as a minister in Paris; Calvin beseeched him to remain at his post (*CO* 16:627–28). The ministers of Geneva also contacted the congregation in Paris by letter (see *CO* 16:629–32), and Calvin wrote to comfort the women in prison there (see *CO* 16:632–34), three of whom were burned on September 27, 1557. When Jean Macard, a minister who had been sent to Paris and who regularly kept Calvin abreast of the situation in France, informed him that one of the imprisoned women, a Madame de Rentigny, had taken part in the mass at the insistence of her husband, Calvin wrote her a letter on April 10, 1558 (*CO* 17:131–32).

Having heard that the king of Navarre, Antoine de Bourbon, had joined the Protestants, Calvin wrote him a letter on December 14, 1557 (*CO* 16:730–34), and encouraged him to take up the cause of the persecuted Protestants in France. At the same time he sent the king a 1544 French translation of his *Supplex exhortatio,* which was first published in 1543 (see pp. 160–61).

One of the first French noblemen to join the Protestants was François d'Andelot, a brother of Gaspard de Coligny. When Henry II asked Andelot during a meal about his view of the mass, his answer led to his immediate imprisonment. Calvin wrote him a couple of encouraging letters (late May 1558—*CO* 17:192–94; and July 12, 1558—*CO* 17:251–53). When Calvin heard that Andelot had disappointed many Protestants by participating in the mass (which was considered apostasy from the evangelical faith), he let Andelot know in a letter that he did not approve of his behavior. Calvin urged him, however, to prove by his actions that one instance of stumbling does not necessarily mean that one has deviated from the right path. Calvin called upon Andelot to follow Christ even in difficult circumstances. In the days to come Andelot would become one of the pillars of the Protestant community.

After suffering several defeats in his struggle against Spain, King Henry II concluded the Peace of Cateau-Cambrésis with Philip II on April 3, 1559. Both monarchs would now fight against the evangelical heresy. One of the results of the peace was the return to France of Admiral Gaspard de Coligny, who after a defeat at Saint-Quentin in 1557 had been taken captive by the Spanish. Coligny had converted to the evangelical faith in 1558 during his captivity in Ghent. On September 4, 1558, Calvin wrote letters of encouragement to both Coligny and his wife Charlotte (*CO* 17:319–20, 321–22). When Coligny was released, he tried to use his influence at the king's court to help the Protestants.

Calvin also played a role in the drafting of the Gallican Confession in May 1559 (see pp. 142–43). But then in June 1559 a strongly worded letter from Henry II directed the courts to persecute the Protestants with full fury. Anne Du Bourg, one of the presidents of the Parlement of Paris, opposed this course of action, was arrested in June 1559 through the personal involvement of Henry II, and was burned on December 21, 1559. In a letter to Ambrosius Blauer (February 1560—*CO* 18:13–16) Calvin tells about Du Bourg's martyrdom in some detail. Henry II had already been dead for some time (July 10, 1559), after being wounded in a joust during a friendly tournament.

Calvin showed how deeply involved he was with the persecuted evangelicals in France by the letters of encouragement that he wrote (see *CO* 17:570–74 for the letter written at the end of June 1559, and *CO* 17:681–87 for the letter of November 1559). In a letter on July 19, 1559, he strongly urged the evangelical congregation in Metz to come out openly for the evangelical faith (*CO* 17:582–84)—they had shown little response to his earlier insistence upon a public confession of their faith. Calvin's original communication (see his letter dated September 10, 1558—*CO* 17:326–29) constituted his reply to the congregation's query whether they should not first be certain of the support of the German princes before they declared their allegiance to the evangelical faith.

In 1559 a group of Protestants devised a plan to destroy the power of the Guises, a distinguished Roman Catholic family with Spanish sympathies. The family was led by Cardinal Charles, archbishop of Reims; by Duke François, who had conquered Metz, Toul, and Verdun for France, had prevented the defeat of France at Saint-Quentin, and had captured Calais from the English;

and finally by Claude. The Guise family exerted a great deal of influence at the royal court through Catherine de Médicis, who since the death of her husband, Henry II, in July 1559 had been serving as regent for her young son Francis II. One of the reasons for the Guise influence was that the king of Navarre, Antoine de Bourbon, had not seized the opportunity after the death of Henry II. (See Calvin's letter of August 13 to Jean Sturm [*CO* 17:594–95], and his letter of October 4 to Peter Martyr Vermigli [*CO* 17:652–53], in which he expresses great concern about the situation of the brethren in France, and in which he says that the king of Navarre could have prevented it. He had made big promises, but his cowardice was the most shameful that one could imagine; not only that, it was downright traitorous, says Calvin.)

Under the leadership of Jean de Barry de La Renaudie, the conspiring Protestants planned an attack on François de Guise, the so-called Conspiracy of Amboise.[47] Calvin was asked for his advice on the planned attack, and he counseled against it. When La Renaudie visited him in December 1559, Calvin rejected the plan with horror.[48] The plot failed on March 15, 1560, because of a betrayal, and the Guises revenged themselves through intense persecution of the Protestants, who were derisively called Huguenots. It is unclear where this name came from. Perhaps it was related to *eyguenot*, an appellation used in Geneva since 1520 for supporters of the party seeking independence from Savoy and pursuing an alliance with other Swiss cities such as Fribourg and Bern. The Huguenots themselves wore the term as a badge of honor.[49]

Calvin, meanwhile, was seeking support abroad for the French brethren. In particular he tried through Jean Sturm and François Hotman (see the letter to them that is dated June 4, 1560—*CO* 18:97–100) to get the German Protestant princes to speak to the French king and to let him know, first, that they were pleased about the plan to convene a national council to rid the church of abuses; second, that they might be willing to help the king; and finally, that in giving their advice they had the king's safety and the peace and welfare of the people in mind.

Calvin also made an effort to get Antoine de Bourbon, king of Navarre (whom Calvin calls Varanne in letters to others), to do more for the Huguenots. Antoine had asked him to send Beza, and Beza left on July 20, 1560, for Nérac, where he preached in public for approximately three months until

---

47. Henri Naef, *La Conjuration d'Amboise et Genève* (Geneva, 1922).

48. See his letter of March 23, 1560, to Jean Sturm (*CO* 18:38–39), his letters of May 11, 1560, to Vermigli (*CO* 18:81–83) and Bullinger (*CO* 18:83–85), and his letter of April 16, 1561, to Coligny (*CO* 18:425–31).

49. See *TRE*, s.v. "Hugenotten."

Francis II called Antoine and his brother Louis de Condé to Paris. Beza returned to Geneva.

When Calvin discovered that many of his letters to individuals in France who were seeking his help were being reproduced and circulated, and even that a part of one letter was quoted in a secret discussion at the king's court, he limited his private correspondence to what was absolutely essential.

After the failure of the Conspiracy of Amboise, the Huguenots encountered great difficulty in improving their position. When Francis II called all the leading figures to meet in Fontainebleau on August 21, 1560, Gaspard de Coligny risked going there as well. Calvin gives a detailed account of the meeting in a letter to Bullinger (dated October 1—*CO* 18:204–8) and relates, among other things, how in Fontainebleau Coligny delivered a request to the king from the Huguenots in Normandy to be allowed to hold worship services in freedom. In December there would be a meeting of the Estates General, and in January the bishops were going to meet to prepare for a general council.

Francis II died on December 5, 1560. His successor to the throne, Charles IX, was still only nine years old. In a memorandum directed to Antoine de Bourbon (*CO* 18:282–85), Calvin indicates what goals he thinks Antoine should be working toward, given the situation in France. In the first place, Louis de Condé, who had been involved in the Conspiracy of Amboise and in October had been taken prisoner in Orléans at Francis II's initiative, ought to be released by judicial pronouncement. Second (and most important), the Estates General must determine who is going to hold the regency, a point Calvin was directing against Catherine. The third matter concerned worship. No one should be compelled to participate in the mass, and it should be possible for those who do not wish to do so to pray and to hear the Word of God.

As it turned out, the power in France fell into the hands of the regent Catherine de Médicis, who restricted the influence of the Guises by giving Coligny and Condé limited freedom of movement and by playing them off against the Guises. The Huguenots had some freedom, but no religious services could be held either in public or at home.

Meanwhile, Jeanne d'Albret, the wife of Antoine de Bourbon, had openly joined the evangelical church after the capture of her brother-in-law, Louis de Condé. Calvin heard from Beza about the step she had taken and wrote her a letter about it on January 16, 1561 (*CO* 18:313–14), expressing his joy at her decision. Thanks to God's great goodness, the seed that the Lord God had planted in her heart long ago had not been choked out. Calvin notes that princes in their high position often do not dare to show that they belong to the flock of the Great Shepherd. He hopes that Jeanne in her position, which she

Jeanne d'Albret

owes to God, will be committed to God with a double bond of obedience. Calvin also urges her to engage in Bible study, for that is something we need, he writes, because of the weakness of our faith.

That same day Calvin also wrote Renée of France (*CO* 18:315–16) and Coligny (*CO* 18:317). Renée's husband, Duke Hercule d'Este, had imprisoned her for a time in 1553–54 in Fort Consandolo because of her evangelical faith, but by participating in the mass she had won her release. Calvin had written her a letter of encouragement on February 2, 1555 (*CO* 15:417–19), and continued to keep in contact with her (see, e.g., his letter of July 26, 1558—*CO* 17:260–62). In October 1559, as the duke lay on his deathbed, he made his wife promise not to correspond with Calvin any more. Her son Alfonso, who succeeded his father, gave his mother the choice of remaining in Ferrara as a follower of the Roman Catholic faith or otherwise going to France. She chose the latter. Calvin wrote her on July 5, 1560 (*CO* 18:147–48), that she was not obligated to keep the oath she had taken. He pointed out to her the dangers that going to France would pose, but he also gave her encouragement. He encouraged her as well in the aforementioned letter of January 16, 1561, in which he asked her, among other things, to do what she could for "the poor members of Jesus Christ."

Renée of France was the mother-in-law of François de Guise, who was murdered on February 13, 1563, in Orléans. Calvin was still corresponding with her in 1564 (see *CO* 20:230–33, 244–49, 278–79). In a letter on January 24, 1564 (*CO* 20:244–49), for example, he deals with the fact that Renée felt aggrieved at statements made by a few ministers about her son-in-law, François de Guise. He writes in some detail about how we must view those who follow the wrong path and do evil. Hate and revenge are not appropriate for Christians. He hopes that Renée will not return in kind the wicked behavior of others, but will manage to show love to those who do not know what love is. He also hopes that her sincerity succeeds in putting to shame the hypocrisy of others.

In the letter to Gaspard de Coligny mentioned earlier, Calvin thanks him for the extraordinary courage he has shown in his efforts in behalf of the Huguenots (e.g., at Fontainebleau). If only many more would help him. Since others are slow, may he pay attention to Christ's words calling us to be ready to follow him without being concerned about what others do. Coligny was at the time in Orléans, where a meeting of the Estates General was being held. On that same day, January 16, 1561, Calvin wrote a letter to Antoine de Bourbon (*CO* 18:311–12), who was also present at that meeting, in which he urged Antoine in a somewhat veiled yet unmistakable way to stand up for the Protestants. The majority of the Estates General declared themselves in favor of freedom of conscience.

It is significant that for several years Geneva offered assistance to the congregations of France by sending them pastors. This began in 1555. On April 22, 1555, the ministers of Geneva received a letter (*CO* 15:575–78) from Jehan Vernou and Jehan Lauvergeat, who at the time were serving as ministers in the Val d'Angrogne (Piedmont). They had been sent out by Geneva at the request of the congregations in that region. On the same day (April 22) the ministers of Geneva decided to send Jacques L'Anglois to France at the request of the congregation in Poitiers. L'Anglois was the first minister officially sent to France, and many more would follow him in the years 1555–62. The records of the meetings of the Genevan ministers contain the names of eighty-eight ministers who went to France during these years, some of whom became martyrs.[50] In August 1555, for example, five ministers on their way to their assignments in France were arrested and imprisoned in Chambéry. One of them, Antoine Laborie, wrote Calvin a letter in which he reported on their session in court. Calvin comforted them by means of letters (see *CO* 15:805–7). On October 12 the ministers died as martyrs.

During this time many congregations in France were appealing to Calvin for ministers. Sometimes they also sought advice. The congregation in Paris, for example, asked not only for a minister, but also about the position they should take with respect to the Council of Trent and with respect to the upcoming meeting of the Estates General (for Calvin's answer see his letter of

50. See Robert M. Kingdon, *Geneva and the Coming of the Wars of Religion in France, 1555–1563* (Geneva, 1956).

February 26, 1562—*CO* 18:376–78). Geneva did comply with Coligny's request for a minister by sending Jean Raymon Merlin, who since his departure from Lausanne in 1560 had served as a minister in Geneva.

The sending of ministers to France continued in spite of the letter (see *CO* 18:337–39) that King Charles IX wrote to the Council of Geneva on January 23, 1561, in which on behalf of the Crown Council he accused Geneva of all the recent unrest in France. He wanted Geneva to recall all her ministers from France immediately. The Council replied (*CO* 18:343–45) that they had not sent any ministers to France and had not been involved in this matter in any way. Rather, it was the ministers of Geneva who had been consulted about this, and they had indeed sent ministers to France to preach the gospel, but they had also opposed armed rebellion and the plundering of churches (see also the letter from Calvin to Bullinger on February 1—*CO* 18:348–50).

In connection with the granting of help to France, we should also mention the involvement of Geneva and Calvin in the colonization plans of Nicolas de Villegagnon, who with the support of Coligny and the French king left for Brazil in July 1555. In 1556 he appealed to Calvin to send some ministers, and Pierre Richer and Guillaume Chartier were selected by Geneva with Calvin's cooperation. Eleven French refugees accompanied them from Geneva. On a little island off the Brazilian coast, called Coligny, worship services were conducted for the colonists, and the gospel was brought to the nationals. Calvin received letters from Villegagnon (*CO* 16:437–40) and from the two ministers (*CO* 16:440–43), who reported on their experiences. They knew that Calvin was thinking about them and asked for his intercession. A rupture developed, however, between Villegagnon, who became a Roman Catholic, and the others, because Villegagnon wanted to exercise spiritual dictatorship; as a result the whole undertaking ended in failure.[51]

An important event in 1561 was the religious colloquy in Poissy. This colloquy was convened at the wish of Catherine de Médicis, who was afraid that internal strife between Roman Catholics and Protestants would weaken the French throne. The colloquy began on September 9 and lasted until October 19. Michel de L'Hospital, the chancellor of France, was responsible for organizing it. The goal was to get Roman Catholics and Protestants to speak with each other on equal terms and to consider how they had deviated from what

---

51. Jean de Léry, one of the eleven individuals from Geneva involved in this undertaking, wrote and published an account of the journey: *Histoire d'un voyage faict en la terre du Brésil autrement dit Amérique* (N.p., 1577; republished as *Le Voyage au Brésil* [Paris, 1927]). For Calvin's view of the apostolate see W. F. Dankbaar, "Het apostolaat bij Calvijn," *NTT* 4 (1949–50): 177–92 (this article is also found in W. F. Dankbaar, *Hervormers en humanisten: Een bundel opstellen* [Amsterdam, 1978], 185–99).

the early church had taught. On this basis they might be able to come to some agreement. Beza represented Geneva at the insistence of Antoine de Bourbon, Condé, and Coligny. Peter Martyr Vermigli was present on behalf of Zurich. The duke of Württemberg sent Johann Brenz, a choice that did not please Calvin at all. Calvin found what Brenz had said about the ubiquity of the body of Christ even worse than the Roman Catholic view. He feared that the ideas of Brenz and his supporters would lead to intense conflict (see Calvin's letter of August 23 to Simon Sulzer—*CO* 18:627–29). A delegation from Germany arrived shortly after the conclusion of the colloquy.

The opening of the colloquy took place in the presence of Charles IX and Catherine. Beza began by reciting the confession of guilt found in the Genevan liturgy, then explained the points on which the Roman Catholics and Protestants agreed and disagreed, and finally presented the Gallican Confession. During the colloquy the Lord's Supper became the principal topic of discussion, but no agreement was reached. In light of what was taking place at the Council of Trent, the Jesuit general Diego Lainez disputed the legitimacy of such a colloquy at all.

Calvin (under the pseudonym Carolus Passelius) and Beza regularly wrote each other during the Colloquy of Poissy, for Calvin wished to keep abreast of what was happening. Remember to write me, he tells Beza on September 10 (*CO* 18:682). He expresses his fear that in an effort to create discord, the Roman Catholics will try to impose the Augsburg Confession on the French Protestants, which in his opinion is not clear in its position and is related more to situations in Germany. He favors maintaining the French confession of faith, which has been accepted by the French Protestants. He also wrote this to Count Eberhard von Erbach when he heard that another delegation from the Palatinate was going to Poissy (see the letter of September 30—*CO* 18:751–53).

After the religious colloquy in Poissy, Beza stayed in France at the behest of the court and several others. At the court he succeeded in obtaining provisional freedom of worship for the Protestants until the persons delegated by the parlements could decide about a further arrangement.

When Beza was confronted with the fact that Antonio Caraccioli, bishop of Troyes and also a delegate to the Colloquy of Poissy, wished to join the Protestants in Troyes without giving up his ecclesiastical status, Beza turned to Calvin for advice (see the letter of November 9—*CO* 19:109–10). Calvin replied by explaining how the question of bishops and other ecclesiastical officers who agree with the pure teaching of the gospel should generally be handled. For him it was a matter of finding a middle ground: not being overly strict, but also not disturbing the order of the church just to please somebody.

First of all, it must be determined whether the person in question is fit to preach. The past must be forgotten. Such a person must be asked to make a new profession of faith and to acknowledge his errors. A bishop who wishes to become a minister must either give up his privileges or, if he wishes to hold on to his property, must content himself instead with a position as a patron of the church (see *CO* 10a:184–86).

On December 24, 1561, Calvin responded to a request by Jeanne d'Albret by writing to her husband, Antoine de Bourbon, and rebuking him for seeking the pope's support in regaining territory that had fallen into Spanish hands (*CO* 19:198–202). Antoine had promised the pope to promote the Roman Catholic faith in France in exchange for his support. If the pope would not support him, he would cross over to the other side.

The Edict of Saint-Germain was issued in France on January 17, 1562. According to the edict, Protestants were granted freedom of conscience and religion, provided that religious meetings were not held in the cities. Meanwhile, the Guises were trying to drive a wedge between the Huguenots and the German princes.

As François de Guise was on his way back from a visit to Duke Christoph von Württemberg on March 1, 1562, he and his soldiers disturbed a religious meeting being led by François de Morel in the vicinity of Vassy. What ensued was a bloodbath. Of the more than 1,200 people in attendance, approximately 60 were killed and another 250 wounded. Civil war now erupted. Calvin sent Jean Budé with letters calling on the German princes to plead the cause of the Protestants in France with King Charles IX by urging him to hold to the Edict of Saint-Germain, according to which worship services outside the cities were permitted (see Calvin's letter of March 25 to Jean Sturm—*CO* 19:359–60).

The Protestants could no longer expect much good from Antoine de Bourbon, who had let himself be won over by the Guises. Calvin had heard from Beza that Antoine had been completely ruined at the court in Paris. He compared Antoine to a Roman emperor who had fallen away from the Christian faith—Julian the Apostate. To Antoine's wife, Jeanne d'Albret, Calvin sent a letter of encouragement on March 22, 1562 (*CO* 19:347–49). The Huguenots now placed themselves under the leadership of Condé and Coligny.

Calvin was able to follow closely the course of the conflict in France, as the detailed information in his letters to Bullinger and Simon Sulzer indicates. After a short stay in Geneva, Beza had returned to France at the request of Condé, and he in particular kept Calvin regularly informed about the course of events there.

In reaction to the bloodbath of Vassy, the Huguenots, led by the minister Jacques Rufi, took possession of the city of Lyons on April 30, 1562. The church of Saint Jean was plundered. Baron François Des Adrets (a general) became the leader in Lyons, and Calvin wrote both him and the ministers in Lyons a letter on May 13 (*CO* 19:409–13) in which he comments on what had happened: it does not befit a minister to take up arms, let alone with pistol in hand to force the mayor to hand over his power. Calvin also criticizes the plundering of the church, which he regards as twice as bad as highway robbery.

While Condé and Coligny were positioning their troops (for the most part soldiers recruited in Germany and Switzerland) around Orléans, François de Guise invaded Normandy, where many Huguenots resided, and besieged Rouen. Antoine de Bourbon died on November 17 of injuries sustained in the conflict. On December 17 a battle was waged at Dreux, which is described by Calvin in some detail in a letter to Bullinger on January 16 (*CO* 19:637–41). During the battle Condé was captured.

Calvin wrote a letter of advice on January 20, 1563 (*CO* 19:643–47), to Jeanne d'Albret, Antoine de Bourbon's widow, who was ruling Navarre for her still underage son. Having introduced the Reformation into her land, she must heed God's command in all difficulties (among other things, the king of Spain was threatening to attack Navarre) and trust that God will help her if she is obedient to him. Calvin had the letter delivered by Jean Raymon Merlin, formerly a professor in Lausanne and since 1560 a minister in Geneva. The ministers and Council of Geneva allowed him to assist the queen in furthering the Reformation in Navarre for as long as she found it necessary.

In response to the queen's request for more ministers, Geneva sent twelve additional young men in May and June, but at the same time asked her to have Merlin returned to Geneva as soon as possible (see Calvin's letter to her on June 1—*CO* 20:34–36). The queen, however, asked the Council of Geneva in August whether Merlin could stay longer.

On March 19, 1563, Condé concluded a peace treaty in Amboise. Its conditions were less favorable to the Huguenots than were those of the Edict of Saint-Germain (January 17, 1562). The people could hold religious meetings only in places specially designated for that purpose—seventy-five places in all, one per canton.

One thing worth noting is the contact that the commander of the besieged city of Lyons, the Huguenot Jean de Soubise, had with Calvin. Soubise had heard from the besiegers that the Peace of Amboise had been drawn up and that he was supposed to surrender the city. He refused to do this, however, without proper authorization. In the meantime he wrote Calvin for advice.

In a letter dated April 5, 1563 (*CO* 19:685–87), Calvin responds to Soubise that this peace, which was arranged without his knowledge, is now a fact and must be accepted regardless of how irksome it is. But Calvin urges him in the meantime to rule the particular affairs in Lyons responsibly. Soubise, however, tried to continue the war on his own. In response to several letters that he had received, Calvin wrote to him (*CO* 20:30–31) that if he wants to have a good conscience, he must have a solid reason for his action. Calvin does not think that there is any such reason, and if Soubise thinks there is, he has no chance for success. In Calvin's opinion, the best thing that Soubise can do is to take his time.

Many Huguenots viewed the agreement at Amboise as a betrayal, for the battle of Dreux had ended inconclusively and François de Guise had been murdered at the siege of Orléans on February 13, 1563. (Coligny, Beza, and Count de La Rochefoucauld were later accused of complicity in the murder, and Coligny published a written defense against the charge.) The opposition was weakened. At first Calvin also expressed his opposition to what Condé had arranged in the Peace of Amboise. In a letter to Bullinger on March 19 (*CO* 19:690–92), he writes that Condé could easily have seen to it that Catherine complied with the conditions already stipulated. But, he thinks, Condé acted in too servile a fashion. After receiving a letter from Condé, however, Calvin wrote him back on May 7 (*CO* 20:12–15) that he believed Condé had done his best and that he hoped that Condé would continue to exert himself in the way that Calvin was encouraging him. Calvin knew that not everything can happen in one day, but he reminded Condé of the expression "the sooner the better."

Along with the letter, Calvin sent a brief confession that he had once hoped Condé would be able to deliver to the emperor in Frankfurt when Maximilian II was crowned king of the Germans (*Confession de foy pour présenter à l'empereur*—*CO* 9:753–72). That had not happened, however, because Condé did not receive the confession in time. Calvin was now sending it to him in the hope that he would stand behind it. That will result, Calvin believes, in winning over many ignorant people in the country. Many Germans in particular, who are alienated from the French in their conception of the Lord's Supper, will show respect if they see that Condé supports this confession. Condé must watch out for those who try to get him to support the Augsburg Confession, which does not take a clear position on the Lord's Supper and has already created a lot of discord in Germany. Calvin (with Beza) wrote Condé one more time about this confession and also urged him to lead a Christian life, since word was getting around that he was having relationships with various women (letter of September 13, 1563—*CO* 20:159–61).

The high esteem in which Calvin was held by the Protestants in France can be seen in letters he received from them asking for advice. Morel, for example, who served as minister in the court of Renée of France in Montargis, presented Calvin with several questions: May a minister loan money to others at interest? May judges and other high-ranking political officials be members of the Consistory? (For Calvin's answers see his letter of January 10, 1562—*CO* 19:245–46.) And Antoine de Crussol, the Protestant governor of Languedoc, asked Calvin whether during the visit of Catherine de Médicis and Charles IX he could rightly accompany them in a procession and on other idolatrous occasions (see Calvin's letter of July 31, 1563—*CO* 20:111–13). These examples could be supplemented with many others, even from outside of France. The letters that Calvin wrote in response to such questions make clear how very pastoral he was in his approach and how sensitive he was to the circumstances in which those whom he was advising found themselves.[52]

Calvin's Last Days

We have seen that after the departure of Calvin's opponents from Geneva in May 1555, the Reformer entered a period marked by much less conflict than before. As we have established, he became more and more involved in affairs outside of Geneva. From 1556 on, however, the state of his health began to decline. He was seriously ill during the winter of 1558–59, although with great effort and with the help of his brother Antoine he was able to prepare a new edition of the *Institutes.* When the Academy of Geneva opened on June 5, 1559, he was somewhat recovered and again took up a variety of activities, but in early 1564 he had to give up many of them because of the poor condition of his health.

On February 2, 1564, Calvin gave his last lecture, on a pericope from Ezekiel. He delivered his last sermon on February 6. On March 27 he made his way a final time to the city hall, where he recommended on behalf of the ministers that Nicolas Colladon become rector. The following day he was present at a Consistory meeting. On March 31 he took part for the last time in a meeting of the ministers. On Easter Sunday (April 2) he was in church and participated in the Lord's Supper.

On April 25 Calvin dictated his will to a notary (for the text see *CO* 20:298–302). He thanked God for his grace and declared that he had done his utmost, according to the measure of grace given him, to preach God's Word purely

52. See also chapter 10; Jean-Daniel Benoit, *Calvin, directeur d'âmes* (Strasbourg, 1947).

Holland's Portrait of Calvin

and to interpret the Scriptures faithfully. He then indicated to whom his few possessions were to be distributed.

On April 27 Calvin wished to bid farewell to the syndics and the members of the Little Council. Since they did not want him to have to come to them, they all went to his house, where he welcomed and addressed them. He thanked them for their friendship and declared that he had always sought to do his best for the city in the service of God, although there was much in which he had fallen short. He thanked them for being patient with his shortcomings, as God had also been, and expressed regrets about his failings. He called upon them to pursue the honor of God in public life. Then he bade farewell to each one personally.[53] The following day he said farewell to the ministers, commending to them Beza, who had been chosen to replace him.[54]

During the following days Calvin still received a number of friends and important persons. Even the aged Farel, to whom Calvin had written a parting note on May 2 (*CO* 20:302–3), visited him. When the ministers held their weekly meeting in Calvin's home on May 19, he was among them one last time. He died on May 27 and was buried the following day.

---

53. See *Discours d'adieu aux mambres du petit conseil* (*CO* 9:887–90).
54. See *Discours d'adieu aux ministres* (*CO* 9:891–94).

2

First Publications

The Foreword to the *Antapologia* of Nicolas Duchemin (1531)
Commentary on Seneca's *De clementia* (1532)
Nicolas Cop's Academic Address (1533)

The Foreword to the *Antapologia* of Nicolas Duchemin (1531)

Calvin became acquainted with Nicolas Duchemin during his student days in Orléans. Then in the summer of 1529 Calvin changed universities. Instead of continuing with the lectures of the more orthodox and traditional Pierre de L'Estoile in Orléans, he and friends François Daniel and Nicolas Duchemin moved to Bourges because the renowned Italian jurist and humanist Andrea Alciati, founder of the historical school of thought, was lecturing there. He had been brought there by Marguerite of Angoulême, who in 1527 had through her second marriage become queen of Navarre, and who as the duchess of Berry was patroness of the university in Bourges.

Alciati was no stranger to the young students. Under the pseudonym Aurelius Albucius he had written the venomous *Apologia* against his colleague de L'Estoile in Orléans. Duchemin, who had attended de L'Estoile's lectures for several years and also lived at his house, composed the *Antapologia* in defense of de L'Estoile before leaving for Bourges.[1] It was published just two years later when Duchemin sent it along with Calvin, who in March 1531 returned to Paris for the publication of his commentary on Seneca's *De clementia* and had Duchemin's treatise printed as well.

In his treatise Duchemin discusses a purely legal question in juridical terms

---

1. The full title was *Nicolai Chemyni Aureliani Antapologia adversus Aurelii Albuci Defensionem pro Andrea Alciato contra D. Petrum Stellam nuper aeditam* (Paris, 1531).

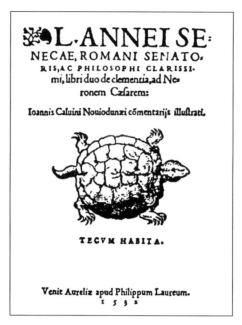

Title page of the commentary on Seneca's De clementia

and accuses Alciati of insincerity in his pseudonymous pamphlet against de L'Estoile. Calvin wrote the foreword to *Antapologia* in the form of a letter that was dated March 6, 1531, and addressed to his friend François de Connan, who was definitely on the side of Alciati. In the foreword (*Praefatio in Nic. Chemini Antapologiam*—*CO* 9:785–86), Calvin states why the treatise was written and why he endorses it. This foreword was Calvin's first publication.[2]

Commentary on Seneca's *De clementia* (1532)

On April 4, 1532, Calvin's first scholarly publication appeared, a commentary on *De clementia* ("On Clemency"), a work of the Roman philosopher Seneca. The full title of Calvin's work read: *L. Annei Senecae, Romani senatoris, ac philosophi clarissimi, libri duo de clementia, ad Neronem Caesarem: Ioannis Calvini Nouiodunaei commentariis illustrati* (*CO* 5:1–162).[3]

2. For an English translation see Ford Lewis Battles and André Malan Hugo, *Calvin's Commentary on Seneca's De Clementia* (Leiden, 1969), 385–86.

3. See H. Lecoultre, "Calvin d'après son commentaire sur le De Clementia de Sénèque," *RThPh* 24 (1891): 51–77; Quirinus Breen, *John Calvin: A Study in French Humanism* (Grand Rapids, 1931), 67–99; André Malan Hugo, *Calvijn en Seneca* (Groningen, 1957); Battles and Hugo, *Calvin's Commentary on Seneca's De Clementia;* and François Wendel, "Le Commentaire sur le *De clementia* de Sénèque," in *Calvin et l'humanisme* (Paris, 1976), 37–62.

Seneca was born around the beginning of the Christian Era in Cordova, Spain, and studied philosophy and rhetoric in Rome. As a philosopher he was a disciple of the strict Stoic school. He was involved in the education of Nero, who would later become emperor. As both Nero's minister and an adherent of Stoic morality, he was placed in the awkward position of not being able to approve of the emperor's conduct.

The church fathers, Augustine in particular, frequently cite Seneca to buttress their arguments. In fact, a fictitious correspondence between Seneca and the apostle Paul was produced, probably in the fourth century, to portray Seneca as a Christian philosopher. Calvin very likely came into contact with Seneca during his first years of study in Paris. It is possible that he was struck by Seneca's appeal to Emperor Nero to show clemency to the heretics in Rome. King Francis I should be able to take a more benevolent position toward the evangelicals! Perhaps what drew Calvin to Seneca was the Christian humanists' sensitivity to Stoic ideas. Calvin himself never offered an explanation.

What is certain is that Erasmus published the works of Seneca in 1521 and an improved edition in 1529. Erasmus, who never put aside his text-critical labors on Seneca, did not consider his edition to be perfect; accordingly, Calvin indicates in the foreword to his commentary on Seneca's *De clementia* that here and there he will correct Erasmus. Moreover, he intends by means of this critical commentary to bring about a certain rehabilitation of Seneca— not so much of his ideas, but of the place that he deserves as a stylist and a philosopher. Above all Calvin hoped through this commentary to establish his reputation as a humanist scholar.

Erasmus's widely read treatise *De ratione studii, ac legendi interpretandique auctores* appeared in Strasbourg in 1521. Methodologically, Calvin shows himself to be a worthy student of Erasmus in his critical commentary on Seneca's treatise. First, he briefly summarizes Seneca's train of thought. Then he provides linguistic and stylistic commentary, followed by illustrations with citations from a large number of Latin (75) and Greek (22) authors. This is not to say that Calvin had read all of these writers; he was able to profit from handbooks published by others. He also quotes several church fathers, particularly Augustine, and cites three passages from the Bible.

In his commentary, Calvin points out the resemblance between the Stoic and Christian conceptions of providence, expresses a preference for monarchy, and suggests that the conscience contains a natural law (cf. ancient philosophy). Calvin dedicated his work on April 4, 1532, to Claude de Hangest, who had become abbot in Noyon and had played an important role in Calvin's acquisition of one or more of his study benefices. Calvin sent a copy of the commentary to Erasmus.

Calvin wrote François Daniel on April 22 (*CO* 10b:19–20) that his commentary on Seneca was out: "Finally, the die is cast." He also informed Daniel that the book, which he had had published at his own expense, was selling poorly. He had requested several professors in Paris to use it in their classes, and perhaps a professor in Bourges would also switch to it. He is sending Daniel a copy of the book and asks that he help with its sale. If Daniel sees any possibilities for that, Calvin will send him a hundred more copies.

Nicolas Cop's Academic Address (1533)

On November 1, 1533 (All Saints' Day), at the official opening of the new academic year and in the presence of professors and ecclesiastical dignitaries, Nicolas Cop, rector of the University of Paris, delivered a sharply worded address (*Concio academica nomine rectoris universitatis Parisiensis scripta*—*CO* 9:873–76; *CO* 10b:30–36; and *OS* 1:4–10).[4] In the introduction he talked about Christian philosophy (*philosophia christiana*) and then went on to expound upon Matthew 5:3 ("Blessed are the poor in spirit"), calling attention to the difference between law and gospel.

What Cop was saying was not entirely new. From what sources, then, was he drawing? According to August Lang, what he had to say about Christian philosophy reminds one of the foreword to the third edition of Erasmus's Greek New Testament.[5] There is a similar connection, according to Lang, between Cop's address and a sermon delivered by Martin Luther on All Saints' Day, 1522, which Martin Bucer translated into Latin and published in Strasbourg in 1526. Finally, there is a relationship between Cop's address and passages in both Philipp Melanchthon's *Loci communes* (1521) and Bucer's commentary on the Gospels (1530).

Much attention has also been devoted to the question of who the real author of Cop's address was—Cop himself or Calvin? Because two old copies

---

4. See Appendix 3, "The Academic Discourse. Delivered by Nicolas Cop on Assuming the Rectorship of the University of Paris on 1 November 1533" (English translation and notes), in John Calvin, *Institutes of the Christian Religion* (1536 edition), ed. Ford Lewis Battles, rev. ed. (Grand Rapids, 1986), 363–72. See also Jean Rott, "Documents strasbourgeois concernant Calvin. I. Un Manuscrit autographe: La Harangue du recteur Nicolas Cop," *RHPhR* 44 (1964): 290–311 (this material can also be found in *Regards contemporains sur Jean Calvin: Actes du colloque Calvin Strasbourg 1964* [Paris, 1965], 28–49); and Joseph N. Tylenda, "Calvin's First Reformed Sermon? Nicholas Cop's Discourse—1 November 1533," *WThJ* 38 (1975–76): 300–318. Tylenda also provides an English translation (with notes) of Cop's address.

5. August Lang, *Die Bekehrung Johannes Calvins* (Leipzig, 1897; reprint, Aalen, 1972). See also the secondary sources listed in note 4.

of the speech have been preserved, a complete one in Cop's hand in Strasbourg and a partial one in Calvin's hand in Geneva, the question arises, Which of the two is the original? In any case, as far as the content of the address is concerned, Cop must have benefited from Calvin's theological knowledge.

One of the results of Cop's speech was that on November 3 two Franciscan monks lodged a complaint of heresy against Cop with the Parlement of Paris. He was called to account but decided at the last moment to secretly leave the city. After consultation with Francis I, who was not in Paris at the time, it was decided to set a price on Cop's head. Persecution of the "cursed Lutheran sect" (the words of Francis I) broke out, followed by the arrests of, among others, the ministers Gérard Roussel and Elie Coraud.

An indication that Calvin had some involvement in Cop's address is that he too secretly departed the city before the authorities could have him arrested. In so doing, he left behind his books and letters.

3

Calvin and the Bible

Bible Translation
Calvin's Commentaries
   The Commentaries on the New Testament
      Commentary on the Epistle to the Romans
      Commentaries on 1 and 2 Corinthians
      Commentary on Galatians, Ephesians, Philippians, and Colossians
      Commentary on 1 and 2 Timothy
      Commentary on Hebrews
      Commentary on Titus
      Commentaries on 1 and 2 Thessalonians and Philemon
      Commentary on James
      Commentary on James, 1 and 2 Peter, 1 John, and Jude
      Commentary on Acts
      Commentary on John
      Commentary on the Synoptic Gospels
   The Commentaries on the Old Testament
      Commentary on Isaiah
      Commentary on Genesis
      Commentary on the Psalms
      Commentary on Exodus through Deuteronomy
      Commentary on Joshua
Calvin's Lectures (*Praelectiones*)
   Lectures on Hosea
   Lectures on the Minor Prophets
   Lectures on Daniel
   Lectures on Jeremiah and Lamentations
   Lectures on Ezekiel

Calvin's Sermons
Contributions to the Weekly Bible Studies (*Congrégations*)

Early on it appeared that Calvin wished to stimulate as much use of the Bible by the common people as possible. Because of the growing interest in the Bible, he had plans to produce an edition of sermons by Chrysostom, believing that these sermons would greatly contribute to the use of Scripture. A hand-written foreword for the edition, dating probably from 1535, is extant in Geneva (for the text see *CO* 9:831–38). According to Calvin, Chrysostom deserves a lot of credit for allowing the Scriptures to speak for themselves and for paying so much attention to the simple meaning of the words.[1]

Bible Translation

Calvin was closely connected to Olivetanus's French translation of the Bible, which came off the press on June 4, 1535. The title page indicates that the text of the translation is based entirely on the Hebrew and Greek, but that does not take away from the fact that Olivetanus made use of other translations as well. As far as the Old Testament is concerned, he relied especially on the translation by Jacques Lefèvre d'Etaples, which had appeared in 1530, although Olivetanus did produce his own translation of the Psalms. He also made frequent use of the work of Lefèvre in translating the apocryphal writings.

At Guillaume Farel's urging, the Waldenses had decided to provide financial support for Olivetanus's Bible translation. They had done so on September 12, 1532, during a meeting of the synod in Chanforans, where they at the same time made the decision to join the Reformation.

In the foreword of February 12, 1535, Olivetanus dedicates his translation not to some important person, but to "the poor church." The translation, which was published by Pierre de Wingle in Serrières near Neuchâtel, was presented to the synod of the Waldenses in Chanforans in September 1535.[2]

---

1. John H. McIndoe gives an English translation of the foreword in "John Calvin: Preface to the Homilies of Chrysostom," *Hartford Quarterly* 5 (1965): 19–26. See also John Robert Walchenbach, *John Calvin as Biblical Commentator: An Investigation into Calvin's Use of John Chrysostom as an Exegetical Tutor* (Pittsburgh, 1974); Alexandre Ganoczy and Klaus Müller, *Calvins handschriftliche Annotationen zu Chrysostomus: Ein Beitrag zur Hermeneutik Calvins* (Wiesbaden, 1981).

2. See *The Cambridge History of the Bible*, vol. 3, *The West from the Reformation to the Present Day*, ed. S. L. Greenslade (New York, 1978), 117–20; Eugénie Droz, "Calvin collaborateur de la Bible de Neuchâtel," in idem, *Chemins de l'hérésie: Textes et documents*, 4 vols. (Geneva, 1970–76), 1:102–17; Jürgen Quack, "Calvins Bibelvorreden (1535–1546)," in idem, *Evangelische Bibelvorreden von der Reformation bis zur Aufklärung* (Gütersloh, 1975), 89–116.

The Latin foreword, which appears only in the edition of 1535, is by Calvin and has as its title *Ioannes Calvinus caesaribus, regibus, principibus, gentibusque omnibus Christi imperio subditis salutem (CO* 9:787–90).[3] In the foreword Calvin pleads for the Bible in the vernacular so that all believers will be able to have a direct knowledge of what Scripture says. He talks about "impious voices" (the Sorbonne) who deprive simple folk of the Word of God or at least of direct contact with the Word. That is in conflict with true piety and with the intention of God, who has always been pleased to reveal himself to the poor and chose his prophets and apostles from among shepherds and sinners. Calvin also criticizes the priests and bishops who, as shepherds of the sheep, withhold the real food (the Word of God) and offer contaminated fare instead (their own ideas). He declares the bishop of Rome and his priests to be guilty because they have hidden the light under a bushel.

A second foreword precedes the New Testament. It is anonymous and written in French, but after 1545 it was associated with Calvin. The heading of this foreword reads: *A tous amateurs de Iésus Christ, et de son S. Evangile, salut (CO* 9:791–822; a Latin version was published by Theodore Beza in 1576 in his *Lettres et avis de Calvin*). In this foreword Christ is extolled as the mediator of the new covenant that is the fulfilment of the old. We cannot do without the gospel. Without it we are not Christians. In their introduction to this foreword, Irena Backus and Claire Chimelli point out its relationship to two other writings.[4] In form it resembles the Latin foreword to the Vulgate published by Robert Estienne in 1532.[5] In content it more closely resembles Heinrich Bullinger's 1534 treatise on the covenant.[6]

The French foreword by Calvin that appears in the edition of 1535 is missing in the editions of 1539 and 1543. We note, however, that a work by Calvin and Pierre Viret that dealt with the Bible and in particular with the relationship between the Old and New Testaments did appear in Geneva in 1543. This work consisted of two letters, the first of which, written by Calvin, showed "how Jesus Christ is the end of the law, and the sum of all that it is necessary

3. See Appendix 4, "John Calvin's Latin Preface to Olivetan's French Bible (1535)," in John Calvin, *Institutes of the Christian Religion* (1536 edition), ed. Ford Lewis Battles, rev. ed. (Grand Rapids, 1986), 373–77.

4. *La Vraie Piété: Divers traités de Jean Calvin et Confession de foi de Guillaume Farel,* ed. Irena Backus and Claire Chimelli (Geneva, 1986), 17–23.

5. *Biblia: Breves in eadem annotationes ex doctissimis interpretationibus et Hebraeorum commentariis* (Paris, 1532).

6. *De testamento seu foedere Dei unico et aeterno Heinrychi Bullingeri brevis expositio* (Zurich, 1534).

to look for in Scripture."[7] Calvin's French foreword of 1535 again appeared in the edition of the Bible published in Geneva in 1544, but with a small addition taken from the letter of 1543. From 1551 on, the title of the foreword read: *Epistre aux fidèles monstrant comment Christ est la fin de la loy.*

Olivetanus's Bible translation of 1535 also contains the clause, *V.F.C. à nostre allié et confédéré le peuple de l'alliance de Sinai, Salut* ("V.F.C. to our ally and confederate, the people of the covenant of Sinai, Greetings"). The initials V.F.C. have been understood as an abbreviation for *Votre Frère Calvin* ("Your Brother Calvin"),[8] but they have also been connected with *V*iret, *F*arel, and *C*alvin. More recently, the research of Bernard Roussel has concluded that *V*(=W)olfgang *F*abricius *C*apito was meant.[9]

Following the edition of 1535, Olivetanus was aware that the French translation of the New Testament could be improved, so he asked for Calvin's cooperation with the project. Calvin promised that he would correct Olivetanus's separate translation of the New Testament before it went to press. In 1540 a revised edition appeared.

Meanwhile, Sebastian Castellio, the rector of the school in Geneva since 1540, also intended to publish a translation of the New Testament. On September 9, 1542, he approached Calvin with the request to approve his translation. Calvin did not want to hold up the edition, but he informed Castellio that quite a few corrections would be necessary. No agreement could be reached. Castellio did not want to have the translation corrected, but he did want to arrange for Calvin to go over it and discuss it with him. Calvin would not go along with that proposal, however, since he had the impression that Castellio would argue endlessly about each suggested correction (see *CO* 13:439—the letter written to Pierre Viret on September 11). Castellio later completed his Bible translation in Basel. The Latin edition appeared in 1551 and the French in 1555.

Calvin also proved to be heavily involved in the revised edition of Olivetanus's translation of the whole Bible. The first revised edition from Calvin's hand dates from 1546. This edition also contains a foreword by Calvin just before the apocryphal writings (*Préface mise en tête des livres apocryphes de*

7. The complete title of the two letters reads: *Deux épistres, l'une demonstre comment nostre Seigneur Iésus Christ est la fin de la loy, et la somme de tout ce qu'il faut chercher en l'Escriture. Composée par M. I. Calvin. L'autre, pour consoler les fidèles qui souffrent pour le nom de Iésus, et pour les instruire à se gouverner en temps d'adversité et de prospérité, et les confirmer contre les tentations et assautz de la mort. Composée par M. P. Viret.*

8. Droz, *Chemins*, 1:108–15 (with a facsimile from the Neuchâtel Bible!).

9. See Dominique Barthélemy, Henri Meylan, and Bernard Roussel, *Olivétan: Celui qui fit passer la Bible d'hébreu en français*, Textes de Calvin et d'Olivétan (Biel, 1986).

l'ancien testament—*CO* 9:827–28). In the editions of 1555 and 1560 this fore-word has been abridged. It is probable that the foreword preceding the Apoc-rypha in Olivetanus's Bible of 1535 was also by Calvin.[10]

Calvin must also have devoted a lot of attention to the second revised edi-tion of the Bible (1551), as his letter to Farel on November 10, 1550, indicates (*CO* 13:655–57). There he reports that for the past four months he has been busy with the revision of Olivetanus's Bible translation because, despite his request, the printers have not found anyone else for the job and there is a lot of demand for this translation. He himself has involved Louis Budé (who at the time was lecturing on the Old Testament at the Collège de La Rive in Geneva) and Theodore Beza in the work. Budé, Calvin writes to Farel, will concentrate on the translation of the Psalms, Proverbs, Ecclesiastes, and Job.

How far Budé actually got we do not know. He died on May 25, 1551, before the new translation was published. He had at least finished his work on the Psalms, which not only appeared in the edition of 1551, but was also published the same year in Geneva as a separate work with notes (*Les Pseaumes de David traduicts selon la vérité hébraïque*). Calvin wrote a foreword for this edition in which he discusses the usefulness both of the Psalms (cf. the more personal foreword to his commentary on the Psalms) and of Budé's translation.[11]

Calvin, Budé, and an unknown third person who was responsible for the Minor Prophets were engaged in revising the translation of the Old Testament for the edition of 1551; Beza worked on the Apocrypha. After 1551 further revi-sions were published in 1553 and 1560. The definitive edition finally appeared in 1588.

Calvin's Commentaries

When Farel successfully detained Calvin in Geneva in 1536, the latter began his work as a lecturer (*sacrarum literarum doctor*) at Saint Pierre on the epistles of Paul. We know that he began sometime before September 5, for it was on that date that Farel asked the Council to provide for the support of "that Frenchman" who had begun giving the required lectures. Sometime before 1537 Calvin also took up his duties as a minister in Geneva, but his instruction of students in the Scriptures was always very important to him.

---

10. See Wilhelm H. Neuser, "Calvins Stellung zu den Apokryphen des Alten Testaments," in *Text-Wort-Glaube: Studien zur Überlieferung, Interpretation und Autorisierung biblischer Texte*, ed. Martin Brecht (New York, 1980), 298–323. Neuser provides a German translation of the forewords of 1535 and 1546 (pp. 311–12).

11. Rodolphe Peter, "Calvin and Louis Budé's Translation of the Psalms," in *Courtenay Studies in Reformation Theology*, vol. 1, *John Calvin*, ed. Gervase E. Duffield (Grand Rapids, 1966), 190–209.

When Calvin went to Strasbourg in 1538, he first became the pastor of the French refugee congregation. But after January 1, 1539, he also lectured on the Gospel of John and 1 Corinthians to students at the gymnasium headed up by Jean Sturm. On February 1, 1539, he was appointed teacher of New Testament interpretation.

Calvin did not limit himself to giving lectures; he also went on to write commentaries. Because he began by writing on the books of the New Testament, we shall devote our attention first of all to his commentaries on the New Testament.[12] We will then turn to those he wrote on the Old Testament.

The Commentaries on the New Testament

Commentary on the Epistle to the Romans

The first commentary Calvin published was on the Epistle to the Romans, which came off the press in Strasbourg in March 1540.[13] The contents are probably a revised summary of lectures he had given in Geneva from 1536 to 1538.

At the beginning of the commentary we find a letter Calvin had written on October 18, 1539, to Simon Grynaeus (see *CO* 10:402), who in 1529 had become a professor of Greek in Basel, and in March 1536 had begun his lectures as a professor of theology with a treatment of the Epistle to the Romans. In the letter Calvin reminds Grynaeus of the conversation they had had a few years earlier about the criteria for a good commentary.[14] They had agreed that the principal virtue of an exegete is *perspicua brevitas,* by which they meant that dogmatic explanations should be kept as brief as possible. Furthermore, an exegete must concentrate on the *mens scriptoris,* that is to say, on making clear what a given writer intended to say. Calvin doubts that he has reached the ideal of a good commentary, but he has always had that ideal in mind. He is well

12. See T. H. L. Parker, *Calvin's New Testament Commentaries* (London, 1971).

13. *Commentarii in Epistolam Pauli ad Romanos.* Improved editions appeared in 1551 and 1556. For the text (of 1556 and the variants from 1551) see *CO* 49:1–292. A new edition of the commentary was produced by T. H. L. Parker: *Iohannis Calvini Commentarius in Epistolam Pauli ad Romanos* (Leiden, 1981). Parker gives the text of the commentary of 1556 with the variants from the editions of 1540 and 1551. A complete French translation of Calvin's commentary on the Epistle to the Romans appeared in 1550 (*Commentaire de M. Iean Calvin sur l'Epistre aux Romains*) after only summaries had been published in 1543 and 1545 (respectively, *Exposition sur l'Epistre de Sainct Paul aux Romains: Extraicte des commentaires de M. I. Calvin,* and *Argument et sommaire de l'Epistre Sainct Paul aux Romains, pour donner intelligence à toute l'épistre en peu de parolles. Par Iehan Calvin*). See also Benoit Girardin, *Rhétorique et théologie: Calvin, le commentaire de l'Epître aux Romains* (Paris, 1979); T. H. L. Parker, "Calvin the Exegete: Change and Development," in *Calvinus ecclesiae doctor,* ed. Wilhelm H. Neuser (Kampen, 1980), 33–46.

14. Hans-Joachim Kraus, "Calvin's Exegetical Principles," *Interpretation* 31 (1977): 8–18; Parker, *Calvin's New Testament Commentaries,* 49–68.

aware that others have written commentaries on Romans, both long ago and more recently. He mentions in particular the outstanding work of Philipp Melanchthon, Heinrich Bullinger, and Martin Bucer. He also notes that exegetes will not always agree with each other, for the Lord God has not given any one person full insight into everything. That ought to lead us to humility and cooperation. An exegete should not allow himself to be guided by a passion for innovation or a desire to polemicize; he must not attack another nor seek to satisfy his own ambition.

In the foreword to his commentary Calvin says that the Letter to the Romans, rightly understood, is a key that gives access to all the hidden treasures of Scripture. Then he gives an overview of the contents of the epistle. In that connection he mentions the fact that we are justified through faith, which is treated in the first five chapters and serves as the main theme of the entire epistle.

Commentaries on 1 and 2 Corinthians

The commentary on the Epistle to the Romans was followed by a number of others. We do not include here the exposition of the Epistle of Jude, which was published by Calvin in 1542 and again in 1545, the second time with an exposition of 1 and 2 Peter.[15] These publications were probably lectures that he had given; moreover, his later commentary on Jude and 1 and 2 Peter does not even mention them. The first real commentaries to follow the one on Romans were those on 1 and 2 Corinthians.[16]

Calvin dedicated the commentary on 1 Corinthians on January 24, 1546, to Jacques de Bourgogne, lord of Falais and Breda. The letter (for the text see *CO* 12:258–60) served also as the foreword to the commentary. De Falais had grown up in the court of Charles V and had joined the Reformation already in his youth. On October 14, 1543, Calvin (under the name Charles d'Espeville) had advised de Falais and his wife Yolande de Brederode to emigrate, because they no longer felt safe in France (*CO* 11:628–32). They both departed for Geneva in 1545, but remained in Strasbourg when de Falais became ill. In the

15. *Exposition sur l'Epistre de Sainct Iudas apostre de nostre Seigneur Iésus Christ. Composée par M. Iean Calvin* (Geneva, 1542; *CO* 55:501–16); and *Exposition sur les deux Epistres de S. Pierre et l'Epistre de S. Iude, traduit de latin* (Geneva, 1545).

16. Latin: *Iohannis Calvini Commentarii in priorem Epistolam Pauli ad Corinthios* (Strasbourg, 1546—*CO* 49:293–574), and *Ioannis Calvini Commentarii in secundam Pauli Epistolam ad Corinthios* (Geneva, 1548—*CO* 50:1–156); French: *Commentaire de M. Iean Calvin, sur la première Epistre aux Corinthiens, traduit de latin en françois* (Geneva, 1547), and *Commentaire de M. Iean Calvin, sur la seconde Epistre aux Corinthiens, traduit de latin en françois* (Geneva, 1547).

foreword Calvin holds de Falais up as an example, for in him we find, in the spirit of Paul, an expression of the gospel manifesting itself in spiritual power.

On January 24, 1556, Calvin wrote a whole new foreword for the new edition of his commentary on 1 Corinthians, for after the debate with Jérôme Bolsec, Calvin and de Falais had become estranged. The new foreword now replaced the original one. But de Falais should not feel distressed by this, writes Calvin, for he has not merely striven to estrange himself from me, but also wishes to have nothing to do with "our church." Calvin makes clear that he does not enjoy removing de Falais's name, for in so doing he is departing from the usual practice.

Calvin dedicated the new edition to Galeazzo Caraccioli di Vico, an Italian of distinguished ancestry, who because of his faith had left Naples and his wife and family, and had settled in Geneva. Calvin holds up di Vico's self-denial as an example. May God give both di Vico and himself, he writes, the gift of perseverance.

Calvin dedicated his commentary on 2 Corinthians on August 1, 1546, to Melchior Wolmar, whose acquaintance he had made as a student in Orléans, where Wolmar taught Greek. It was Calvin's intention to have the commentary printed by Wendelin Rihel in Strasbourg, something to which he felt obligated, he writes Farel (see *CO* 12:391), because Rihel had helped him out when he was in financial straits. Having sent the manuscript of the commentary on 2 Corinthians to Strasbourg, Calvin worried about it for a whole month because he thought that it had disappeared on the way (so he wrote to Farel; see *CO* 12:380–81). In the future, therefore, before sending anything away, he would first make a copy for himself. It is not clear whether the commentary on 2 Corinthians was actually published in Strasbourg in 1546. At any rate, the French edition appeared in 1547 in Geneva, where the Latin edition was also published a year later. All of Calvin's subsequent commentaries were also printed in Geneva.

Commentary on Galatians, Ephesians, Philippians, and Colossians

In 1548 Calvin's commentary on the epistles of Paul to the Galatians, Ephesians, Philippians, and Colossians came off the press in Geneva.[17] Calvin dedicated the commentary on February 1, 1548, to Christoph, duke of Württemberg (*CO* 12:658), who also had control over the territory of Mont-

---

17. Latin: *Ioannis Calvini Commentarii in quatuor Pauli Epistolas: Ad Galatas, ad Ephesios, ad Philippenses, ad Colossenses* (Geneva, 1548—*CO* 50:157–268; 51:137–240; and 52:1–132); French: *Commentaire de M. Iean Calvin, sur quatre Epistres de Sainct Paul: Assavoir, aux Galatiens, Ephésiens, Philippiens, Colossiens* (Geneva, 1548).

béliard, where in 1543 and 1544 Pierre Toussaint and others had encountered problems when the duke tried to introduce Lutheran practices there. Calvin says that he was urged to write the dedication to the duke by Pierre Toussaint, who had spoken about the duke with praise. Calvin believed that by reading his commentary, the duke, who knew Latin, would be encouraged to continue on the right course. He also held up the duke as an example because he had weathered every storm with calm and composure. Calvin did not mention the problems in the past with Lutheran practices.

Commentary on 1 and 2 Timothy

Calvin's contact with England began in 1548. On July 25 he dedicated his commentary on the epistles to Timothy[18] to Edward Seymour, duke of Somerset, who from 1547 to 1549 served as the guardian of young King Edward VI, administered the government (*CO* 13:16–18), and with Thomas Cranmer's support introduced the Reformation into England. Calvin praises the duke for his zeal for reform and hopes that Seymour can finish his work in that area according to the pattern of church government that Paul lays out for Timothy.

In thanks for this dedication, Calvin received a ring from Anne Stanhope, the duke of Somerset's wife, for which he sent a letter of thanks on June 17, 1549 (*CO* 13:300–302), to Anne Seymour, the duke's highly educated daughter. He asked her to convey his gratitude and at the same time urged her to stay the good course of following Christ.

Commentary on Hebrews

Calvin requested permission from the Council on March 25, 1549, to print his commentary on the Epistle to the Hebrews. He assured them that he did not desire to have any book printed that was not based on Scripture. Permission was granted, and his commentary appeared in both Latin and French the same year.[19]

In the foreword of May 23, 1549, Calvin dedicates the commentary to King Sigismund August of Poland (*CO* 13:281–86). He writes that the Letter to the Hebrews contains a full discussion of the eternal divinity of Christ, his exalted teaching office, and his unique priesthood, which are the salient points of celestial wisdom. Since the teaching of the book explains the power and office of Christ to us so vividly, it is incumbent upon the church to honor the epistle

---

18. Latin: *Ioannis Calvini Commentarii in utramque Pauli Epistolam ad Timotheum* (Geneva, 1548—*CO* 52:241–396); French: *Commentaire de M. Iean Calvin, sur les deux Epistres de Sainct Paul à Timothée, traduit du latin* (Geneva, 1548).

19. Latin: *Ioannis Calvini Commentarii in Epistolam ad Hebraeos* (Geneva, 1549—*CO* 55:1–198); French: *Commentaire de M. Iean Calvin, sur l'Epistre aux Ebrieux* (Geneva, 1549).

as a treasure without equal. In the dedication Calvin remembers the little book that Johann Eck wrote on the mass and dedicated to the father of the king. He hopes that people will realize that what Eck calls a sacrifice stands in clear contradiction to the priesthood of Christ. He also appeals to Sigismund to promote the Reformation in Poland.[20]

Commentary on Titus

In 1550 Calvin's commentary on Titus appeared in Geneva in both Latin and French.[21] Calvin wrote the foreword on November 29, 1549, dedicating the commentary to Guillaume Farel and Pierre Viret, whom he calls "true servants of Jesus Christ, his well-beloved brothers, and colaborers in the work of our Lord Jesus Christ" (for the foreword see *CO* 13:477–78).

Commentaries on 1 and 2 Thessalonians and Philemon

On February 17, 1550, Calvin wrote the foreword (see *CO* 13:525–26) to his commentary on 1 Thessalonians, dedicating it to Mathurin Cordier, who had taught him Latin. In the foreword Calvin expresses his gratitude to Cordier for the instruction he had received, and goes on to say that he wishes everyone who profits from his commentaries to know that to a certain degree they have his schoolmaster Cordier to thank. The commentary itself was not printed until 1551, when it appeared in a complete edition of the epistles of Paul.[22] The same was true of the commentary on 2 Thessalonians, which Calvin dedicated on July 1, 1550, to Benoit Textor (see *CO* 13:598), the family doctor.[23]

The aforementioned 1551 edition of Paul's epistles (*In omnes Pauli epistolas atque etiam in Epistolam ad Hebraeos*), with a foreword by Theodore Beza, also contains Calvin's commentary on the Epistle to Philemon (*CO* 52:437–50), which had not been published previously. A French translation of this commentary was included in the 1556 French edition of the epistles of Paul, the Epistle to the Hebrews, and the General Epistles.

Commentary on James

The commentary on the Epistle to James came off the press in 1550.[24] This commentary was the product of the meetings that the ministers held on Fri-

---

20. This dedication of the commentary on the Epistle to the Hebrews to King Sigismund marked the beginning of Calvin's contact with Poland. See Oscar Bartel, "Calvin und Polen," in *Regards contemporains sur Jean Calvin: Actes du colloque Strasbourg 1964* (Paris, 1965), 253–68.

21. Latin: *Commentarii in Epistolam ad Titum* (Geneva, 1550—*CO* 52:397–436); French: *Commentaire de M. Iean Calvin, sur l'Epistre à Tite* (Geneva, 1550).

22. *Commentarii in priorem Epistolam ad Thessalonicenses* (*CO* 52:133–80).

23. *Commentarii in posteriorem Epistolam ad Thessalonicenses* (*CO* 52:181–218).

24. *Commentaire de M. Iean Calvin, sur l'Epistre de Sainct Jacques* (Geneva, 1550—*CO* 55:377–436).

days and would appear again in early 1551 in a commentary that also contained an exposition of 1 and 2 Peter, 1 John, and Jude.

Commentary on James, 1 and 2 Peter, 1 John, and Jude

On January 24, 1551, Calvin dedicated his commentary on James, 1 and 2 Peter, 1 John, and Jude to King Edward VI of England (*CO* 14:30–37).[25] In the dedication he writes extensively about the Council of Trent. In an accompanying piece (*CO* 14:38–41) he states that he trusts that the king will accept the dedication. Here Calvin holds up King Josiah as an example of the restoration of pure religion. There are indifferent things that one may tolerate, but the rule should always be that the clarity of the gospel not be obscured by all sorts of ceremonies. Examples of abuses are prayers for the souls of the dead, intercession of the saints (which supplants prayer to God), and the swearing of an oath in the name of a saint. Calvin requests the king to take action against whatever corrupts true Christianity. He also points out the importance of good training for prospective ministers and, in that connection, of the reformation of the university. He had this commentary personally delivered to England by Nicolas de La Fontaine, along with his commentary on Isaiah, which he had also dedicated to the king a short time before.

Commentary on Acts

The commentary on Acts came out in two parts.[26] On February 29, 1552, Calvin dedicated the commentary on Acts 1–13 to Christian III, king of Denmark (see *CO* 14:292–96). In the dedication he attacks the heralds of the Antichrist in Rome, who continually have the word *church* on their lips, but lead the common people astray. We can talk about the kingdom of Christ only if we proclaim the gospel by which Christ gathers and leads his church, and if we regard as the true people of Christ the fellowship of believers bound to each other by faith. This commentary was printed in 1552 in both Latin and a French translation.

Calvin dedicated the commentary on Acts 14–28 on January 25, 1554, to Crown Prince Frederick of Denmark, who had been appointed coregent by his father (see *CO* 15:14–17). In the dedication Calvin commends the prince's

25. Latin: *Ioannis Calvini Commentarii in Epistolas Canonicas, unam Petri, unam Ioannis, unam Iacobi, Petri alteram, Iudae unam* (Geneva, 1551—*CO* 55:201–500); French: *Commentaires de M. Iean Calvin sur les Canoniques* (Geneva, 1551).

26. Latin: *Commentariorum Ioannis Calvini in Acta Apostolorum, liber 1* (Geneva, 1552—*CO* 48:1–317); French: *Le Premier Livre des Commentaires de M. Iean Calvin, sur les Actes des Apostres* (Geneva, 1552); Latin: *Commentarius Ioannis Calvini in Acta Apostolorum, liber posterior* (Geneva, 1554—*CO* 48:317–574); French: *Le Second Livre des Commentaires de M. Iean Calvin, sur les Actes des Apostres* (Geneva, 1554).

father for so effectively introducing the Reformation into his country. He thinks it profitable to direct the prince's attention to Luke's description of the origin of the church, so that the prince might be encouraged in the carrying out of his obligation as a Christian prince to protect the kingdom of Christ. The Latin and French editions of the commentary both appeared in 1554.

Calvin dedicated the second edition of his commentary on Acts on August 11, 1560, to Nicolaus Radziwil, count palatine in Vilnius (*CO* 18:155–61), who had strongly promoted the Reformation among the Polish nobility, had the Bible translated into Polish, and had evangelical preachers called from Germany. Calvin had also corresponded with him before (see *CO* 15:428–29, 906–8; *CO* 17:181–82).

Commentary on John

On January 1, 1553, Calvin wrote the foreword to his commentary on the Gospel of John. Both the Latin and the French editions were published in Geneva in 1553.[27] Calvin dedicated the commentary to the syndics and the Council of Geneva (see *CO* 47:iv–vi). In the dedication he refers to Geneva as a refuge center for Christians who have been driven out from other places. That is significant in light of Christ's statement that he regards the taking in of strangers as something done personally to him. In the midst of confusion may the Council know that Christ will be nearby protecting those cities where the gospel can be proclaimed and his people are allowed to live. Calvin also expresses the hope that even after his death the Council and the people will profit from what he has written. It would be unfortunate if the instruction that has gone forth from Geneva to other nations would bear less fruit in the city itself than far beyond its borders. On January 5 Calvin delivered a copy of the commentary to the Council.

Commentary on the Synoptic Gospels

Calvin wrote the dedication for his commentary on the first three Gospels on August 1, 1555. The Latin edition appeared in 1555, as did the French.[28] The dedication (see *CO* 15:710–12) was addressed to the Council of Frankfurt in

---

27. Latin: *In Evangelium secundum Iohannem, Commentarius Iohannis Calvini* (Geneva, 1553—*CO* 47:1–458); French: *Commentaire sur l'Evangile selon Sainct Iean* (Geneva, 1553).

28. Latin: *Harmonia ex tribus Evangelistis composita, Matthaeo, Marco et Luca; adiuncto seorsum Iohanne, quod pauca cum aliis communa habeat. Cum Calvini Commentariis* (Geneva, 1555—*CO* 45); French: *Concordance qu'on appelle Harmonie, composée de trois Evangelistes, asçavoir S. Matthieu, S. Marc, et S. Luc; item, l'Evangile selon Sainct Iehan: Le Tout avec les Commentaires de M. Iehan Calvin* (Geneva, 1555). See also Dieter Schellong, *Calvins Auslegung der synoptischen Evangelien* (Munich, 1969).

response to efforts by Joachim Westphal to have the English refugee congregations that had existed in Frankfurt since 1554 expelled from the city. At the end of 1554 Westphal had published his *Collectanea sententiarum D. Aurelii Augustini de coena Domini* in Frankfurt and dedicated it to the Council of the city. In this work he cites Augustine as a major support for the Lutheran conception of the Lord's Supper.

In the commentary on the Synoptics, Calvin discusses the text primarily on the basis of the sequence in Matthew, but within this framework he also deals with Mark and Luke. In so doing, he is following in the footsteps of Martin Bucer, who published a commentary on the Synoptic Gospels in 1527. Calvin writes in the introduction to the commentary that at first glance many will probably not agree with the way he treats the material. But it is clear, he adds, that none of the three Gospels can be interpreted without comparison with the other two. To prevent having to page back and forth, therefore, it seemed to him that it would be helpful to place the three Gospels side by side in a table as it were, so that one could clearly see where they do and do not agree with each other.

Calvin also writes in the introduction that the authors of the Gospels were guided through their thoughts to show above all that Christ is truly the Son of God, the Redeemer whom God had promised to the world. In what they write they do not intend in any way to do away with the Law and the Prophets. Calvin is directing this comment against the Anabaptists, for whom (he says) the Old Testament has now become superfluous. He goes on to say that the Gospel writers point directly to Christ and urge us to seek in him the fulfilment of what the Law and the Prophets proclaim. We read the gospel with profit, therefore, only if we learn to see the connection between it and the promises from an earlier time.

The Commentaries on the Old Testament

Commentary on Isaiah

The commentary on Isaiah, which appeared in 1551,[29] was the first commentary in which Calvin engaged in the interpretation of the Old Testament.[30] It was not put together by Calvin himself, however, since he did not have enough time to devote to it then. In 1549 Nicolas Des Gallars (Gallasius) had attended Calvin's lectures on Isaiah, taken notes, and then developed them at home, letting Calvin read the finished product for possible corrections. Calvin dedi-

---

29. Latin: *Ioannis Calvini Commentarii in Isaiam prophetam* (Geneva, 1551); French: *Commentaires sur le prophète Isaïe. Par M. Iean Calvin* (Geneva, 1552).

30. On Calvin's Old Testament commentaries see T. H. L. Parker, *Calvin's Old Testament Commentaries* (Edinburgh, 1986); Wulfert de Greef, *Calvijn en het Oude Testament* (Amsterdam, 1984).

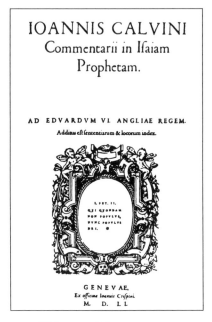

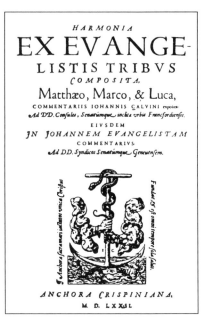

Title page of the commentary on Isaiah (1551)

Title page of the commentary on the four Gospels

cated the commentary on December 25, 1550, to King Edward VI of England (*CO* 13:669–74), noting that the commentary was not from his own hand, but had been carefully compiled from lectures (*praelectiones*) that he had given. The question might thus be raised whether the dedication to the king can be considered a real gift. But, says Calvin, the prophet Isaiah was of royal blood and had been in the service of Christ, the supreme King. He is therefore a figure worthy of the king.

Furthermore, Calvin hopes that the commentary will please the king. Isaiah had served five kings, and Calvin will leave it to Edward VI himself to decide which of them to emulate. He recalls that Isaiah speaks of the glorious situation to which the people could look forward after the return from exile and the rebuilding of the temple. Later, after the coming of Christ, the knowledge of the true God spread throughout the world. Calvin hopes that the king, in accordance with Isaiah 49:23, will cooperate in the reform of the church in his kingdom, now that the Lord God has reestablished his church after a very difficult period.

When the commentary on Isaiah had sold out, Calvin was urged to have it reprinted. He himself, however, wanted to write a new commentary, which subsequently appeared in Geneva in 1559.[31] Compared with the edition of 1551, it was much more extensive. In the foreword to the French edition of 1572 we read that through Calvin's diligent work on this commentary, the material had increased by a third over the edition of 1551.

In the introduction to the commentary Calvin treats the office of the prophets, whom he views as interpreters of the law. They must not add anything to the law, but must faithfully interpret it and uphold its authority. What Moses says about warnings and promises in general, the prophets apply specifically to their own time. Moreover, they also speak more clearly about Christ and his grace. Finally, Calvin draws a line from the prophets' task to the proclamation of the Word in our own day. It is true, he notes, that we today do not receive revelation from God in the sense of predictions about the future. But it is worthwhile comparing the time of the prophets and the present so as to become acquainted with God's judgments in particular events and incidents. God never changes. What he regarded as evil then still holds for today. That is important to remember if pious teachers (*pii doctores*) wish to speak about the preaching of the prophets with any benefit.

The commentary of 1551 had been dedicated to King Edward VI of England, but he had died in 1553 and had been succeeded by his sister Mary, who persecuted the Protestants. When Mary died in 1558, she was succeeded by her sister Elizabeth, whose reign the church in England was expecting to greatly benefit the Reformation. Peter Martyr Vermigli wrote to Calvin on December 1, 1558 (*CO* 17:391), that now that Jezebel had died, one could hope that the walls of Jerusalem would be rebuilt.

In a letter on January 15, 1559 (*CO* 17:413–15), Calvin dedicated the new edition of his commentary on Isaiah to Queen Elizabeth, although he retained the dedication to Edward VI as well. He hoped that after the difficult period just ended the queen would vigorously take up the work of reform once again, that evangelical writings might again appear in England, and that refugees would be able to return. He pointed out to her that, according to Isaiah 49:23, queens are called to be nurses of the church.

The queen, however, refused the dedication (*CO* 17:566), the reason being that during his stay in Geneva, John Knox had written a caustic treatise, *The First Blast of the Trumpet against the Monstrous Regiment and Empire of Women*, in which he had rejected female rulership. Calvin deals with the refusal of the

---

31. *Ioannis Calvini Commentarii in Isaiam prophetam. Nunc demum ab ipso authore recogniti, locupletati, magnoque labore et cura expoliti. Additi sunt duo indices: prior rerum et sententiarum, posterior vero locorum utriusque Testamenti, quos in his commentariis ipse author interpretatur, aut opposite ad sensum suum accommodat* (Geneva, 1559— *CO* 36:19–37:454).

dedication in a letter to William Cecil, Baron Burleigh (*CO* 17:490–92), the queen's first secretary, to whom Calvin had also written on January 29, 1559, pleading for the return of the exiles (*CO* 17:419–20). Knox had asked Calvin in a personal conversation a few years earlier how he felt about the rulership of women, and Calvin had answered (see the letter to Heinrich Bullinger of May 28, 1554—*CO* 15:125) that it was against the natural order and, like slavery, for example, was the result of the fall. But sometimes there are women so gifted that it seems clear from the blessings they bestow during their reigns that they rule under divine auspices. God, then, puts to shame the slothfulness of men if he chooses to manifest his glory more plainly through women. Calvin writes further that he had pointed out to Knox the examples of Huldah and Deborah, and that he had also cited Isaiah's reference to queens as nurses of the church. Finally, he had said that women sometimes come to the throne by right of succession and that it seemed better to him to drop the whole question. Governments that are established through God's special providence must not be overthrown. In addition, Calvin declares that he did not know anything about the publication of the treatise by Knox and after the publication had stated that he was not pleased with it. He did not think it right to make a big fuss about it, however, and said rather that the matter ought to be ignored. Calvin regrets that the queen will not accept his dedication because of Knox's treatise. Because the work has been imputed to him, he feels that he has been falsely accused. Cecil replied in a letter dated June 22 (*CO* 17:565–66)—he suggests that the relation between Calvin and England continues to be damaged by Knox.

Commentary on Genesis

Calvin's commentary on Genesis appeared in 1554, followed in the same year by a French translation.[32] He had already been hard at work in 1550 exegeting Genesis for his students, but putting this material into written form did not proceed so smoothly because of the press of other duties (see his letters to Guillaume Farel—*CO* 13:623, 655).

---

32. Latin: *In primum Mosis librum, qui Genesis vulgo dicitur, Commentarius Iohannis Calvini* (Geneva, 1554—*CO* 23:1–622); French: *Commentaire de M. Iean Calvin sur le premier livre de Moyse dit Genèse* (Geneva, 1554). See also Lewis F. Lupton, "Calvin's Commentary on Genesis," in idem, *A History of the Geneva Bible*, vol. 5, *Vision of God* (London, 1973), 107–17; Richard Stauffer, "L'Exégèse de Genèse 1, 1–3 chez Luther et Calvin," in Centre d'études des religions du livre, *In principio: Interprétations des premiers versets de la Genèse* (Paris, 1973), 245–66 (this article is also found in Richard Stauffer, *Interprètes de la Bible: Etudes sur les réformateurs du XVIe siècle* [Paris, 1980], 59–85); Claude-Gilbert Dubois, "Jean Calvin, commentaire sur le premier livre de Moyse," in idem, *La Conception de l'histoire en France au XVIe siècle (1560–1610)* (Paris, 1977), 307–15.

Calvin dedicated the commentary to the three sons of Johann Friedrich, elector of Saxony, who had died in March 1554. In the foreword of July 31 (*CO* 15:196–201), he points out to the princes the significance of the unity of the church in obedience to the Word of God. Over against Rome it is important that the small number of those who desire to adhere to the pure doctrine of Christ be one, even though their ceremonial differences are great.

At the suggestion of the Lutheran theologians, the princes did not accept the dedication, because Calvin deviated from the Lutheran doctrine of the Lord's Supper and had allegedly insulted Luther in several places in the commentary (see the letter from Chancellor Francis Burckhardt to Calvin—*CO* 15:260–61). Calvin responded in a letter on February 27, 1555 (*CO* 15:454), in which he expressed his disappointment, for in his view such a position could only harm the interests of the entire church.

Commentary on the Psalms

In 1557 Calvin's commentary on the Psalms appeared in Geneva, followed by a French edition. Because the latter did not correspond very closely to the Latin original, however, a more accurate French translation was published in 1561.[33]

In Calvin's foreword of July 22, 1557, which contains various biographical data, he relates that he had first expounded on the Psalms for "our little school," a practice which, according to Nicolas Colladon (*CO* 21:75), he had begun in 1552. From 1555 until August 1559 the Psalms were also discussed during the weekly Bible studies (*congrégations*). In addition, Calvin often chose a psalm for the Sunday afternoon sermon. At the repeated insistence of friends, he moved on to the writing of a commentary on the Psalms.

Commentary on Exodus through Deuteronomy

Calvin's commentary on Genesis appeared again in 1563, this time in a single volume with the commentary on Exodus through Deuteronomy.[34] On

33. Latin: *In librum Psalmorum, Iohannis Calvini Commentarius* (Geneva, 1557—*CO* 31 and 32); French: *Le Livre des Pseaumes exposé par Iehan Calvin* (Geneva, 1558); *Commentaires de M. Jean Calvin sur le livre des Pseaumes. Ceste traduction est tellement reveue et si fidèlement conferée sur le latin, qu'on le peut juger estre nouvelle* (Geneva, 1561). See also S. H. Russell, "Calvin and the Messianic Interpretation of the Psalms," *SJTh* 21 (1968): 37–47; John Robert Walchenbach, *The Influence of David and the Psalms on the Life and Thought of John Calvin* (Pittsburgh, 1969); Hans-Joachim Kraus, "Vom Leben und Tod in den Psalmen: Eine Studie zu Calvins Psalmenkommentar," in idem, *Biblisch-theologische Aufsätze* (Neukirchen, 1972), 258–77; and Willem Balke, "Calvijn over de geschapen werkelijkheid in zijn *Psalmencommentaar*," in Willem Balke et al., eds., *Wegen en gestalten in het gereformeerd protestantisme: Een bundel studies over de geschiedenis van het gereformeerd protestantisme aangeboden aan Prof. Dr. S. van der Linde* (Amsterdam, 1976), 89–103.

34. *Mosis libri V. cum Ioannis Calvini Commentariis: Genesis seorsum; reliqui quatuor in formam harmoniae digesti* (Geneva, 1563—*CO* 24:1–25:416).

July 31, 1563, he dedicated the book to Henri de Bourbon, prince of Navarre (and later King Henry IV of France), who was ten years old. In 1554 Calvin had dedicated his commentary on Genesis to the three sons of Johann Friedrich of Saxony, but they had rejected it. In a new dedication (*CO* 20:116–22) Calvin used Henri's mother (Jeanne d'Albret) as one of several examples of those who had proven that in difficult circumstances a woman's courage can exceed that of a man.

It is striking that in his exposition of Exodus through Deuteronomy Calvin does not follow the sequence of the chapters. In the introduction he explains why he has made a new division of the material. It was definitely not his intention to improve upon Moses. Rather, he arranged the contents of these books of the Bible differently in order to help the reader to understand the Bible better.

Calvin makes a distinction in his commentary between historical narrative and instruction. He first gives an exposition of a number of Bible passages relating to the history of the period (*CO* 24:9–208). Then comes the instruction, the heart of which is formed by the Ten Commandments. Before discussing the Ten Commandments, however, he examines texts having to do with the central meaning of the law. Following the exposition of each commandment is a discussion of those Scripture passages that have to do specifically with that commandment or mention related religious practices and precepts concerning society. After the exposition of the Ten Commandments, there are both a discussion of Bible passages that can be regarded as a summary of the law and an exposition of those passages containing promises and warnings connected with, respectively, the keeping and breaking of the law. The commentary concludes with the exposition of additional historical material.

Calvin himself produced a French translation of the commentary in order to correct the errors in the Latin edition. This translation came out in 1564.[35]

Commentary on Joshua

Calvin tried to keep working on the publication of his commentaries as long as possible. He wrote Threcius on November 30, 1563 (*CO* 20:199), that others had been asking him to provide an interpretation of the Book of Joshua. Though he was trying to limit himself in the exposition of this book of the Bible, he had not yet been able to proceed any further than chapter 3. Meanwhile, he revised the French translation of his commentary on Genesis and

---

35. *Commentaires de M. Iean Calvin, sur les cinq livres de Moyse. Genesis est mis à part, les autres quatre livres sont disposez en forme d'harmonie . . .* (Geneva, 1564).

prepared a French translation of the commentary on Exodus through Deuteronomy. Still he succeeded in finishing his commentary on Joshua.

The commentary on Joshua came off the press right after Calvin's death. The French translation appeared first, probably so that the large circle of French readers could have immediate access to the foreword, in which Theodore Beza provided a description of Calvin's life and death. The Latin commentary followed soon thereafter.[36]

Calvin's Lectures (*Praelectiones*)

Calvin had lectured on the New Testament at the gymnasium in Strasbourg, where he covered the Gospel of John and 1 Corinthians. In Geneva he gave exegetical lectures on the Old Testament, addressing in Latin the students, ministers, and other interested persons. He thoroughly prepared for these lectures even though he had nothing written in front of him during the classes themselves; he could not find the time to carefully write everything down. Hence we are not familiar with the contents of his lectures up until approximately 1557. Nicolas Colladon does tell us in his biography of Calvin, however, what material Calvin treated (see *CO* 21:71–96): in 1549 he was engaged in the interpretation of Isaiah, followed a year later by Genesis and after that the Psalms. How long he spent on these biblical books we do not know, for the next bit of information we have concerns the edition of the lectures on Hosea. All his lectures subsequent to those on Hosea were also published.

It is striking that in later translations of Calvin's commentaries and lectures, the differences in character between the two are often not distinguished. Calvin himself wrote the commentaries, following as closely as possible the criteria that he had established for a good commentary (see p. 94). Thus in a commentary Calvin always gives a very concise interpretation of the text. In the lectures, however, he generally discusses the text in somewhat more detail than in his commentaries. But even in the lectures he wishes to engage in actual exposition of Scripture and to avoid dogmatic excursus as much as possible. Exceptions to this are his exposition of Habakkuk 2:4 ("the just shall live by faith") and the lecture he gave on election in connection with the interpretation of Malachi 1:2–6a (concerning God's electing love for Israel; see, respectively, *CO* 43:526–36 and 44:401–9). Considering the different value that

---

36. French: *Commentaires de M. Iean Calvin, sur le livre de Iosué. Avec une préface de Théodore de Besze contenant en brief l'histoire de la vie et mort d'iceluy . . .* (Geneva, 1564); Latin: *Ioannis Calvini in librum Iosue brevis commentarius, quem paulo ante mortem absolvit. Addita sunt quaedam de eius morbo et obitu . . .* (Geneva, 1564—*CO* 25:417–570).

Calvin himself placed on his commentaries and his lectures, we do him an injustice if we do not clearly distinguish between them.

Lectures on Hosea

In 1556, and perhaps even earlier, Calvin began his exposition of Hosea. All the lectures on Hosea were published in Geneva in 1557, both in Latin and in French.[37] These were the first lectures that Jean Budé and Charles de Jonvillers wrote down verbatim.

Calvin writes in the foreword that originally he was not at all keen about the publication of these lectures. Since he had too little time to give to their preparation, he felt that they were not suitable for publication. But he also could not find the time to write a commentary on Hosea, so he agreed to publish the lectures as an experiment. It appears from a letter to Heinrich Bullinger (dated February 17, 1557—CO 16:412–13) that Calvin was not very happy with the publication. But the experiment proved to be successful, and all his subsequent lectures, therefore, were published in both Latin and French.

Lectures on the Minor Prophets

Calvin's lectures on the Minor Prophets appeared in Latin in 1559 and in French translation in 1560.[38] The degree to which he was involved in the publication can be seen in what Nicolas Colladon relates (CO 21:88). When in September 1558 Calvin had not yet finished his exposition of Malachi because of illness, he gave the last lectures at home for the benefit of the printer. He dedicated these lectures on February 23, 1560, to King Gustavus Vasa (CO 17:445–48), who in 1523 had become the first king of an independent Sweden and with the help of others had introduced the Lutheran Reformation there. In the dedication Calvin mentions that the lectures, which he refers to as being far from ready, are being published at the insistence of others after the apparent success of the printing of his lectures on Hosea, which he had permitted on an experimental basis. Genuine simplicity, as befits the true edification of God's children, is what the proper interpretation of Scripture requires. He hopes that his work will benefit others. Given the positive reactions that his

---

37. Latin: *In Hoseam prophetam, Io. Calvini Praelectiones a Ioanne Budaeo et sociis auditoribus assiduis bona fide exceptae* (Geneva, 1557—CO 42:182–514); French: *Leçons de Iean Calvin sur le prophète Hosée, recueillies fidèlement de mot à mot par Iehan Budé et autres ses compaignons auditeurs* (Geneva, 1557).

38. Latin: *Ioannis Calvini Praelectiones in duodecim prophetas (quos vocant) minores. . .* (Geneva, 1559—CO 42:176–44:498); French: *Leçons et expositions familières de Iean Calvin sur les douze petits prophètes . . .* (Geneva, 1560).

earlier published work received, he would like nothing more than to devote the rest of his life to exegetical work, if his other duties would allow it.

A few days later Calvin composed a letter to Crown Prince Eric (*CO* 17:450–51) in which he asked the prince to put in a good word for him with his father. It was to no avail, however; the delivery of the book was not met with appreciation.

Lectures on Daniel

On August 18, 1561, Calvin wrote the dedication for the edition of the lectures he had delivered on Daniel. The dedication (*CO* 18:614–24) is addressed to all pious servants of God who are trying to establish the kingdom of Christ in France in the right way. Calvin wishes to encourage his brothers in France in their struggle by holding up Daniel as an example. The Latin edition of the lectures on Daniel came off the press in 1561, and the French translation appeared a year later.[39]

Lectures on Jeremiah and Lamentations

On July 23, 1563, Calvin dedicated his lectures on Jeremiah and the Lamentations of Jeremiah to Frederick III, elector of the Palatinate (see *CO* 20:72–79), who had joined the Calvinists in 1560 and reformed his territory accordingly. In the dedication Calvin devotes a lot of attention to the way in which we commune with Christ in the celebration of the Lord's Supper. In addition, he warns about the apostate François Baudouin. The Latin edition of the lectures came out in Geneva in 1563, followed by the French translation in 1565.[40]

Lectures on Ezekiel

On February 2, 1564, Calvin presented his last lecture—on a passage from Ezekiel. These lectures, which go no further than Ezekiel 20:44, were published in 1565 in both Latin and French.[41]

---

39. Latin: *Ioannis Calvini Praelectiones in librum prophetiarum Danielis, Ioannis Budaei et Caroli Ionuillaei labore et industria exceptae. Additus est e regione versionis Latinae Hebraicus et Chaldaicus textus* (Geneva, 1561—*CO* 40:529–41:304); French: *Leçons de M. Iean Calvin sur le livre des prophéties de Daniel, recueillies fidèlement par Iean Budé et Charles de Ionviller, ses auditeurs* (Geneva, 1562).

40. Latin: *Ioannis Calvini Praelectiones in librum prophetiarum Ieremiae et Lamentationes, Ioannis Budaei et Caroli Ionuillaei labore et industria exceptae* (Geneva, 1563—*CO* 37:469–39:646); French: *Leçons ou commentaires et expositions de Iean Calvin, tant sur les Révélations que sur les Lamentations du prophète Iérémie . . .* (Lyons, 1565).

41. Latin: *Ioannis Calvini in viginti prima Ezechielis prophetae capita Praelectiones, Ioannis Budaei et Caroli Ionuillaei labore et industria exceptae* (Geneva, 1565—*CO* 40:21–516); French: *Leçons ou commentaires et expositions de M. Iean Calvin sur les vingt premiers chapitres des Révélations du prophète Ezéchiel, qui sont les derniers leçons qu'il a faites avant sa mort . . .* (Geneva, 1565).

Calvin's Sermons

Although Calvin's first task in Geneva was to lecture on the New Testament, he also began his work as a minister sometime before 1537.[42] When he settled in Strasbourg in 1538, he became pastor of the French refugee congregation there, and from the beginning of 1539 also served as a teacher in the gymnasium. He returned to Geneva in 1541, and when he conducted his first church service since coming back, he continued with his exposition of Scripture (*lectio continua*) at the very place where he had left off three years before. Except for a brief address on the ministerial office, he chose not to pay any attention to what had happened; the banishment had been merely an interruption in his duties.

Calvin preached frequently. It was intended originally that he preach twice on Sundays and once each on Mondays, Wednesdays, and Fridays, but early on already he was conducting services every day. The Council decided on September 11, 1542, that he should not preach more than once on Sundays (*CO* 21:302).

The only extant sermons from the years before 1549 are the two preached on the Wednesdays of November 4 and 11, 1545. They were published in 1546 on the basis of notes taken by Calvin's colleague, Jean Cousin (*CO* 32:455–80), but without Calvin's consent, since he was not accustomed to having sermons printed. These sermons, which were based on Psalm 115 and Psalm 124, had to do with a political incident in October 1545. The Roman Catholic Duke Heinrich von Braunschweig-Wolfenbüttel, whose territory had with the emperor's consent been taken away from him in 1542 by the princes of the Smalcald League, had attempted to reconquer it from the Protestant princes of Hesse and Saxony. On October 21 he and his son had been captured. With the danger of this situation in mind, Calvin on November 4 preached the sermon on Psalm 115; a week later, after the danger had passed, he preached the sermon on Psalm 124.

Four sermons that Calvin preached in 1549 (on Psalm 16:4; Hebrews 13:13; and Psalm 27:4 and 8 respectively) were revised and published in 1552 along with a brief exposition of Psalm 87. In the foreword that he wrote for this edition on September 20, 1552, he says that the sermons contain material that is useful for that time because they deal with the relation of a Christian to the papacy. That is also borne out in the headings that he gives to each of the sermons. In the sermon on Psalm 16:4 Christians are admonished to avoid idol-

42. On Calvin's sermons see T. H. L. Parker, *The Oracles of God: An Introduction to the Preaching of John Calvin* (London, 1947); idem, *Calvin's Preaching* (Edinburgh, 1992). See also note 51.

atry. The sermon on Hebrews 13:13 is an appeal to endure persecution for the sake of following Christ and the gospel. In the sermon on Psalm 27:4 he discusses how much believers should appreciate belonging to a church where they have the freedom to worship God in the right way. And in the sermon on Psalm 27:8 he indicates what we should be doing to regain the freedom to serve God in pure fashion in the Christian church.

On July 4, 1552, Calvin sent to Edward VI of England the brief exposition of Psalm 87 that was appended to the sermons. This exposition had originally been a sermon as well. In a letter sent to Edward at the same time (*CO* 14:34–43) Calvin talks about the religious duties of a king: "It is a grand thing to be king, especially of such a country, but I have no doubt that you place an incomparably greater value on being a Christian. Thus God has conferred upon you the still greater, inestimable privilege of being a Christian king, indeed of being allowed to serve him as 'lieutenant' in the maintenance of the kingdom of Jesus Christ in England." Calvin urges the king on in the serving of Christ. The good understanding between Edward VI and Calvin can be seen from the fact that the king paid Calvin a hundred crowns as thanks for the writings he had received. Edward also sent along a piece he had written in French in his own hand against the papacy.

On August 25, 1549, the deacons, who cared for the French-speaking poor in the congregation in Geneva, made a decision of great significance for the transmission of Calvin's sermons when they appointed Denis Raguenier as stenographer. His job was to take down Calvin's sermons in shorthand, transcribe them, and then give them to the deacons, who would eventually have them printed and use the proceeds for refugee relief. The oldest known sermon recorded by Raguenier is that of Sunday, August 25, when Calvin began his sermons on Acts. By his own count, Raguenier recorded 2,042 of Calvin's sermons. After Raguenier's death in 1560 or 1561, his work was carried on by others.

On Sundays Calvin would preach from the New Testament, although once in a while he would break the sequence in the afternoon service and choose a psalm for his text, especially one that had not yet been set to verse.[43] The catalogue compiled by Raguenier records the following series of sermons preached on Sunday:

95 sermons on Acts 1–15 (begun on August 25, 1549)
94 sermons on Acts 16–28 (begun on November 27, 1552)

43. See Parker, *Calvin's Preaching*, 163–71, where he summarizes Calvin's sermons on 1 and 2 Timothy, and refers to several sermons on the Psalms.

72 sermons on the Psalms (begun on November 17, 1549)
22 sermons on Psalm 119 (begun on January 8, 1553)
46 sermons on 1 and 2 Thessalonians (begun on March 26, 1554)
55 sermons on 1 Timothy (begun on September 16, 1554)
31 sermons on 2 Timothy and 17 sermons on Titus (begun on April 21, 1555)
110 sermons on 1 Corinthians (begun on October 20, 1555)
66 sermons on 2 Corinthians (begun on February 28, 1557)
43 sermons on Galatians (begun on November 14, 1557)
48 sermons on Ephesians (begun on May 15, 1558)

On the other days of the week (Calvin preached on these days only every other week) he treated various books of the Old Testament in *lectio continua.* When Raguenier began his work as stenographer, Calvin had already preached 180 sermons on Jeremiah 1–28; Raguenier recorded another 91 on Jeremiah 29–51. According to Raguenier's catalogue, he also recorded the following:

25 sermons on Lamentations (begun on September 6, 1550)
28 sermons on Micah (begun November 12, 1550)
17 sermons on Zephaniah (begun on February 6, 1551)
65 sermons on Hosea (begun on April 2, 1551)
17 sermons on Joel (begun on September 5, 1551)
43 sermons on Amos (begun on October 28, 1551)
5 sermons on Obadiah (begun on February 5, 1552)

Calvin began preaching on Jonah in March 1552, but because Raguenier became sick, he was able to record only 6 of the sermons on Jonah. Next Calvin moved on to Nahum and Habakkuk. Raguenier was unable to take up his task again until July 18, 1552, and by then Calvin had reached Daniel 5. Raguenier recorded the remaining 47 sermons on Daniel. Subsequent series included:

174 sermons on Ezekiel (begun on November 21, 1552)
159 sermons on Job (begun on February 26, 1554)
200 sermons on Deuteronomy (begun on March 20, 1555)
343 sermons on Isaiah (begun on July 16, 1556)
123 sermons on Genesis (begun on September 4, 1559)

According to Nicolas Colladon, after Raguenier's death Calvin preached on Judges, 1 Samuel (107 sermons begun on August 8, 1561), 2 Samuel (87 ser-

mons begun on February 3, 1562), and 1 Kings. It is not known how far he got
with 1 Kings. He gave his last sermon in this series on February 2, 1564.

Calvin was not involved in the publication of his sermons, with one exception—his *Quatre sermons traictans des matières fort utiles pour nostre
temps. . . avec briefve exposition du Pseaume LXXXVII.* Otherwise he let the ste-
nographers do their work without taking a further look at it; as with the tran-
scription of his lectures, he did not collaborate on this project. The only thing
that should yet be mentioned is that he composed a foreword for the edition
of 65 sermons on the Gospels (see *CO* 46:iv). A large number of Calvin's sermons were published, some during his lifetime and others later. We offer the
following survey:

Deux sermons faitz en la ville de Genève. . . . Geneva, 1546.[44]

*Quatre sermons traictans des matières fort utiles pour nostre temps . . . avec
briefve exposition du Pseaume LXXXVII.* Geneva, 1552.

Homiliae quatuor . . . explanatio Psalmi LXXXVII. . . . Geneva, 1553 (a Latin
translation by Claude Baduel of the preceding entry).

Vingtdeux sermons, auxquels est exposé le Pseaume centdixneufième. . . .
Geneva, 1554.[45]

*Deux sermons prins de la première Epistre à Timothée au second chapitre, . . .
où il est traicté d'un seul moyenneur de Dieu et des hommes.* Geneva, 1555.

*Six sermons, à sçavoir Quatre exhortatifs à fuir idolatrie. . . et deux où il est
traicté du seul moyenneur de Dieu et des hommes.* Geneva, 1555.[46]

Homiliae sive Conciones VII. Geneva, 1556 (a Latin translation by Claude
Baduel of *Quatre sermons* and three sermons from *Vingtdeux sermons*).

Sermons sur les dix commandemens de la loy. Geneva, 1557.

*Sermons sur le dixième et onzième chapitre de la première Epître Sainct Paul
aux Corinthiens. . . .* Geneva, 1558.

*Plusieurs sermons touchant la divinité, humanité, et nativité de nostre Seigneur
Iésus Christ. . . .* Geneva, 1558.[47]

44. These are the two sermons on Psalm 115 and Psalm 124 mentioned on p. 110. See also *SC*
7:xxxvi–xxxvii and, for the text of the sermons, *CO* 32:451–80.

45. See Emil Blaser, "Vom Gesetz in Calvins Predigten über den 119. Psalm," in *Das Wort sie sollen lassen stehn: Festschrift für D. Albert Schädelin* (Bern, 1950), 67–78.

46. These are the *Quatre sermons . . .* and *Deux sermons . . .* mentioned earlier.

47. This collection contains a Bible study on John 1:1–5 and 26 sermons: 1 on Luke 2:1–14; 9 on
Matthew 26:36–28:10; 4 on Acts 1:3–11; 4 on Acts 2:1–4, 13–24; 1 on 2 Thessalonians 1:6–10; and 7 on
Isaiah 52:13–53:12. See also *SC* 7: l–liv. T. H. L. Parker has translated the seven sermons on Isaiah
52:13–53:12 into English: *Sermons on Isaiah's Prophecy of the Death and Passion of Christ* (London,
1956).

Dixhuict sermons ausquels, entre autres poincts, l'histoire de Melchisédech et la matière de la iustification, sont déduites, avec l'exposition de trois cantiques, assavoir de la V. Marie, de Zacharie et de Simeon . . . , par Iean Bonnefoy. . . . Geneva, 1560.

Trois sermons sur le sacrifice d'Abraham. . . . Geneva, 1561.

Sermons sur les deux Epistres S. Paul à Timothée, et sur l'Epistre à Tite. Geneva, 1561.

Sermons sur le V. livre de Moyse, nommé Deutéronome. Geneva, 1562.

Treze sermons traitans de l'élection gratuite de Dieu en Iacob, et de la réiection en Esau. . . . Geneva, 1562.[48]

Sermons sur le cantique que feit le bon Roy Ezéchias après qu'il eut esté malade et affligé de la main de Dieu. . . . Geneva, 1562.

Soixantecinq sermons sur l'harmonie ou concordance des trois Evangelistes. . . . Geneva, 1562.

Sermons sur l'Epistre S. Paul apostre aux Ephésiens. Geneva, 1562.

Three Notable Sermons Made by the Godly and Famous Clerke Maister John Calvin upon the Ps. 46. Trans. W. Warde. London, 1562.[49]

Sermons sur le Livre de Iob. . . . Geneva, 1563.[50]

Sermons sur l'Epistre S. Paul apostre aux Galatiens. Geneva, 1563.

Quarantesept sermons sur les huict derniers chapitres des prophéties de Daniel. . . . La Rochelle, 1565.

Sermons sur le livre de Moyse, nommé Deutéronome. Geneva, 1567.

In librum Iobi conciones. Geneva, 1593.

Homiliae in I. librum Samuelis. Ex Gallicis Latinae factae et nunc primum in lucem editae. Geneva, 1604.

"Sermon sur Ezéchiel 2/1–5" and "Sermon sur Actes 3/17–20," in *Calvin d'après Calvin: Fragments extraits des oeuvres françaises du réformateur,* ed. C. O. Viguet and D. Tissot (Geneva, 1864), 281–97, 310–25.

Supplementa Calviniana: Sermons inédits. Edited by Erwin Mülhaupt et al. Neukirchen-Vluyn, 1936–. Already published are vol. 1, *Predigten über das 2. Buch Samuelis;* vol. 2, *Sermons sur le Livre d'Isaïe chapitres 13–19;*

---

48. These sermons had already been published in Geneva in 1560 as *Traité de la prédestination éternelle de Dieu, par laquelle les uns sont éleuz à salut, les autres laissez en leur condemnation.* Calvin's *Responses à certaines calomnies et blasphèmes* of 1557 (directed against Castellio—see p. 178) is appended to the sermons in the edition of 1562.

49. See Richard Stauffer, "Eine englische Sammlung von Calvinpredigten," in *Der Prediger Johannes Calvin: Beiträge und Nachrichten zur Ausgabe der Supplementa Calviniana,* ed. Karl Halaski (Neukirchen, 1966), 47–80.

50. See Susan E. Schreiner, " 'Through a Mirror Dimly': Calvin's Sermons on Job," *CTJ* 21 (1986): 175–93.

vol. 5, *Sermons sur le Livre de Michée;* vol. 6, *Sermons sur les livres de Jérémie et des Lamentations;* vol. 7, *Psalmenpredigten, Passions-, Oster-, und Pfingstpredigten.*

The *Calvini Opera* includes 874 of Calvin's sermons. The prayers after the sermons are usually left out, and there are no notes. The editors of the *Opera* did not place a lot of value on the sermons, but that attitude has since changed. Many of the sermons preserved in manuscript are, along with the closing prayer and notes, being published today in the *Supplementa Calviniana,* which will complete the *Opera* by adding another 670 sermons. Unfortunately, no more of Calvin's sermons can be published after that because not all the manuscripts of the sermons have been preserved. In 1806 many of the sermons kept in the library of Geneva were sold to a bookdealer because of a lack of storage space, and some of them have disappeared without a trace.[51]

The following is a summary of the sermons that appear in the *Opera*:

4 sermons on Psalm 16:4; Hebrews 13:13; Psalm 27:4; and 27:8, with the exposition of Psalm 87 (*CO* 8:369–452)

3 sermons on Genesis 14:13–24 (*CO* 23:641–82)

4 sermons on Genesis 15:4–7 (*CO* 23:683–740)

3 sermons on Genesis 21:33–22:15 (*CO* 23:741–84)

13 sermons on Genesis 25:11–27:36 (*CO* 58:1–206)

200 sermons on Deuteronomy (*CO* 25:573–29:232)

107 sermons (Latin) on 1 Samuel (*CO* 29:233–30:734)

2 sermons on Psalm 115 and Psalm 124 (*CO* 32:451–80)

22 sermons on Psalm 119 (*CO* 32:481–752)

159 sermons on Job (*CO* 33:1–35:514)

4 sermons on Isaiah 38:9–22 (*CO* 35:517–80)

7 sermons on Isaiah 52:13–53:12 (*CO* 35:581–688)

47 sermons on Daniel 5–12 (*CO* 41:305–42:174)

65 sermons on Matthew, Mark, and Luke (*CO* 46:1–826)

9 sermons on Matthew 26:36–28:19 (*CO* 46:829–954)

1 sermon on Luke 2:1–14 (*CO* 46:955–68)

51. See Bernard Gagnebin, "L'Histoire des manuscrits des sermons de Calvin," in *SC* 2:xiv–xxviii. On the planning of the edition of the sermons in the *SC*, see *Der Prediger Johannes Calvin,* ed. Halaski. One should also consult the introductions of each published part of the *SC*. For a survey of articles and books on Calvin's preaching see Richard Stauffer, *Dieu, la création et la Providence dans la prédication de Calvin* (Bern, 1978), 309–16. This is supplemented by Wulfert de Greef, "Das Verhältnis von Predigt und Kommentar bei Calvin, dargestellt an dem Deuteronomium Kommentar und den -Predigten," in *Calvinus servus Christi,* ed. Wilhelm H. Neuser (Budapest, 1988), 195–204.

1 sermon on John 1:1–5 (*CO* 47:461–84)
4 sermons on Acts 1:1–11 (*CO* 48:585–622)
5 sermons on Acts 2:1–4, 13–21 (*CO* 48:624–64)
19 sermons on 1 Corinthians 10 and 11 (*CO* 49:577–830)
43 sermons on Galatians (*CO* 50:269–51:136)
48 sermons on Ephesians (*CO* 51:241–862)
1 sermon on 2 Thessalonians 1:6–10 (*CO* 52:219–38)
55 sermons on 1 Timothy (*CO* 53)
31 sermons on 2 Timothy (*CO* 54:1–370)
17 sermons on Titus (*CO* 54:373–596)

The following sermons have been published in the *Supplementa*:

87 sermons on 2 Samuel (*SC* 1)
66 sermons on Isaiah (*SC* 2)
28 sermons on Micah (*SC* 5)
25 sermons on Jeremiah 14:19–18:23 and 2 sermons on Lamentations 1:1–5 (*SC* 6)
10 sermons on Psalms 80:9–20; 147:12–20; 148:1–14; 149:4–9; 65:6–14; 46:7–12; 48:2–8; and 48:9–15; 2 sermons on Matthew 28:1–10; 1 sermon on Acts 2:1–10; and 6 sermons on Matthew 26:40–27:66 (*SC* 7)

Not yet published are:

89 sermons on Genesis 1:26–20:6[52]
67 sermons on Isaiah 30–41
57 sermons on Isaiah 42–51
55 sermons on Ezekiel 1–15
69 sermons on Ezekiel 23–48
44 sermons on Acts 1–7
58 sermons on 1 Corinthians 1–9
Several sermons on isolated texts (see *SC* 1:vii–ix)

Sermons not yet recovered are:

Sermons on Isaiah 1–12 and 54–56
Sermons on Jeremiah 1–14 and 19–52

52. See Richard Stauffer, "Les Sermons inédits de Calvin sur le Livre de Genèse," *RThPh* 97 (1965): 26–36.

23 sermons on Lamentations 1:6–5:22
28 sermons on Zephaniah, Obadiah, and Jonah
65 sermons on Hosea
17 sermons on Joel
43 sermons on Amos
Sermons on Ezekiel 16–22
46 sermons on 1 and 2 Thessalonians
Sermons on 1 Corinthians 12–16
66 sermons on 2 Corinthians

Contributions to the Weekly Bible Studies (*Congrégations*)

Sometime before November 21, 1536, Guillaume Farel and Calvin introduced the so-called *congrégations* into Geneva, for on November 21 Farel wrote to the ministers in Lausanne on behalf of his colleagues (*CO* 10b:71–73) that they were holding colloquia in Geneva every Friday morning at seven o'clock. These were the so-called *congrégations,* in which about sixty ministers from Geneva and its vicinity participated. The ministers, who were permitted to miss only for a valid reason, took turns presenting an exposition of a part of Scripture, which was then discussed. Citizens from the city were also allowed to come and listen. The ministers met together afterwards to discuss practical matters. In the letter mentioned above, Farel expresses the hope that their colleagues in Lausanne and vicinity will want to establish the same practice to strengthen their unity. This, in fact, they did for a brief time until it was forbidden by Bern (*CO* 10b:145).

In instituting the *congrégations,* Farel and Calvin were following the example of Zurich, where exegetical presentations had been given in the choir area of the Grossmünster (cathedral) since June 19, 1525. These so-called prophesyings had as their goal the theological molding of ministers and of the students from the upper classes of the Latin school.[53]

The objective and procedures of the weekly Bible studies mentioned in Farel's letter were elaborated on in *Les Ordonnances ecclésiastiques* of 1541 and were expanded somewhat on that foundation in *Les Ordonnances ecclésiastiques* of 1561.[54] We know that during the *congrégations* books of the Bible were discussed in *lectio continua.*[55] A few of the presentations by Calvin at the Friday

53. See Ulrich Gäbler, *Huldrych Zwingli: His Life and Work,* trans. Ruth C. L. Gritsch (Philadelphia, 1986), 99–101.
54. For the 1541 text see *CO* 10a:18 or *OS* 2:332–33.
55. For a summary see Jean Calvin, *Deux congrégations et Exposition du catéchisme*, ed. Rodolphe Peter (Paris, 1964), xv–xvi.

meetings (where French was the language spoken) were published. At the beginning of a collection of sermons that dealt with the divinity, humanity, and birth of our Lord Jesus Christ and that was published in Geneva in 1558,[56] for example, we find a study of John 1:1–5 that Calvin had presented at a *congrégation* (for the text see *CO* 47:461–84).

A presentation by Calvin on election, *Congrégation sur l'élection éternelle de Dieu*, was also published. The background to this particular *congrégation*, which was held on Friday, December 18, 1551, and was devoted entirely to the subject of election, was the appearance on the scene of Jérôme Bolsec. Bolsec, who hailed from Paris, had been a Carmelite monk but had gone over to the Reformation and, after fleeing Paris, had set up practice as the court physician of Jacques de Bourgogne, lord of Falais, at his estate outside Geneva. Bolsec had caused problems with his statements about free will and predestination at the *congrégation* held on May 15, 1551, and could not be dissuaded by the other ministers. At the *congrégation* on October 16, 1551, where minister Jean de Saint-André introduced the discussion on John 8:47 ("He who belongs to God hears what God says. The reason you do not hear is that you do not belong to God"), Bolsec used the occasion to protest against the predestinarian interpretation of the text. With an appeal to the early church and Augustine, he accused Calvin of making God the author of sin. He also urged the assembly not to let themselves be deceived by the ministers.

Calvin responded in a long address to what Bolsec had said. The chief of police, who was also present, immediately had Bolsec arrested, and he was charged with unbiblical teaching and disturbing the unity of the assembly.

During the proceedings against Bolsec (see *CO* 8:141–248), de Falais, among others, came to his defense. On November 14 the ministers of Geneva wrote a letter asking their colleagues in Basel, Bern, and Zurich for their opinion about the matter (*CO* 8:205–8); and on November 21 the Council of Geneva asked the churches in Basel, Bern, and Zurich for advice about the question of predestination (*CO* 8:223–24). In the replies received, Bolsec's teaching was rejected, but Calvin was disappointed with them. He wrote to Christophe Fabri and Farel (*CO* 14:213–14) that he had again experienced how meager the help was from the ministers in Basel. He was even more disappointed with Zurich (see the letter to Farel—*CO* 14:218–19) and with the personal letter he received from Heinrich Bullinger (for the text of the letter see *CO* 14:214–15). It also bothered him that edicts had been issued forbidding ministers in the vicinity to write the ministers in Geneva directly. On the other hand, although

56. *Plusieurs sermons de Iehan Calvin touchant la divinité, humanité, et nativité de nostre Seigneur Iésus Christ* (Geneva, 1558).

DEVX

CONGREGA-
TIONS PROPOSEES
PAR M. IEAN CALVIN, DV SE-
cond chapitre de l'Epiftre de fainct Paul aux Galatiens, verfet onzieme.

*Item l'expofition du quarantetroifieme Dimanche du Cate-
chifme, où eft expofée la derniere requefte de l'oraifon de
noftre Seigneur Iefus Chrift.*

ceux qui l'edifient trauaillent en

Si le Seigneur n'edifie la maifon,

Pfeaume cxxvii.

De l'Imprimerie de Michel Blanchier.

M. D. LXIII.

AVEC PRIVILEGE.

Title page for two congrégations
on Galatians 2:11

TREZE

SERMONS
DE M. I. CALVIN,

Traitans de l'election gratuite de
Dieu en Iacob, & de la reiection en Efau.
Traité auquel chacun Chreftié pourra
voir les bontez excellentes de Dieu enuers les fiens, & fes iugemens merueil-
leux enuers les reptouuez.

↯ Recueillie de fes predications
l'an mil cinq cens foixante.

Rom. 8 t. 33.

*O profondes richeffes de la fapience &
cognoiffance de Dieu, que fes iugemens font
incompr ehenfibles, & fes voyes impofsibles
à trouuer!*

M. D. LXI I.

*Title page for the thirteen sermons
on the election of Jacob and
reprobation of Esau*

---

the ministers in Neuchâtel (Farel among them) had not been asked for advice, they did write a letter sharply condemning Bolsec (*CO* 14:221–24).

At the heart of Calvin's December 18 presentation on election was the issue of the universality of salvation, which he denied in view of particular election. All the ministers endorsed Calvin's exposition, which was subsequently published in 1562.[57] The Council of Geneva decided on December 21, 1551, to permanently banish Bolsec. He was no longer allowed to enter the city, but he did remain on de Falais's estate, which lay in Bernese territory.[58]

Finally, we turn our attention to two presentations by Calvin, on Galatians 2:11–16 and Galatians 2:15–21, which he gave at the end of 1562 or the begin-

---

57. *Congrégation faite en l'église de Genève par M. Iean Calvin. En laquelle la matière de l'élection éternelle de Dieu fut sommairement et clairement déduite et ratifiée d'un commun accord par ses frères ministres* (Geneva, 1562; for the text see *CO* 8:85–140).

58. When Bolsec had to leave Bern as a result of Calvin's insistence that Bern take measures against him, he fled to Paris. He returned to the Roman Catholic Church and in 1577 wrote a biography of Calvin (*Histoire de la vie, moeurs, actes, doctrine, constance et mort de Jean Calvin, jadis ministre de Genève* [Lyons, 1577]) that was full of shameless lies and slander. It was dedicated to the archbishop of Lyons.

ning of 1563. They were published along with an exposition of the petition, "Lead us not into temptation, but deliver us from evil." This exposition he based on Lord's Day 43 of the catechism.[59] We close by noting that in Geneva there are still a few manuscripts of presentations by Calvin that await publication in the *Supplementa Calviniana*: presentations on Exodus 1:1–8 (September 1, 1559); Joshua 1:1–5 (June 4, 1563); Joshua 11 (September 1563); and Isaiah 1:1–4 (January 21, 1564).[60]

59. The title of the 1563 edition reads: *Deux congrégations proposées par M. Iean Calvin, du second chapitre de l'Epistre de Sainct Paul aux Galatiens, verset onzième. Item l'exposition du quarantetroisième dimanche du Catéchisme, où est exposée la dernière requeste de l'oraison de nostre Seigneur Iésus Christ.* For a reprint of this edition with introduction and notes see Calvin, *Deux congrégations*, ed. Peter.

60. Also surviving are accounts of Calvin's observations on presentations by others. For a summary see Calvin, *Deux congrégations*, ed. Peter, xix. See also Danielle Fischer, "Michel Cop: Congrégation sur Josué 1/6–11 du 11 juin 1563, avec ce qui a été ajouté par Jean Calvin" (première impression du manuscrit original, avec une introduction et des notes), *FZPhTh* 34 (1987): 205–29.

4

Building Up the Church

In this chapter we shall devote our attention to Calvin's publications that have to do with the building up of the church. We look first of all at what he and the other ministers in Geneva considered to be important aspects of the building up of the congregation. Next we turn to what he wrote concerning the liturgical structure of public worship and the instruction of the youth. We also include in this category those writings of Calvin in which he provides special assistance to believers—sometimes solicited, sometimes not. Finally, we focus our attention on those publications in which he deals with matters of church order.

Fundamental Issues in Congregational Nurture

Under Guillaume Farel's leadership the entire citizenry of Geneva had decided for the Reformation on May 21, 1536. The result was that much had to be done to nurture the congregation. When Farel coerced Calvin into staying in Geneva in 1536, he expected that Calvin would devote his energy to the continuation of the Reformation in the city, and this, in fact, Calvin did. In this section we shall concentrate on a few publications in which he (and others) articulate the fundamental things that must occur in the building up of the congregation.

Articles concernant l'organisation de l'église et du culte à Genève (*1537*)

We examine first of all the *Articles concernant l'organisation de l'église et du culte à Genève (Articles concerning the Organization of the Church and of Worship in Geneva).*[1] This was a written document presented by the three ministers of Geneva (Elie Coraud, Farel, and Calvin) to the Council on January 16, 1537. In the *Articles* they state the points that they consider of primary importance for the further reformation of the church in the city. There are four issues in particular that they regard as important for a church of order and law: the frequent celebration of the Lord's Supper, along with a concern for keeping it holy through possible excommunication; the singing of psalms; the instruction of the youth; and marriage laws. The first three points come up for discussion in the sections that follow. We begin our detailed discussion with the celebration of the Lord's Supper and matters related to it. (As far as the fourth point [marriage laws] is concerned, the Council was asked to designate a few of its members who, along with a few ministerial advisors, were to draft regulations for approval by the Council. These regulations were to state how the

---

1. For the text see *CO* 10a:5–14; *OS* 1:369–77, *Articles concernant l'organisation de l'église et du culte à Genève, proposés par les ministres;* for an English translation see *Calvin: Theological Treatises,* ed. J. K. S. Reid (London and Philadelphia, 1954), 48–55. See also Johannes Plomp, *De kerkelijke tucht bij Calvijn* (Kampen, 1969), 144–56.

most common cases involving marriage matters ought to be adjudicated, since the papacy had taken such a capricious approach to them.)

The *Articles* devote a great deal of attention to the celebration of the Lord's Supper and the related issues of discipline and excommunication. The Lord's Supper should be celebrated at least every Sunday. Because that is such a radical step for the congregation, however, an arrangement is suggested whereby the Lord's Supper will be administered once a month in each of the churches in turn. That way each congregational member can participate in the Lord's Supper once per month. At the same time, there ought to be a regulation that ensures that the celebration of communion is not desecrated. Those who show by their way of life that they do not belong to Christ ought to be admonished and possibly expelled from the church until they confess their guilt and amend their lives. This pattern is in accordance with Scripture (Matthew 18; 1 Timothy 1; and 1 Corinthians 5).

One of the problems is that discipline and excommunication have been usurped from the congregation by the bishops. The *Articles* propose to follow Scripture by restoring these prerogatives to the congregation. The Council is asked to appoint members of the congregation of upright life and testimony as "deputies" in the various districts of the city to monitor the behavior of the other members of the congregation. If anyone misbehaves, a deputy is to tell a minister, and together they are to admonish the member concerned. The name of any member who does not heed their admonition is to be revealed to the congregation; if there is still no improvement, excommunication will follow. The individual should attend church services but will not be allowed to participate in the celebration of the Lord's Supper as long as there is no amendment of life.

This supervision does not necessarily have to begin with the deputies; the members of the congregation also have a responsibility for each other. If their admonition of a fellow church member produces nothing, then a deputy should be contacted.

In taking measures against someone, the church can go no further than excommunication. If an excommunicate does not take that discipline to heart, it is suggested that the Council might possibly take further action.

Before a system of discipline and excommunication can be implemented, it ought to be clear who does and who does not belong to the church of Jesus Christ. Therefore, all the inhabitants of the city should be asked to declare their allegiance to the faith of the church. It would be appropriate for the members of the Council as Christian leaders to be the first to take this step. Then a few Council members can be designated along with the ministers to ask the residents of the city to do the same thing. This can be a one-time measure, so that it becomes clear what each person professes to believe and the church can begin in the proper way. (Such a proposal was nothing new—there had been precedents in both Basel and Bern in 1534.)

Finally, in the *Articles* the ministers urgently request the members of the Council to support the proposals if they are deemed to be in accordance with the Word of God. The Council should then also carry out what falls under their responsibility for a proper conduct of affairs in the city. They should not let themselves be discouraged by the weight of the task. What is done in obedience to God, say the ministers, he will also cause to succeed, as the members of the Council have been permitted to experience up to the present time.

In the *Articles* the ministers express their desire to seek the good of the church and the city in cooperation with the members of the Council. They attempt to give to both church and city their own sphere of responsibility. We have in mind here especially the right of excommunication, which, according to the ministers, belongs to the church. That was an unusual thing in Switzerland at that time, for in many other cities measures had been taken to place the matter of excommunication in the hands of the civil authorities rather than the church.

On January 16 the Council dealt with the *Articles* and approved them without any great difficulty. A few modifications were made, however, some in the proposals concerning the celebration of the Lord's Supper and concerning marriage matters. With respect to the former, the Council decided that the celebration of the Lord's Supper would take place four times a year. And although the ministers might give their opinion on matters concerning marriage, these matters would remain under the jurisdiction of the Little Council.

About a month after the *Articles* were accepted, the *Instruction et confession de foy* appeared in Geneva. This was a catechism and confession of faith used in the Geneva church.[2] The Latin edition of this work came out in Basel in March 1538 under the title *Catechismus, sive christianae religionis institutio, communibus renatae nuper in evangelio Genevensis ecclesiae suffragiis recepta, et vulgari quidem prius idiomate, nunc vero Latine etiam, quo de fidei illius sinceritate passim aliis etiam ecclesiis constet, in lucem edita, Ioanne Calvino autore* (*CO* 5:313–62; *OS* 1:426–32).[3] It is striking that the title speaks of a catechism or *institutio*. It appears, then, that the original intent of the work, namely, to

2. For the text see *CO* 22:25–74; *OS* 1:378–417, *Instruction et confession de foy dont on use en l'église de Genève*. For an English translation see *Instruction in Faith (1537)*, trans. and ed. Paul T. Fuhrmann (Philadelphia, 1949; reprint, Louisville, 1992).

3. For an English translation see Ford Lewis Battles, *John Calvin: Catechism 1538* (Pittsburgh, 1976).

serve as an instructional booklet for the youth, had receded into the background, for it seemed now to be serving more as a confession of faith, as the foreword by Calvin also bears out. Those churches that have heard about the opposition in Geneva to the ministers must know that the church of Geneva is one with other churches in the faith.

The *Confession de la foy* (a separate document) was published in Geneva in 1536 or 1537 without mention of either the name of the author or the date of publication.[4] If we go by the complete title of the work, this confession of faith is an extract from the catechism that had appeared shortly before. Apparently, the aforementioned *Instruction et confession de foy* had not been considered suitable for the inhabitants of Geneva as a confession of faith. So it was the intention that all inhabitants of the city, as well as those living outside of Geneva but under her jurisdiction, endorse the latter confession and promise to hold to it. Nevertheless, it is not entirely clear which of the two documents appeared first. Olivier Labarthe thinks that it was the *Confession de la foy*.[5]

It has long been accepted on the authority of Nicolas Colladon and Theodore Beza that Calvin was responsible for the confession of faith. But Labarthe has pointed out the great resemblance between the confession of faith and two earlier works by Farel, so that the confession of faith could be attributed to him.[6]

The confession of faith consists of twenty-one articles. The first article states that Scripture alone is the rule of faith and that we should be guided only by what is taught there.

In Geneva the process of declaring agreement with the confession did not go smoothly at all. More than once the ministers had to push the Council to do what they had promised. The members of the Council did set a good example at the end of July 1537, but not many of the other citizens followed it. Because the Council interpreted this nonacceptance of the *Confession* as resistance to the Reformation and to the related reforming of society in the city,

---

4. See *CO* 22:85–96; *OS* 1:418–26, *Confession de la foy, laquelle tous bourgeois et habitans de Genève et subiectz du pays doyvent iurer de garder et tenir, extraicte de l'instruction dont on use en l'église de la dicte ville*. See also *Le Catéchisme français de Calvin publié en 1537, réimprimé pour la première fois d'après un exemplaire nouvellement retrouvé, et suivi de la plus ancienne Confession de foi de l'église de Genève, avec deux notices*, ed. Albert Rilliet and Théophile Dufour (Geneva, 1878). For an introduction to and modern French text of the confession of faith, see *La Vraie Piété: Divers traités de Jean Calvin et Confession de foi de Guillaume Farel*, ed. Irena Backus and Claire Chimelli (Geneva, 1986), 41–53; for an English translation see *Calvin: Theological Treatises*, ed. Reid, 26–33.

5. Olivier Labarthe, *La Relation entre le premier catéchisme de Calvin et la première confession de foi de Genève*, thèse de licence, University of Geneva, 1967.

6. The two earlier works by Farel are *Summaire et briefve déclaration d'aucuns lieux fort nécessaires à ung chascun chrestien pour mettre sa confiance en Dieu et ayder son prochain*, 3d ed. (Neuchâtel, 1534), and *La Manière et fasson qu'on tient en baillant le sainct baptesme . . .* (Neuchâtel, 1533).

there was little else it could do but decide that those who refused to subscribe to the confession should be banished. This meant that the measures concerning discipline and excommunication that the ministers had proposed in the *Articles* were now being imposed by the civil government. The Council was interfering in what were usually ecclesiastical affairs. When the Council then also ordered the ministers to adopt several of the customs of the church in Bern regarding feast days, baptism, and the Lord's Supper, the tension only increased. The final result was that on April 23, 1538, the Council decided to banish Farel and Calvin from Geneva.

Articles Designed for the Restoration of Peace in Geneva (1538)

On April 25 Calvin and Farel left Geneva. They went first to Bern and then several days later to Zurich, where a synod in session urged them not to abandon Geneva. The two ministers drew up a memorandum of fourteen articles in which they laid out what had to happen before they would be ready to take up their work in Geneva again (*CO* 10b:190–92).[7] They wanted, among other items, the introduction of discipline, a division of the city into districts to facilitate contact between the ministers and the members of the congregation, a sufficient number of ministers, no interference by the Council in the appointment of ministers, and the celebration of the Lord's Supper at least once a month. A letter to Geneva from the Council of Bern produced nothing (for the text of the letter see *CO* 10b:187–88; for the answer, *CO* 10b:194–95). Nor did a delegation that went with Calvin and Farel from Bern to Geneva. Calvin and Farel were not allowed into Geneva; the delegation was.

Liturgical Structure of Public Worship

Early on, Calvin had begun to reflect on the liturgical structure of public worship, as can be seen in the first edition of the *Institutes* (1536).[8] When he

---

7. The heading in *CO* reads: *Articuli a Calvino et Farello propositi ad pacem Genevae restituendam*.

8. On the subject of Calvin and liturgy see T. Brienen, *De liturgie bij Johannes Calvijn* (Kampen, 1987), and the secondary sources he mentions, including H. Hasper, *Calvijns beginsel voor den zang in den eredienst* (The Hague, 1955). We should also mention Kilian McDonnel, "Conception de la liturgie selon Calvin et l'avenir de la liturgie catholique," *Concilium* 42 (1969): 75–84; Nicolaus Mansson, *Calvin och gudstjästen* (Calvin and Worship) (Stockholm, 1970); Richard Stauffer, "L'Apport de Strasbourg à la Réforme française par l'intermédiaire de Calvin," in Richard Stauffer, *Interprètes de la Bible: Etudes sur les réformateurs du XVIe siècle* (Paris, 1980), 153–65; Bruno Bürki, "Jean Calvin avait-il le sens liturgique?" in *Communio sanctorum: Mélanges offerts à Jean-Jacques von Allmen* (Geneva, 1982), 157–72; Markus Jenny, *Luther, Zwingli, Calvin in ihren Liedern* (Zurich, 1983); Rodolphe Peter, "Calvin and Liturgy, according to the *Institutes*," in *John Calvin's Institutes: His Opus Magnum* (Potchefstroom, 1986), 239–65.

writes there about the sacraments (baptism and the Lord's Supper), he expresses the opinion that the Lord's Supper ought to be administered at least weekly. He goes on to indicate what the order of worship should be in a church service in which communion is celebrated (see *CO* 1:139–40; *OS* 1:161). The Lord's Supper is to be administered after the sermon, and either psalms are to be sung or Scripture is to be read during the celebration itself.

On January 16, 1537, after Calvin had become a minister in Geneva, he and the other ministers submitted to the Council the *Articles concerning the Organization of the Church and of Worship in Geneva.* We have seen that in this document the ministers identify a number of significant points for the regulation of worship, such as the frequent celebration of the Lord's Supper and the singing of psalms. The Lord's Supper should be celebrated at least every Sunday, but because the people are not yet up to celebrating it that often, it is proposed that it be held once per month, in each of the three churches in turn, with the understanding that the whole congregation is allowed to participate each time.

As far as psalm singing is concerned, the ministers observe that according to the example of the early church and the testimony of Paul, it is a good thing to sing in church with both heart and mouth. The ministers expect the singing of psalms to have a positive influence on the prayers and on the glorification of the name of God. A number of qualified children are to be selected to lead the congregation in the singing of the psalms. The members of the Council are asked to see to it that no one disturb the order of things once these proposals have been implemented in the gathering of the congregation.

Already in 1538, as minister of the newly formed congregation of French refugees in Strasbourg, Calvin had to deal directly with the liturgical structure of public worship. As yet no celebration of the Lord's Supper had taken place. That occurred for the first time in November 1538, and from then on it was celebrated once per month. In place of confession, Calvin was influenced by Matthäus Zell and Martin Bucer to institute the practice that those who desired to participate in the Lord's Supper should apply to him for possible further instruction, admonition, or consolation. Calvin did this not to limit Christian freedom, but to protect the sanctity of the sacrament (see his letter to Guillaume Farel that is dated May 1540—*CO* 11:41).

As far as the liturgical structure of public worship itself was concerned, Calvin was able to make use of what was already present in Strasbourg. He adopted many of the prayers and drew up a form for baptism.[9] Congregational singing in particular was one of the first issues that he really became

---

9. See *CO* 9:894 (*Discours d'adieu aux ministres*).

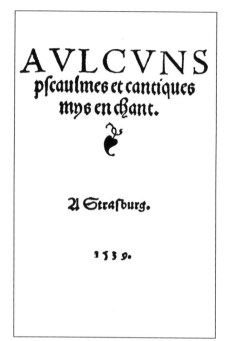

Title page and page 3 of Aulcuns pseaulmes . . .

involved in, having been inspired in that direction by the singing in the other churches in Strasbourg. The first psalm that he set to verse was Psalm 46, for which he chose a melody composed by Wolfgang Dachstein, organist at Saint Thomas Church, for the German versification of Psalm 25. Matthias Greiter, cantor of Saint Thomas Church, not only wrote songs but also composed the melodies for them. Calvin selected several of Greiter's psalm melodies and wrote a French text of other psalms for them. This is the way the versifications and melodies of Psalms 25, 36, 91, and 138 originated. He also worked on a versification of the Song of Simeon, the Ten Commandments, and the Apostles' Creed.

Through Farel, Calvin received another thirteen psalm versifications prepared by Clément Marot. These were for Psalms 1, 2, 3, 15, 19, 32, 51, 103, 114, 115, 130, 137, and 143. At the beginning of 1539 Calvin published these psalms along with those that he himself had set to verse earlier; the title of this booklet was *Aulcuns pseaulmes et cantiques mys en chant.*[10]

10. There is a copy of this little book in the Bayerische Staatsbibliothek and a facsimile in Hasper, *Calvijns beginsel,* 456–71; see also *Calvin's First Psalter,* ed. Richard R. Terry (London, 1932).

In 1542 Calvin published two works on the structure of public worship. The booklet *La Forme des prières et chantz ecclésiastiques, avec la manière d'administrer les sacremens, et consacrer le mariage, selon la coustume de l'église ancienne* (*CO* 6:161–210; *OS* 2:11–58) was printed in Geneva with no mention of Calvin as the author.[11] An edition also appeared in Strasbourg under another title, which begins with the words *La Manyère*.[12] This edition also differs in that, among other things, the Decalogue is sung in two parts, and the Apostles' Creed is set to music.

In these two very similar works, Calvin says that there are three important elements of public worship: preaching, prayers, and the administration of the sacraments. He pays a lot of attention to the prayers, which include the singing. The vernacular ought to be used and not Latin. Music is a gift of God, suitable for public worship, but it must be adapted to a worship setting.[13]

An order of worship that Calvin provides for the Sunday service gives extensive attention to intercession. He also provides an order of worship for a special weekday service, in which the accent falls on prayers that are determined by the circumstances (plague, war, etc.).[14] The order of worship for the Sunday service in *La Forme des prières* looks like this:

Invocation

Call to confession and prayer

Assurance of pardon

Hymn (in the second edition of *La Forme des prières* [1545] the singing of the first table of the law also occurs here)

Prayer for obedience

Hymn (in the 1545 edition the singing of the second table of the law also occurs here; meanwhile, the minister mounts the pulpit)

---

11. Pierre Pidoux produced a facsimile edition, *La Forme des prières et chantz ecclésiastiques . . .* , which appeared in Kassel and Basel in 1959. Ford Lewis Battles has provided an English translation of the "Letter to the Reader" with which *La Forme des prières* begins: "John Calvin, *The Form of Prayers and Songs of the Church*, 1542, 'Letter to the Reader,'" *CTJ* 15 (1980): 160–65.

12. The title reads: *La Manyère de faire prières aux églises françoyses. Tant devant la prédication comme après, ensemble pseaulmes et cantiques françoys qu'on chante aus dictes églises, après sensuyt l'ordre et façon d'administrer les sacramentz de baptesme, et de la saincte cène de nostre Seigneur Iésu Christ, de espouser et confirmer le mariage devant l'assemblée des fidèles. Avecques le sermon tant du baptesme que de la cène. Le tout selon la parolle de nostre Seigneur* (for the text see the various printings of the Genevan editions).

13. See H. H. Wolf, "Die Bedeutung der Musik bei Calvin," *MGKK* 41 (1936); Arnold Geering, "Calvin und die Musik," in *Calvin-Studien 1959*, ed. Jürgen Moltmann (Neukirchen, 1960), 16–25; Charles Garside, Jr., *The Origins of Calvin's Theology of Music, 1536–1543* (Philadelphia, 1979).

14. On November 11, 1541, the Council established Wednesday as a special prayer day.

Prayer (concluded with the Lord's Prayer)
Hymn
Prayer for illumination of the Holy Spirit
Scripture reading
Sermon
Prayer (including intercession)
Explanation of the Lord's Prayer
Hymn
Benediction (Numbers 6:24–26)

With regard to the sacraments, Calvin cites Augustine's reference to them as visible words. But there must not only be something to see; for a good understanding of these things an explanation must be heard. True consecration takes place by the declaration and reception of the word of faith (Augustine).

Baptism is to take place in the Sunday afternoon service or in a weekday service after the sermon, and ordinary water should be used (no salt, oil, etc.). As far as the Lord's Supper is concerned, Calvin first points out that the big difference between communion and the mass has to do with the fact that the celebration of the former goes back to its institution by Christ. On the Sunday before, attention ought to be focused on the upcoming celebration so that each person can prepare, so that the children will participate in the celebration only if they have had proper instruction and have made a profession, and so that the "strangers" can personally ask for further instruction beforehand. Calvin places a strong emphasis on the worthy celebration of the Supper and adds verses 27–29 to the account of the institution of the Lord's Supper in 1 Corinthians 11:23–26. This is followed by a warning that states who exactly are to be excluded from the celebration. Then the members of the congregation are challenged to examine themselves as the apostle bids them to do.

Calvin further states, however, that our faith is not perfect. The Lord's Supper is a medicine for poor, sick people. The members of the congregation must place their hope in the promise of Jesus Christ, who desires to have fellowship with us, so that he lives in us and we in him. Calvin challenges the congregation to lift up their hearts (*sursum corda*) to where Jesus Christ is in heavenly glory and from where he will come for their deliverance. We have the bread and wine as signs and testimonies as we spiritually seek the truth in those places where, according to God's Word, we will find it.

The celebration of the Lord's Supper is to follow the sermon and to be preceded by the congregation's singing of the Apostles' Creed while the minister prepares the table. The Lord's Prayer and a communion prayer are recited. Then after instruction about the meaning of the Lord's Supper, the celebration itself takes place, with the deacons distributing the bread and wine.

La Forme des prières also explains how the confirmation of a marriage should proceed. The work ends with a brief explanation of the task of the minister regarding the visitation of the sick.

In 1545 a new edition of *La Forme des prières et chantz ecclésiastiques* appeared, which was practically the same as *La Manyère* of 1542.[15]

On June 10, 1543, Calvin wrote a foreword to the edition of the psalms that had been set to verse by Marot and were now to be published in Geneva together with *La Forme des prières et chantz ecclésiastiques*, which was first published in 1542. Marot himself had published a versification of thirty psalms in 1542 in Lyons. The edition of 1543 contains forty-nine psalms, even though the title refers to fifty: *Cinquante pseaumes en françois par Clém. Marot*. This edition includes the thirty psalms published earlier (revised and improved) and a number of other songs, including the Song of Simeon, the Ten Commandments, the Apostles' Creed, the Lord's Prayer, the greeting of the angels (which the Council asked to be omitted when the book was reprinted!), and table prayers for before and after meals. Calvin's versifications gave way to those of Marot as the latter gained acceptance.

Marot died in Turin on September 12, 1544. His versifications were being sung in the services in Geneva, and the question now was who would set to verse the remaining 101 psalms. When Calvin discovered by chance in 1548 that Theodore Beza had set Psalm 16 to verse, the ministers asked Beza to continue with Marot's work. His psalm versifications appeared intermittently until the work was finished in 1561. King Charles IX of France gave the Huguenots permission to import the psalter from Geneva, so during May 1562 the Genevans worked full-time on the printing of the psalm versifications by Marot and Beza.[16] Twenty-seven thousand copies were shipped to France.

Instruction of the Youth

The *Articles* presented by the ministers to the Council of Geneva on January 16, 1537, dealt in part with the instruction that the church should

---

15. The title of this edition reads: *La Forme des prières et chantz ecclésiastiques, avec la manière d'administrer les sacremens, et consacrer le mariage, selon la coustume de l'église ancienne. . .* (Strasbourg, 1545).

16. Clément Marot and Theodore Beza, *Les Pseaumes en vers français, avec leurs mélodies* (Geneva, 1986). This is a facsimile of the Genevan edition of 1562.

give the children.[17] This instruction is important, we read, for their profession of faith. The ministers are to draw up a brief and simple summary of the faith that all children must learn. A few times a year the children should meet with the ministers to be examined and to receive further instruction until they are sufficiently trained. The Council should see to it that parents train their children in the catechism and have them meet with the ministers at the appointed time.

About a month after the *Articles* were submitted to the Council and were accepted with a few minor changes, the aforementioned *Instruction et confession de foy dont on use en l'église de Genève* (*CO* 22:25–74; *OS* 1:378–417) appeared. It was intended to meet the *Articles'* call for a brief and simple summary of the faith suitable for the instruction of children.

The original text of the catechism must have been in Latin, but the first published edition was written in French. A Latin edition was printed in Basel in 1538: *Catechismus, sive christianae religionis institutio* (*CO* 5:313–62; *OS* 1:426–32). The contents of this catechism follow the *Institutes* of 1536.

In the French congregation in Strasbourg and later also in Geneva, Calvin made catechetical use of *L'Institution puérile de la doctrine chrestienne faicte par manière de dyalogue* (*OS* 2:152–56), which he probably wrote between 1538 and 1541.[18] Calvin also wrote a new catechism in a very short time in November 1541: *Le Catéchisme de l'église de Genève, c'est a dire le Formulaire d'instruire les enfants en la chrestienté* (*CO* 6:1–134), which was published in early 1542.[19] In this catechism one notices the influence of Martin Bucer that Calvin had come under in Strasbourg. Bucer had composed a *Kurtze schrifftliche erklärung für die kinder und angohnden, der gemeinen artickeln unsers christlichen glaubens, der zehen gebott, des Vatter unsers . . .* (Strasbourg, 1534), which he followed with a less detailed catechism in 1537: *Der kürtzer Catechismus und erklärung der XII stücken Christlichs glaubens. Des Vatter unsers unnd der Zehen gepotten . . .* (Strasbourg, 1537).[20]

Compared with what Calvin had written earlier, the material in his later catechism was handled in a new way. He now employed the question-and-

---

17. On the subject of Calvin and instruction of the youth see M. B. van 't Veer, *Catechese en catechetische stof bij Calvijn* (Kampen, 1941); Willem Verboom, *De catechese van de Reformatie en de Nadere Reformatie* (Amsterdam, 1986).

18. Willem Verboom, "De catechese in Genève," in *De catechese van de Reformatie*, 53–65.

19. See Jean-Pierre Pin, "Pour une analyse textuelle du catéchisme (1542) de Jean Calvin," in *Calvinus ecclesiae doctor*, ed. Wilhelm H. Neuser (Kampen, 1980), 159–70; Jaques Courvoisier, "Les Catéchismes de Genève et de Strasbourg," *BSHPF* 85 (1935): 105–21.

20. For the text see *Martin Bucers Deutsche Schriften*, vol. 6.3, *Martin Bucers Katechismen aus den Jahren 1534, 1537, 1543*, ed. Robert Stupperich (Gütersloh, 1987).

answer form (373 questions and answers) and, strikingly, treated the Apostles' Creed before the Ten Commandments. No original copy of this catechism has survived, but the content is the same as the Latin edition of 1545. On November 28, 1545, Calvin dedicated the Latin translation of his catechism (*Catechismus ecclesiae Genevensis, hoc est, formula erudiendi pueros in doctrina Christi* [Strasbourg, 1545]—*CO* 6:1–146; *OS* 2:72–151) to the "faithful ministers of Christ who preach the pure doctrine of the gospel in East Friesland."[21] People in East Friesland, where his writings were being read, had asked him for this dedication. In the dedication Calvin states that he has written this catechism in Latin in order to bring to expression the unity of the churches. They may be far apart from each other in distance, but they are one with each other in the confession of the same faith.

In 1551 the booklet *L'ABC françois* appeared in Geneva.[22] This little book was intended to be used in school for the catechizing of the youngest children, who would learn not only the alphabet, but also the Lord's Prayer, the Apostles' Creed, and the Ten Commandments. We also find various prayers, which come, for the most part, from Calvin and are intended for a variety of occasions. In addition, the booklet contains a short explanation by Calvin of what children who want to participate in the Lord's Supper need to know: a large number of Bible verses as well as twenty-one questions and answers that Calvin drew up with a view to participation in communion. Four times a year, before each celebration of the Lord's Supper, the children were given an opportunity in a church service to answer the questions. Demonstrating a satisfactory knowledge of the faith there was considered as a profession of faith.[23] In these questions and answers Calvin followed the order of his catechism. After 1553 they also appeared in the edition of the catechism under the title *La Manière d'interroguer les enfans qu'on veut recevoir à la cène de nostre Seigneur Iésus Christ* (see *CO* 6:147–60).

Special Assistance

In this section we focus our attention on several treatises that Calvin wrote to help others. We reflect here, in the first place, on what he wrote about the

21. For an English translation (with introduction) see *Calvin: Theological Treatises*, ed. Reid, 83–139.

22. Rodolphe Peter, "The Geneva Primer or Calvin's Elementary Catechism," in *Calvin Studies V: Papers Presented at a Colloquium on Calvin Studies at Davidson College* . . . , ed. John H. Leith (Davidson, N.C.: 1990), 135–61.

23. See *Les Ordonnances ecclésiastiques* (of both 1541 and 1561)—*CO* 10a:28 and 115–16; see also Calvin's letter of November 11, 1560, to Kaspar Olevianus (*CO* 18:236).

meaning of the Lord's Supper. Next we take up what he wrote to help out those of evangelical persuasion in France, who were in a difficult position and more than once were at a loss to know how to act in their situation. Calvin called them Nicodemites and later even used the term *pseudo-Nicodemites.* In the context of special assistance we also look at his warnings against astrology (*Advertissement contre l'astrologie*) and at his work on offenses (*De scandalis*).

Treatises on the Lord's Supper

Petit traicté de la saincte cène (1541)

At others' insistence, Calvin wrote a treatise in 1540 (while still in Strasbourg) in which he explained for people in the pew the basic meaning of the Lord's Supper.[24] Many did not know what to think amid all the confusing discussion about the Lord's Supper. Because this little book was intended for lay people, Calvin wrote it in French. He published it in Geneva in 1541, and Nicolas Des Gallars provided a Latin translation in 1545 (*Libellus de coena Domini*).[25]

In the title of the French edition of 1541, Calvin calls the little book a *Short Treatise on the Holy Supper of Our Lord Jesus Christ.* As the full title indicates, his intent was to demonstrate the true teaching, benefit, and use of the Lord's Supper, as well as to indicate the reasons why "the moderns," by whom he meant Martin Luther, Ulrich Zwingli, and Johannes Oecolampadius, had written so differently about it.

At the beginning of the treatise, Calvin says that he wishes to accommodate the common people by explaining the basic meaning of the Lord's Supper. Not only that, but others have requested such an explanation. Then he goes into the institution of the Lord's Supper by Jesus Christ, who established the sacrament to signify and seal the promises of the gospel, to train us to recognize his exceeding goodness toward us, and to urge us to lead a Christian life (Calvin mentions particularly unity and brotherly love).

24. On the subject of Calvin and the Lord's Supper, see *TRE*, s.v. "Abendmahl in der Reformation"; and Willem Balke, "Het avondmaal bij Calvijn," in *Bij brood en beker: Leer en gebruik van het heilig avondmaal in het Nieuwe Testament en in de geschiedenis van de westerse kerk*, ed. Willem van 't Spijker et al. (Goudriaan, 1980), 178–225.

25. *Petit traicté de la saincte cène de nostre Seigneur Iésus Christ. Auquel est demonstré la vraye institution, proffit et utilité d'icelle. Ensemble la cause pourquoy plusieurs des modernes semblent en avoir escrit diversement* (*CO* 5:429–60; *OS* 1:503–30). Francis M. Higman provides an introduction and the text in John Calvin, *Three French Treatises* (London, 1970). For a modern French edition see Jean Calvin, *Petit traité de la sainte cène,* ed. H. Châtelain and P. Marcel (Paris, 1959). For an introduction and modern French text of *Petit traité* see *La Vraie Piété: Divers traités de Jean Calvin et Confession de foi de Guillaume Farel,* ed. Irena Backus and Claire Chimelli (Geneva, 1986), 123–51. For an English translation (with introduction) see *Calvin: Theological Treatises,* ed. Reid, 140–66.

Next Calvin deals with the benefits of celebrating the Lord's Supper and further explains how we participate in communion with Christ. He goes on to discuss the right way to celebrate the sacrament and then examines a few of the errors with respect to its meaning, for instance, the conception of the Lord's Supper as a sacrifice by which we obtain the remission of sins, and transubstantiation. In this context he also attacks the mass.

Finally, Calvin takes up the debate about the Lord's Supper that Protestants had been conducting recently. He talks about "the dispute that has arisen in our day" (the religious colloquy in Marburg in 1529), which he looks upon unfavorably. The devil has stirred up this controversy to impede the advance of the gospel or even to obstruct it altogether.

With regard to this discussion, Calvin mentions particularly Luther on the one hand, and Zwingli and Oecolampadius on the other. He indicates what their positive contributions were, but he also mentions the weaknesses in their ideas. Luther emphasized the bodily presence of Christ in the Lord's Supper, but did not state how this differs from the Roman Catholic conception. Luther should also have said that what is involved is not the veneration of the sacrament but the veneration of God. Moreover, he should have expressed himself more clearly and precisely. Zwingli and Oecolampadius, on the other hand, stood over against the Roman Catholic conception by placing a strong emphasis on the bodily presence of Christ in heaven. They too spoke of the body and blood of Christ in connection with the Lord's Supper, but they made no association between the sign and the truth signified, thereby leaving the impression that they intended to push real communion with Christ in the Lord's Supper into the background.

Both sides erred, says Calvin, in that they did not listen to each other patiently and were not really committed to finding the truth together. But that is not to say that we should not be thankful for what the Lord God has given us in these men. As far as the dispute is concerned, the storm has died down somewhat; and Calvin expresses the hope that before long all those involved will draw up a generally accepted formula, which is so greatly needed.

Calvin ends with the confession that in the celebration of the Lord's Supper believers partake of the body and blood of Christ. How this happens one person may be able to describe better than another. But this much is certain: we must raise our hearts upwards to heaven, so that we not think that Christ is enclosed in the elements of bread and wine. So as not to diminish the efficacy of the sacraments, we must remember, says Calvin, that we partake of Christ by the secret and incomprehensible power of God. It is the Holy Spirit who effects our partaking of Christ; that is why we use the term *spiritual.*

A Brief and Clear Summary of the Lord's Supper (1560)

In November 1560, at the request of Albert Rizaeus Hardenberg, minister in Bremen, Calvin wrote a small treatise on the Lord's Supper entitled *Breve et clarum doctrinae de coena Domini compendium* (*CO* 9:681–88). The treatise was not published; a copy of the manuscript can be found in the library in Geneva. Because of his Reformed view of the Lord's Supper, Hardenberg had no end of trouble with his Lutheran colleagues, who even drove him out of Bremen (see also Calvin's letter to Hardenberg that is dated November 7, 1560—*CO* 18:233–34).

Writings to the Nicodemites and Pseudo-Nicodemites in France

Petit traicté (1543)

In a "short treatise" (*Petit traicté*) in 1543, Calvin deals with the crisis of conscience that many in France who had come to the Reformation faith were experiencing.[26] In the full title of the treatise he indicates what the struggles were: How should one of the faithful who knows the truth of the gospel act among Roman Catholics? Should the Protestants in France declare their faith openly, or should they keep it a secret in their Roman Catholic environment?

Before giving his opinion on the mass, Calvin makes clear that the way in which we serve the Lord God is not an insignificant matter. Confession of the name of God in one's heart cannot be separated from a similar confession with one's mouth. We may never detract from the honor of God; this requires every believer to confess one's faith openly. Calvin points to Cyprian, who refused to worship an idol even though he could have saved his life by doing so.

Calvin concludes the little treatise with the following advice: if at all possible, emigrate. If that is not possible, stay away entirely from Roman Catholic church services. Those who do not have the willpower for that and participate in the church services out of fear of others, should continually confess their guilt before God, so that their consciences do not fall asleep. Moreover, they should pray to God for deliverance and then look for means to get out of their situation.

According to the official title of the *Petit traicté*, a letter was added as a postscript in which the same set of questions is discussed. This was a letter that Calvin had already written on September 12, 1540, to a friend who had asked him how to act when living in the midst of Roman Catholics.

---

26. *Petit traicté, monstrant que c'est que doit faire un homme fidèle congnoissant la vérité de l'évangile quand il est entre les papistes. Avec une épistre du mesme argument* (*CO* 6:537–88; *Recueil des opuscules* [Geneva, 1566], 758–89).

Martin Luther (woodcut by Lucas Cranach the Younger)

Excuse à Messieurs les Nicodémites (1544)

In the treatise *Excuse à Messieurs les Nicodémites* (1544) Calvin again turned his attention to the problems of Reformation believers living in a Roman Catholic setting. According to the complete title, they had complained about his being too rigorous.[27] Calvin begins by offering his apology to those who were hurt by the *Petit traicté* of 1543. But he will not say anything good about them because they have not really chosen between God and the devil. Since they refer to Nicodemus, Calvin will from now on call them Nicodemites. What they do not understand is that they must deny themselves, and that if they are to serve God, they must forget the world. With respect to Nicodemus,

---

27. *Excuse de Iehan Calvin, à Messieurs les Nicodémites, sur la complaincte qu'ilz font de sa trop grand'rigueur* (CO 6:589–614; *Recueil des opuscules*, 789–803). See also *Three French Treatises*, ed. Higman, 131–53 (introduction, 21–26).

Calvin notes that initially, when Nicodemus was still in ignorance, he went to Jesus by night, but later he openly displayed his faith as a disciple at Jesus' burial. As a Christian, Nicodemus did not fear persecution.

In 1549 Calvin's *De vitandis superstitionibus* appeared, which was a Latin translation of *Petit traicté* and *Excuse à Messieurs les Nicodémites.*[28] The Latin title of *Excuse* indicates that he is addressing pseudo-Nicodemites, a name that suggests that he did not regard the Nicodemites as true followers of Nicodemus.[29]

Correspondence regarding *Petit traicté* and *Excuse*

Following the publication of his *Petit traicté* and *Excuse*, Calvin received a letter at the end of 1544 from Antoine Fumée, a member of the Parlement of Paris (*CO* 11:826–30), asking him to find out the opinions of Luther, Philipp Melanchthon, and Martin Bucer concerning these two treatises in which Calvin had disapproved of the conduct of the so-called Nicodemites. Fumée stated that he was prepared to cover the travel costs to have the letters delivered.

On January 21, 1545, Calvin wrote a letter to Luther (*CO* 12:7–8), "the very illustrious teacher of the Christian church, my much revered father," in which he asks Luther to read the letter and the two booklets and then to offer his own opinion. For the people in France who are upset by what Calvin has written and are at a loss to know what to do would like to hear what Luther thinks about it. They wish thereby to find strength for what they have to do. Calvin writes that he would very much like to fly to Luther to enjoy a few hours together with him. He would then want to handle personally with Luther not just this question, but other matters as well. "But what is not afforded us here on earth will, I trust, before long be imparted to us in the kingdom of God."

Calvin did not send this letter directly to Luther but to Melanchthon (see *CO* 12:9–12). He asks Melanchthon for his opinion on the same matter and requests that he first read the two treatises and the letter intended for Luther and then use his own discretion about what to do next. Realizing that Luther

---

28. *De vitandis superstitionibus, quae cum sincera fidei confessione pugnant, libellus Ioannis Calvini. Eiusdem excusatio, ad pseudonicodemos. Philippi Melanctonis, Martini Buceri, Petri Martyris responsa de eadem re. Calvini ultimum responsum, cum appendicibus* (Geneva, 1549).

29. Cf. Calvin's commentary on John 19:38–39, where he says that those who appeal to Nicodemus are like him in one respect: they strive to bury Christ (*CO* 47:423–24). See also Eugénie Droz, "Calvin et les nicodémites," in *Chemins de l'hérésie: Textes et documents*, 4 vols. (Geneva, 1970–76), 1:131–71; Hans Scholl, *Reformation und Politik: Politische Ethik bei Luther, Calvin und Frühhugenotten* (Stuttgart, 1976), 66–86; Carlos M. N. Eire, "Calvin and Nicodemism: A Reappraisal," *SCJ* 10 (1979): 45–69; idem, *War against the Idols: The Reformation of Worship from Erasmus to Calvin* (Cambridge, 1986), chapter 7; Francis M. Higman, "The Question of Nicodemism," in *Calvinus ecclesiae Genevensis custos*, ed. Wilhelm H. Neuser (Frankfurt am Main, 1984), 165–70.

is easily irritated, Calvin does not want to go ahead with something that after-wards might turn out to have been wrong.

Melanchthon did not dare to send Calvin's letter to Luther because Luther, according to Melanchthon in a letter to Calvin (*CO* 12:61), was suspicious of so many things and would not want his answers to questions like Calvin's spread everywhere. Meanwhile, in a letter on February 12, 1545, Calvin informed Pierre Viret of what he had done and sent him copies of several let-ters, including those to Luther and Melanchthon (*CO* 12:32–33).

In 1545 a little book appeared in Geneva containing reprints of Calvin's *Petit traicté* of 1543 and *Excuse* of 1544. A new edition in 1546 included the let-ters (*Conseils*) written by Melanchthon, Bucer, and Peter Martyr Vermigli when the French evangelicals, upset by Calvin's view of the Nicodemites, asked them about their positions. All three stood behind Calvin. In later reprints Calvin also added both a postscript to these letters (*Le Conseil et con-clusion de M. Iean Calvin*) and two letters that he had written to some unnamed Protestants in France (*Recueil des opuscules*, 803–20; the second let-ter, dated July 14, 1546, was written to Valérand Poullain). I have already referred to the 1549 Latin edition of the two treatises (*De vitandis superstition-ibus*; see n. 28). In the reprint of 1550, we find the position taken by the Zurich ministers on June 17, 1549 (*Recueil des opuscules*, 821–24), for the *Consensus Tig-urinus* had been achieved shortly before. Heinrich Bullinger had sent the state-ment of their position to Calvin along with the request that it be included in the reprint.

Calvin's position that the French Protestants had the choice of either dying as martyrs in France or confessing their faith elsewhere became known far and wide in Europe through the translation of his *Petit traicté* and *Excuse* into var-ious languages (German, Czech, English, Dutch, and Italian). It certainly con-tributed to the fact that many people, French and others (some five thousand during the period 1549–59), sought refuge in Geneva.[30]

Another result of the circulation of Calvin's *Petit traicté* and *Excuse* was that in 1560 Theodore Coornhert published his little book *Verschooninghe van de Roomsche afgoderye*, in which he opposed the view expressed by Calvin in his two treatises. Coornhert was in agreement with the pseudo-Nicodemites and tried to win others over to the same point of view. That involved fighting for

---

30. See Droz, "Calvin et les nicodémites," which refers to a couple of works by Albert Autin, *Un Episode de la vie de Calvin: La Crise du nicodémisme, 1535–1545* (Toulon, 1917), and *L'Echec de la Réforme en France* (Paris, 1918), and to Ewald Rieser's *Calvin—Franzose, Genfer oder Fremdling? Untersuchung zum Problem der Heimatliebe bei Calvin* (Zurich, 1968), especially 98–119 ("Exil oder Mut zum Martyrium").

RESPONSE
A VN CERTAIN HO-
lïdois, lequel fous ombre de
faire les Chreftiens tout fpi-
rituels, leur permet de polluer leur corps en toutes ido
latries.

Ifcrite par M. IEAN CALVIN aux
fideles du pays bas.

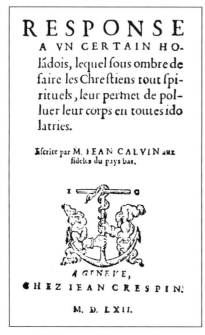

A GENEVE,
CHEZ IEAN CRESPIN.
M. D. LXII.

DES SCANDALES
qui empefchent au-
iourdhuy beaucoup de gens
DE VENIR A LA PVRE
doctrine de l'Euangile, & en desbauchét d'autres.

TRAICTE COMPOSE
nouuellement par Iehan Caluin.

I. COR. II.
QVI EST ICANDALIZE, QVE
IE N'EN SOYE BRVLLE?

A GENEVE.
De l'imprimerie de Iehã Crefpin.
M. D. L.

Title page of Response à un
certain Holandois ...

Title page of
Des scandales

reform, disdaining ceremonies (what matters is what is internal, not external), and placing heavy demands on witnessing to Christ. The conclusion was that those who followed Calvin or Menno Simons could not possibly be martyrs and necessarily denied reformational ideas.

Calvin responded in 1562 with the publication in Geneva of his *Response à un certain Holandois.*[31] He was responding not merely because he had been attacked personally, but especially because Coornhert's view both failed to appreciate those who had been martyred and could harm the advance of the Reformation in the Netherlands.

Finally, we turn our attention to the foreword that Calvin wrote for the edition of his *Quatre sermons. . . avec briefve exposition du Pseaume LXXXVII* (Geneva, 1552). In the foreword (*SC* 7:xxxviii–xxxix) he says that he had written two treatises to show that the way the Nicodemites were acting was not

---

31. *Response à un certain Holandois, lequel sous ombre de faire les chrestiens tout spirituels, leur permet de polluer leurs corps en toutes idolatries. Escrite par M. Iean Calvin aux fidèles du pays bas* (Geneva, 1562—*CO* 9:581–628; *Recueil des opuscules,* 1850–84). See also S. van der Linde, "Calvijn en Coornhert," *ThR* 2 (1959): 176–87; Frederik L. Rutgers, *Calvijns invloed op de Reformatie in de Nederlanden, voor zooveel die door hemzelven is uitgeoefend* (Leiden, 1899; reprint, Leeuwarden, 1980).

right. Still, people were asking him for advice as if he had never written anything. This edition of sermons has to do with that subject (see pp. 110–11).

Advertissement contre l'astrologie *(1549)*

In 1549 Calvin published a little treatise in which he warned against astrology: *Advertissement contre l'astrologie*.[32] He had dictated the text of the work to his secretary, François Hotman, who also prepared a Latin translation that was published on March 1, 1549, and dedicated to Laurent de Normandie.[33]

The church fathers, particularly Augustine, had rejected pagan astrology, but in the sixteenth century the focus on the classics had led to a growing interest in it. Calvin must have been familiar with the work *Advertissement sur les jugemens d'astrologie, à une studieuse damoyselle*, which had appeared in Lyons in 1546. Mellin de Saint-Gelais, who was very likely the author, advocated the rehabilitation of astrology. It is well known that in the years 1546–49 Calvin tried to get the Council of Geneva either to do away with the almanacs that still bore evidence of old superstitions or to replace them with better ones.

In this publication Calvin speaks out against the superstition that the course of one's life can be determined from the stars. For Calvin the course of life for human beings depends above all on God, who operates in their lives according to his wisdom, justice, and goodness.

De scandalis *(1550)*

Calvin had been planning for a long time to write a little book on "scandals" (i.e., stumbling blocks or offenses). In September 1546 he informed Guillaume Farel by letter (*CO* 12:380) that he had begun the writing, but had then stopped because he could not find the right tone and because of the demands of other work. When the book was completed in 1550,[34] he gave the following charac-

---

32. *Advertissement contre l'astrologie qu'on appelle iudiciaire, et autres curiositéz qui regnent aujourd'huy au monde* (Geneva, 1549—*CO* 7:509–42; *Recueil des opuscules*, 1118–37). See also Jean Calvin, *Advertissement contre l'astrologie judiciaire*, ed. Olivier Millet (Geneva, 1985), and "A Warning against Judiciary Astrology and Other Prevalent Curiosities," trans. Mary Potter, *CTJ* 18 (1983): 157–89.

33. *Admonitio adversus astrologiam, quam iudiciariam vocant; aliasque praeterea curiositates nonnullas, quae hodie per universum fere orbem grassantur* (Geneva, 1549).

34. The Latin edition, *De scandalis quibus hodie plerique absterrentur, nonnulli etiam alienantur a pura evangelii doctrina* (*CO* 8:1–84; *OS* 2:162–240), was the first to appear, but the French edition was also published in 1550 in Geneva: *Des Scandales qui empeschent auiourdhuy beaucoup de gens de venir à la pure doctrine de l'évangile, et en débauchent d'autres . . .* (*Recueil des opuscules*, 1145–1219). See also the important critical edition—Jean Calvin, *Des Scandales*, ed. Olivier Fatio and C. Rapin (Geneva, 1984). A modern French text with notes can be found in Jean Calvin, *Trois traités comprenant en un volume*, ed. Albert-Marie Schmidt (Paris, 1934). For an English translation see John Calvin, *Concerning Scandals*, trans. John W. Fraser (Grand Rapids, 1978).

terization of it in a letter to Farel (dated August 19—*CO* 13:623): in proportion to the abundance of material on this subject, the booklet on scandals is not only short but very concise. It all comes down to this, that impudent people have no right to slander and discredit the gospel under the pretext that it creates stumbling blocks; the weak, however, must be strengthened in order to overcome with a steadfast faith whatever stumbling blocks Satan places in the way. If someone is diverted from the right path, or takes offense, or falls away, he himself is to blame and can offer no excuses. At the same time, however, I show how dreadful the punishment of God is for those who create stumbling blocks.

Calvin's booklet on "scandals," then, was a polemical writing, yet was intended especially to fortify the faith of those who had to contend with various arguments that were being brought against the gospel. These attacks were coming from, among others, (1) those in humanist circles who disdained the gospel and believed they were not really learned if they did not mock God, and (2) those in Roman Catholic circles who wished to do the Reformation harm.

In the work itself Calvin lists three kinds of offenses. One can take offense at the gospel itself, particularly at the work of Christ and what he says about self-denial, for the latter runs counter to our own ideas. Second, offense can be created by things that accompany the arrival of the gospel but conflict with it, such as all sorts of confusion, impiety, and sects. Under the third form of offense Calvin mentions various kinds of backbiting over reformed practices, including slander at the hands of both public opinion and Roman Catholics.

In a foreword that he wrote on July 10, 1550, Calvin dedicated *De scandalis* to Laurent de Normandie. Normandie hailed from France but since 1548 had resided in Geneva, where he was a bookseller. In the foreword Calvin says that he finds it appropriate to dedicate this particular booklet to Normandie, because he had experienced a number of setbacks in his life, one right after the other. A few months after his flight from France, he had lost his father, wife, and little daughter to death within the space of half a year. His faith was especially tested by those who sharpened the pain of his setbacks with slanderous language. In all of that, he stood firm through the power of God's Spirit. Calvin thinks that Normandie in so doing is an example that verifies what is taught in this writing.

Confession of Faith: The Gallican Confession (1559)

We have already dealt with Calvin's relation to the *Instruction et confession de foy* of 1537. In this section, therefore, we shall limit ourselves to Calvin's involvement in the drafting of the French confession of faith, the Gallican Confession (1559).

The first national synod was held secretly in Paris from May 25 to 29, 1559. Participating were approximately twenty ministers and elders representing seventy-two congregations. The president of the synod was François de Morel, minister in Paris and successor to Jean Macard, whom Calvin had called back to Geneva because of the dangerous situation. Morel had written Calvin shortly before that a synod would be meeting in Paris and that there were plans to draw up a confession of faith (see *CO* 17:502–6; for Calvin's answer of May 17, see *CO* 17:525, 527).

The synod approved the Gallican Confession, a confession of faith consisting of forty articles. At the last moment, Calvin had had Nicolas Des Gallars take a draft of thirty-four articles to Paris, and it appears from a letter from Morel to Calvin (dated June 5—*CO* 17:540–42) that the synod made only insignificant changes in the draft that Calvin had hastily written (for the text see *CO* 9:739–52): they expanded Calvin's treatment of the Word of God from one article to five.

Before approving the Gallican Confession, the synod adopted a church order. This *Discipline ecclésiastique* used as its source *Les Ordonnances ecclésiastiques*, which had been adopted in Geneva in 1541. It was also based on a simple church order composed by a number of ministers in Poitiers in 1558 after an incident in the rue St. Jacques (see p. 68). The Belgic Confession of Faith (1561) is an adaptation of the Gallican Confession.[35]

It was also decided at the first national synod not to publish the confession and church order for the time being, since the situation in France was so dangerous. When at last they were published, two editions of the Gallican Confession appeared: one in 1559, consisting of thirty-five articles and with a foreword addressed to "the poor believers" in France and all who wish to listen (see *CO* 9:731–52); and the other in 1560, consisting of forty articles and preceded by a letter to the king (for the text of the letter see *CO* 9:737–40).[36]

The official text was established in 1571 at a synod in La Rochelle.[37] As for the confession of faith that Calvin drew up for the French Reformed churches for delivery in 1562 to the emperor in Frankfurt, we refer the reader to the biographical section (p. 78).

---

35. J. N. Bakhuizen van den Brink, *La Confession de foi des églises réformées de France de 1559, et la Confession des Pays-Bas de 1561*, vol. 5.6 of *Bulletin des Eglises Wallones* (Leiden, 1959).

36. See J. N. Bakhuizen van den Brink, *Protestantse pleidooien*, vol. 2, section 3, *Frankrijk en Calvijn* (Kampen, 1962), 81–96.

37. Jacques Pannier, *Les Origines de la Confession de foi et la Discipline des églises réformées de France* (Paris, 1936).

Church Order and Visitation

Les Ordonnances ecclésiastiques *(1541)*

When Calvin returned to Geneva in 1541, he planned to stay only temporarily. His wife had remained behind in Strasbourg. After the Council immediately granted his request to draw up a written church order, however, he promised the Council that, as far as he was concerned, he would always be the servant of Geneva. Six members of the Council were assigned to the task. Calvin and the four other ministers of Geneva also formed part of the committee. Meanwhile, arrangements were made for Calvin's wife and their belongings to be brought over to Geneva. On September 26 the committee presented its draft to the Little Council. The Council of Two Hundred endorsed it on November 9, and on November 20 it was taken up and approved by the General Council.

The new church order (*Les Ordonnances ecclésiastiques: Projet d'ordonnances sur les offices ecclésiastiques*—*CO* 10a:15–30; *OS* 2:328–61) did not retain everything that Calvin had in mind.[38] Quarterly celebration of the Lord's Supper, for example, was instituted in place of monthly communion in each of the city's three churches.[39] Moreover, there is no mention of the complete independence of the Consistory (*consistoire*), which was to be made up of the ministers and twelve elders chosen by the city councils and (although this is not found in the church order!) to be presided over by a syndic-elder. Calvin supported the laying on of hands at the ordination of a minister, but that too was rejected by the Council, which was afraid of the superstition associated with it (reported in the *Ordonnances*; see *CO* 10a:18).

A newly chosen minister had to swear an oath in the Council, the text of which was drafted by Calvin in 1542 and formally established by the Council. Until 1561, the elders had to swear the oath also. In it one promised, among other things, to remain loyal to the Council and to keep the laws; in so doing, however, one always retained the freedom to preach God's Word according to his command. Furthermore, the regulations concerning discipline and excommunication appear to present problems in practice between the Council and the Consistory, because it is not stated clearly enough who has the right of excommunication, the church or the civil government (see pp. 43–45).

---

38. For an English translation (with an introduction) see *Calvin: Theological Treatises*, ed. Reid, 56–72; see also Plomp, *De kerkelijke tucht,* 166–90.

39. Perhaps Geneva here was following Zurich, where it had been decided in 1525 to celebrate the Lord's Supper four times a year (Easter, Pentecost, September 11, and Christmas), and Bern, where the practice of quarterly communion had been introduced in 1528.

It is significant that the new church order speaks of four offices: minister, doctor or teacher, elder, and deacon. The main tasks of the minister are the proclamation of the Word of God, the administration of the sacraments, and (with the elders) the maintenance of discipline. A new minister is admitted to his office after the other ministers have made a selection, the Little Council has given its approval, and the congregation has concurred. The ministers are to meet together once a week (*"compagnie des pasteurs"*) for study, mutual correction, and planning of their work.

The task of the "doctors" is concerned with the instruction of believers in sound doctrine, so that the purity of the gospel is not tainted by ignorance or false ideas.[40] But with this office Calvin is also thinking of those who are involved in education and train the young for the office of minister or an office in civil service. In this regard Calvin has in mind a system of higher education like the one he had seen in Strasbourg, although it was not until 1559 that the Academy of Geneva was founded and opened.

The elders have as their duty the supervision of the Christian life (*disciplina christiana*).[41] They are nominated by both the Little Council and the ministers and chosen by the Council of Two Hundred from the various councils of the city (two from the Little Council, four from the Council of Sixty, and six from the Council of Two Hundred). They serve for one year but can be reelected (which is also considered desirable). The Consistory meets once a week and tries through dialogue and admonition to resolve current conflicts in the congregation. This might be followed by denial of admission to the Lord's Supper and banning from the church. But it is not clear whether the Consistory only gives advice to the Council, which then has the right of excommunication, or whether the Consistory operates as an independent ecclesiastical body. Whoever has been summoned and refuses to show up at a meeting of the Consistory will be reported to the Council and will have to appear there.

Deacons are responsible for the poor and sick, many of whom are accommodated in the "hospital," which is under the deacons' charge.[42] There they bake bread and distribute it also among those who, though they do not stay in

---

40. W. F. Dankbaar, "Het doctorenambt bij Calvijn," in idem, *Hervormers en humanisten: Een bundel opstellen* (Amsterdam, 1978), 153–83 (this article originally appeared as "L'Office des docteurs chez Calvin," *RHPhR* 44 [1964]: 364–88); John T. McNeill, "John Calvin: Doctor Ecclesiae," in *The Heritage of John Calvin*, ed. John H. Bratt (Grand Rapids, 1973), 9–22 (this article is also found in *Readings in Calvin's Theology*, ed. Donald K. McKim [Grand Rapids, 1984], 11–20); G. H. M. Posthumus Meyjes, "Het doctorenambt in Middeleeuwen en Reformatie," *Rondom het Woord* 15.3 (Sept. 1973): 21–45.

41. Albertus van Ginkel, *De ouderling* (Amsterdam, 1975); and Elsie Anne McKee, *Elders and the Plural Ministry: The Role of Exegetical History in Illuminating John Calvin's Theology* (Geneva, 1988).

42. Elsie Anne McKee, *John Calvin: On the Diaconate and Liturgical Almsgiving* (Geneva, 1984).

the hospital, have need of assistance because of their poverty. The deacons, who also meet together once a week, are chosen in the same way as the elders.

Calvin's view of the four offices was strongly influenced by what he had seen in Strasbourg, where they had *Kirchenpfleger* (elders) and the *Kirchenkonvent* (church assembly). Martin Bucer speaks of four offices both in his commentary on the Gospels and in his commentary on the Epistle of Paul to the Romans (he later speaks of three offices).[43]

In addition to an explanation of the four offices, the *Ordonnances* contain regulations concerning baptism, the Lord's Supper, marriage, burial, visitation of the sick and of prisoners, instruction of the youth, and discipline.

Order for Visitation *(1546)*

In January 1546 an order for visitation was adopted in Geneva, the *Ordre sur la visitation des ministres et paroisses dépendantes de Genève* (included in *Les Ordonnances ecclésiastiques* in 1561; see *CO* 10a:98–99; *OS* 2:335–36).[44] Already in *Les Ordonnances ecclésiastiques* of 1541 we find a few articles that serve to promote unity among the ministers, but it was difficult to involve the ministers outside of Geneva in mutual deliberation. The result was that Calvin pleaded in the Council in May 1544 for the introduction of a visitation order for the congregations outside of Geneva. In the regulations adopted in 1546, both the goal and the method of visitation are laid out. As the title indicates, this visitation order was for the ministers and parishes that lay outside of the city of Geneva but fell under her jurisdiction.

Supplement to Les Ordonnances ecclésiastiques *(1547)*

In May 1547 the Council of Two Hundred in Geneva adopted ordinances for the exercise of discipline in the congregations outside of Geneva. The *Ordonnances sur la police des églises de la campagne* (*CO* 10a:51–58) had been drafted by the ministers and presented to the Council in February 1547.[45] The intent of these *Ordonnances* was to provide a supplement to *Les Ordonnances ecclésiastiques* of 1541. The latter had stated that its ordinances also applied to the congregations outside Geneva, but supplementary provisions became nec-

---

43. H. Strohl, "La Théorie et la pratique des quatre ministères à Strasbourg avant l'arrivée de Calvin," *BSHPF* 84 (1935): 123–44; Willem van 't Spijker, *De ambten bij Martin Bucer* (Kampen, 1970), 391–410; and Dankbaar, "Het doctorenambt."

44. For an English translation (with an introduction) see *Calvin: Theological Treatises*, ed. Reid, 73–75; see also Plomp, *De kerkelijke tucht*, 276–79.

45. For an English translation (with an introduction) see *Calvin: Theological Treatises*, ed. Reid, 76–82; see also Plomp, *De kerkelijke tucht*, 209–12.

essary because adherence to the old Roman Catholic traditions was stronger outside of Geneva than in the city proper. These supplementary ordinances were not inserted into the revised edition of *Les Ordonnances ecclésiastiques* in 1561.

Les Ordonnances ecclésiastiques *(1561)*

A revised edition of *Les Ordonnances ecclésiastiques* appeared in 1561.[46] The revision contains only a few modifications involving adjustments to the current situation. In addition, after the regulations concerning the weekly Bible studies, the discipline of ministers, and fraternal censure, the *Ordre sur la visitation des ministres et paroisses dépendantes de Genève* is inserted, in which the goal and method of visitation in Geneva and her dependent congregations are explained.

46. For the text see *CO* 10a:91–124; see also Plomp, *De kerkelijke tucht,* 190–209, 275–79; and "Die Genferkirchenordnung (1561)," in *Die Kirche im Zeitalter der Reformation,* ed. Heiko A. Oberman (Neukirchen, 1981), 246–49.

5

Debating with Roman Catholics

Epistolae duae (1537)

After completing his work on the publication of the *Institutes* in 1536, Calvin traveled with Louis Du Tillet to Ferrara. Using his earlier pseudonym, Charles d'Espeville, he stayed there for several weeks among kindred spirits at the court of the reform-minded Duchess Renée, who was the daughter of King Louis XII of France, the sister-in-law of King Francis I, and since 1527 the wife of Hercule d'Este, duke of Ferrara.[1]

In Ferrara Calvin met evangelical refugees from France, including the French poet Clément Marot, and wrote letters to his friends in France. Two

---

1. H. Lecoultre, "Le Séjour de Calvin en Italie d'après des documents inédits," *RThPh* 19 (1886): 168–92; C. A. Cornelius, *Der Besuch Calvins bei der Herzogin Renata von Ferrara im Jahr 1536* (1893).

of these letters were published in Basel in 1537.[2] At the beginning of the *Epistolae duae* is a letter to the reader that Calvin wrote in Geneva on January 12, 1537, in which he identifies himself with the prophet Ezekiel, whose words many listened to, but did not put into practice because they did not know that a prophet was in their midst (Ezekiel 33:31, 33).

Letter to Nicolas Duchemin

The first letter (*CO* 5:239–78; *OS* 1:289–329) is written to Nicolas Duchemin, who had secured an ecclesiastical position in the diocese of Le Mans.[3] In the letter Calvin speaks out against the Roman Catholic worship service and particularly against the mass, which is "to be detested most of all." Furthermore, he disapproves of those who do not publicly reveal their decision to become an evangelical, since failure to reveal is accompanied by ongoing clandestine participation in the Roman Catholic worship service. As we have seen, Calvin later calls these people Nicodemites (see p. 137).

Letter to Gérard Roussel

The letter to Gérard Roussel (*CO* 5:279–312; *OS* 1:329–62) is addressed to "an old friend, now a prelate," for Roussel had received an appointment as bishop in the diocese of Oléron.[4] In the letter, which includes a detailed discussion of the office of bishop, Calvin sharply confronts Roussel and calls upon him to take a radical step; compromising and waiting around is not an option. Calvin later heard from Guillaume Farel (in a letter dated April 16, 1540—see Herminjard 6:209) that Roussel was still continuing to preach the gospel.

Religious Colloquy in Lausanne (1536)

In October 1536 Farel and Pierre Viret took Calvin along to participate in a

---

2. *Epistolae duae de rebus hoc saeculo cognitu apprime necessariis. . . ;* the French text can be found in *Recueil des opuscules*, 57–131. For several bibliographical marginal notes (especially on the translations of the letters), see Rodolphe Peter, "Etudes critiques: Notes de bibliographie calvinienne à propos de deux ouvrages récents," *RHPhR* 51 (1971): 79–87. See also Eugénie Droz, "Calvin et les nicodémites," in *Chemins de l'hérésie: Textes et documents*, 4 vols. (Geneva, 1970–76), 1:131–71; Alexandre Ganoczy, *The Young Calvin*, trans. David Foxgrover and Wade Provo (Philadelphia, 1987), 112, 274–76, 289–91.

3. The Latin heading above this letter reads: *De fugiendis impiorum illicitis sacris, et puritate Christianae religionis observanda.* In 1554 a French translation by someone in Calvin's circle appeared in Geneva under the title *Traité des bénéfices. . . .* The same text is found in the *Recueil des opuscules* under the title *Comment il faut éviter et fuir les cérémonies et superstitions papales, et de la pure observation de la religion chrestienne.*

4. Calvin entitled this letter *De Christiani hominis officio in sacerdotiis papalis ecclesiae vel administrandis, vel abiciendis.*

public religious colloquy in Lausanne, where at Bern's invitation Reformation ministers and spokesmen for the local Roman Catholic church were to discuss ten articles drawn up by Farel (for the text see *CO* 9:701–2).[5] On October 1 Farel opened the colloquy, where the central question was whether or not to introduce the Reformation into Lausanne and its environs. When on October 5 the presence of Christ in the Lord's Supper was being discussed and someone from the Roman Catholic side accused the Reformers of contempt for the authority of the church fathers and of introducing a new doctrine, Calvin spoke up for the first time. He surpassed Farel and Viret in his knowledge of the church fathers and refuted the accusations.

Calvin once again became the spokesman on October 7 when the doctrine of transubstantiation came up for discussion. He emphasized that the Reformers were not introducing new teaching; the church fathers knew nothing of a doctrine of transubstantiation. In the discussion about the Lord's Supper, Calvin made quite an impression with his knowledge of the church fathers. For his input during the colloquy see *Deux discours de Calvin au colloque de Lausanne* (*CO* 9:877–86).[6]

Correspondence with Louis Du Tillet (1538)

When Calvin was in Strasbourg in 1538, he heard that Louis Du Tillet, who had already left Geneva in 1537, had rejoined the Roman Catholic Church in France. It took a long time before Du Tillet publicly disclosed this, but on September 7, 1538, he wrote Calvin a letter about the matter (*CO* 10b:241–45), suggesting that Calvin had been called to his office not by God but by men, and also appealing to him to return to the true (Roman Catholic) church. Calvin replied to Du Tillet on October 20 and explained the way things had gone (*CO* 10b:269–72). If he had been dealing only with men, he would not have accepted his office. But before God he felt duty-bound to take it on. Du Tillet responded once again with a very long letter (*CO* 10b:290–302) that Calvin never answered because of its contents.[7]

5. For an English translation of the articles see *Calvin: Theological Treatises*, ed. J. K. S. Reid (London and Philadelphia, 1954), 35–37. See also Ch. Subilia, *La Dispute de Lausanne* (Lausanne, 1885); Henri Meylan and R. Deluz, *La Dispute de Lausanne* (Lausanne, 1936); Arthur Piaget, ed., "Les Actes de la dispute de Lausanne, 1536, publiés intégralement d'après le manuscrit de Berne," in *Mémoires de l'Université de Neuchâtel* 6 (1928); Georges Bavaud, *La Dispute de Lausanne (1536): Une Etape de l'évolution doctrinale des réformateurs romands* (Fribourg, 1956); Eric Junod, ed., *La Dispute de Lausanne (1536): La Théologie réformée après Zwingli et avant Calvin* (Lausanne, 1988).

6. For an English translation see *Calvin: Theological Treatises*, ed. Reid, 38–46.

7. See Alexandre Crottet, *Correspondance française de Calvin avec Louis Du Tillet, 1537–1538* (Lausanne/Paris, 1850).

EPISTRE
DE IAQVES SADO-
LET CARDINAL, EN-
uoyée au Senat & Peuple de Geneue:
Par laquelle il tafche lés reduire
foubz la puiffance de l'E-
uefque de Romme.

Auec la Refponfe de Iehan Caluin:
tranflatées de Latin en Françoys.

Imprimé a Geneue par Michel du Bois.
M D. XL.

DE AETERNA DEI
PRÆDESTINATIONE,
qua in falutem alios ex hominibus elegit,a-
lios fuo exitio reliquit: item de prouidentia
qua res humanas gubernat,

Confenfus Paftorũ Geneuenfis Ec-
clefiæ,à Io. Caluino expofitus.

GENEVÆ,
Ex officina Ioannis Crifpini.
M. D. LII.

Title page from Sadoleto's letter
and Calvin's response

Title page of De aeterna
Dei praedestinatione

Responsio ad Sadoletum (1539)

Following the banishment of Calvin and Farel, the Roman Catholics tried to profit from the troubled situation in Geneva. The former bishop of Geneva, Pierre de La Baume, saw a possibility of returning to the city. Discussion of the matter at a bishops' conference in Lyons led to the decision to send the Council and citizens of Geneva an open letter with the challenge to return to "obedience to the bishop of Rome." Cardinal Sadoleto, bishop of Carpentras, was designated as the best one to write the letter. He had already written a similar kind of letter twice before, once in 1537 to Philipp Melanchthon in Wittenberg, and again in 1538 to Jean Sturm in Strasbourg.

Sadoleto's letter to the Council and the population of Geneva is dated March 18, 1539.[8] In it he regrets that the inhabitants of Geneva have broken

8. See G. von Schultesz-Rechberg, *Der Kardinal Jacobo Sadoleto: Ein Beitrag zur Geschichte des Humanismus* (Zurich, 1909); W. H. Beekenkamp, "Calvijn en Sadoleto," *Veritatem in Caritate* 4 (1959): 21–27; Richard M. Douglas, *Jacopo Sadoleto, 1477–1547: Humanist and Reformer* (Cambridge, 1959); Jean Cadier, "Sadolet et Calvin," *RHPhR* 45 (1965): 72–92; Ganoczy, *Young Calvin*, 126, 246, 254–59, 279–81, 294–97; Helmut Feld, "Um die reine Lehre des Evangeliums: Calvins Kontroverse mit Sadoleto 1539," *Catholica* 36 (1982): 150–80.

away from "our mother, the church." According to him, a Christian ought to be guided by the Roman Catholic Church, which establishes the norms for a Christian life. He attacks the ministers of Geneva, especially Farel, portraying them as deceivers and innovators.

On March 27, the Council of Geneva discussed the missive, which they had received the day before along with a cover letter, and they decided to send it to Bern because of the relationship between the two cities. The Council of Bern in turn asked the Bernese ministers to answer the letter, but when the latter could not see their way clear to do it, they turned to Calvin. Calvin received a copy of Sadoleto's letter via Simon Sulzer, along with a request to compose a response to it. His colleagues in Strasbourg also urged him to answer Sadoleto. He wrote his *Responsio ad Sadoletum* (*CO* 5:385–416; *OS* 1:457–89) in August in six days' time.[9] In it he discusses which of the two sides serves God in the only legitimate way. He points out that the church is founded not upon human agreement but upon the Word. Calvin and his followers are not destroying the church but trying to renew it. He discusses the relation of the Spirit and the Word, justification by faith, and the sacraments, and concludes by pointing out that the unity of the church is found in Christ.

Sadoleto's letter and Calvin's response were published in Strasbourg in September. The Genevan Council decided on January 30, 1540, to permit the publication of both a Latin and a French edition so that the common people might become acquainted with the contents.[10]

Religious Colloquies in Haguenau, Worms, and Regensburg

In the years that Calvin was associated with the congregation in Strasbourg, he participated in the religious colloquies carried on by Protestants and

9. *Jacobi Sadoleti Romani Cardinalis Epistola ad senatum populumque Genevensem, qua in obedientiam Romani pontificis eos reducere conatur. Ioannis Calvini Responsio* (Strasbourg, 1539). See also note 10.

10. The *Epistre de Iaques Sadolet Cardinal, envoyée au senat et peuple de Genève, par laquelle il tasche les reduire soubz la puissance de l'évesque de Romme. Avec la Response de Iehan Calvin. Translatées de latin en françoys* appeared in Geneva in 1540 (French text in *Recueil des opuscules*, 131–75). The French translation was not from Calvin's hand. On the French editions see *La Vraie Piété: Divers traités de Jean Calvin et Confession de foi de Guillaume Farel*, ed. Irena Backus and Claire Chimelli (Geneva, 1986), 57–119, where Backus gives an introduction to Sadoleto's letter and Calvin's reply, and where a modern French translation of both of these writings can be found. For an English translation (with an introduction) see *Calvin: Theological Treatises*, ed. Reid, 219–56; John Calvin and Jacopo Sadoleto, *A Reformation Debate*, ed. John C. Olin (New York, 1966; reprint, Grand Rapids, 1976).

Roman Catholics in Haguenau, Worms, and Regensburg.[11] These assemblies also served as the occasion for several of his writings.

On April 19, 1539, princes from both parties concluded the *Frankfurter Bestand*, which opened the way for a religious colloquy in Speyer. Because of the plague, however, the colloquy was held not in Speyer but in Haguenau, located approximately ten kilometers from Strasbourg. On June 28, 1540, the negotiations began. Among those participating were Calvin and Wolfgang Capito, who were representing Strasbourg. Melanchthon could not attend because of illness. Much time had to be spent on the form that the colloquy would take, and it was finally decided that each of the two parties would be represented by eleven persons with voting privileges. The colloquy would reconvene in three months in Worms, and the basis for discussion would be the *Confessio Augustana* (Augsburg Confession). Calvin gives an account of the Haguenau colloquy in a letter to Du Tailly, a French refugee residing in Geneva (*CO* 11:64–67).

Calvin and Jean Sturm left Strasbourg for Worms on October 24. The colloquy was supposed to begin on October 28, but Granvelle, the emperor's representative, could not get there before November 22. In the meantime, the Protestant theologians—among them Melanchthon, Bucer, and Calvin—deliberated together from November 8 to 18 about matters that would come up for discussion during the colloquy.

Granvelle opened the colloquy in Worms with an address on November 25. The two parties did not formally meet together, however; negotiations were carried on from a distance, with a few of the presiding officials serving as intermediaries. In December Calvin wrote Farel an extensive letter on the way things were going in Worms (*CO* 11:135–40; an earlier [November 13] report by Calvin, which was also intended for Farel, has been lost). On December 29 Granvelle proposed that a public debate be held between the two parties, each represented by one person.

On January 1, 1541, during his stay in Worms, Calvin wrote the poem

---

11. For the texts of the religious colloquies in 1540–41, see *Die Vorbereitung der Religionsgespräche von Worms und Regensburg 1540/41*, vol. 4 of *Texte zur Geschichte der evangelischen Theologie*, ed. Wilhelm H. Neuser (Neukirchen, 1974). We note also C. Augustijn, *De godsdienstgesprekken tussen Rooms-Katholieken en Protestanten van 1538 tot 1541* (Haarlem, 1967); Wilhelm H. Neuser, "Calvins Beitrag zu den Religionsgesprächen von Hagenau, Worms und Regensburg (1540/41)," in *Studien zur Geschichte und Theologie der Reformation: Festschrift für Ernst Bizer,* ed. Luise Abramowski et al. (Neukirchen, 1969), 213–37. See also Bernhard Lohse, "Wiedervereinigungsversuche zwischen Katholiken und Protestanten," in *Handbuch der Dogmen- und Theologiegeschichte,* ed. Carl Andresen, 3 vols. (Göttingen, 1980–84), 2:102–8 (especially the secondary literature mentioned on p. 102).

Epinicion Christo cantatum "just for fun."[12] This "Victory Song for Christ" was a poem with clear allusions to the events in Worms. It was not originally intended for publication, but Calvin had let friends read it, and it was circulated without his knowledge. When in 1544 people began asking him for the text of the poem, he discovered that it had been included on a list of forbidden works drawn up in Toulouse by the Dominican Vidal de Becanis. Calvin then went ahead with the publication of the poem, which appeared in Geneva in 1544 as the "Victory Song for Christ." Conrad Badius, who had also been in Worms in 1540–41, republished Calvin's song in Geneva in 1555, attaching it to a French version that he had prepared: *Chant de victoire, chanté à Jésus Christ en vers latins par M. Iean Calvin, l'an M.D.XLI, le premier jour de janvier, à la diète qui pour lors se tenoit à Wormes. Nouvellement traduit en rithme françoise, en vers alexandrins, par Conrad Badius, de Paris* (*Recueil des opuscules*, 195–200).

The colloquy in Worms finally got under way on January 14 with a public debate between Johann Eck and Melanchthon on original sin. It was interrupted on January 18, however, by an imperial edict ordering that it be continued at the diet in Regensburg (see Calvin's letter of January 31 to Farel—*CO* 11:145–47).

In March, before the diet in Regensburg had yet begun, Calvin published under the pseudonym Eusebius Pamphilius a tart commentary on the fatherly advice of Pope Paul III to Emperor Charles V (*Consilium admodum paternum Pauli III, pontificis Romani, datum imperatori in Belgis per cardinalem Farnesium pontificis nepotem pro Lutheranis. Anno 1540. Et Eusebii Pamphili eiusdem consilii pia et salutaris explicatio*—*CO* 5:461–508; French: *Recueil des opuscules*, 438–71). In the time between the discussions in Frankfurt and Haguenau, the pope had tried to prevent the emperor from calling a colloquy and had described the Protestants as a more dangerous enemy than the Turks. In the treatise Calvin supports the idea of a council under the leadership of the emperor.

On April 5 Charles V opened the diet, which met in Regensburg from April 27 to May 31. There the colloquy that had broken off in Worms was to continue. The Roman Catholics were represented by, among others, Gasparo Contarini, who was the papal envoy, Albertus Pighius, and Eck. On the Protestant side were Melanchthon, Bucer, and Calvin. Melanchthon had strongly insisted on Calvin's presence, "on account of his great name among scholars."

---

12. *Epinicion Christo cantatum ab Ioanne Calvino. Calendis Ianuarii anno 1541* (*CO* 5:417–28; *OS* 1:495–98). See also E. A. de Boer, *Loflied en hekeldicht: De geschiedenis van Calvijn's enige gedicht. Het Epinicion Christo cantatum van 1 januari 1541* (Haarlem, 1986).

From April 27 to May 25 the two sides discussed religious issues, with the so-called *Regensburger Buch* instead of the *Confessio Augustana* serving as the starting point.[13] This book contained articles that, at Granvelle's initiative, had been drawn up in private discussions during the colloquy in Worms, particularly by Johann Gropper (Roman Catholic) and Bucer (for the text see *CO* 5:516). The discussions in Regensburg produced agreement on original sin, free will, and justification, but problems arose over the issue of the church and especially over the Lord's Supper (see Calvin's account in letters to Farel on May 11 and 12 and in July—*CO* 11:215–18, 251–52).

Before the diet had come to an end (when the "result" of the colloquy was being discussed there), Calvin chose, against the wishes of Bucer and Melanchthon, to return to Strasbourg. The stay in Regensburg had lasted too long for him, and he felt that he should be back in Strasbourg. He arrived there on June 25.

Calvin's reflections on what had transpired in Regensburg were published along with the acts of Regensburg (*Les Actes de la iournée imperiale, tenue en la cité de Regespourg, aultrement dicte Ratispone, l'an mil cinq cens quarante et un, sur les différens qui sont auiourdhuy en la religion*—*CO* 5:509–684), for he was in favor of being open. Some people want to keep everything secret, he says, but as he sees it, God did not give his Word to be buried or to be imprisoned among a small number of scholars (*CO* 5:682, 513). As for the result of the diet in Regensburg, Calvin wrote to Viret on August 13 (*CO* 11:261–63) that it had ended just as he had always expected—with no religious peace and the transfer of the problems to a council.[14]

Dispute against Abuses (*Traité des reliques,* 1543)

In 1543 Calvin's *Traité des reliques* appeared, a work in which he attacks the veneration of relics.[15] The complete title of this work in English translation

---

13. The text of the *Regensburger Buch* can be found in *CR* 4:190–238. A critical edition appears in *Acta Reformationis Catholicae ecclesiam Germaniae concernentia saeculi XVI,* ed. Georg Pfeilschifter, 6 vols. (Regensburg, 1959–74), 6:24–88.

14. See Wilhelm H. Neuser, "Calvins Urteil über den Rechtfertigungsartikel des Regensb. Buches," in *Reformation und Humanismus: Robert Stupperich zum 65. Geburtstag,* ed. Martin Greschat et al. (Witten, 1969), 176–94.

15. Full title: *Advertissement très utile du grand proffit qui reviendroit à la chrestienté, s'il se faisoit inventoire de tous les corps sainctz, et reliques, qui sont tant en Italie, qu'en France, Allemaigne, Hespaigne, et autres royaumes et pays* (*CO* 6:405–52; *Recueil des opuscules,* 726–58). See also John Calvin, *Three French Treatises,* ed. Francis M. Higman (London, 1970) for the French text with notes. Nicolas Des Gallars (Gallasius) produced a Latin translation (Geneva, 1548). See also *Institutes* 1.11. Irena Backus provides an introduction and a modern French translation with notes in *La Vraie Piété,* ed. Backus and Chimelli, 155–202.

reads: *A Very Useful Account of the Great Profit That Christianity Will Again Receive If It Takes Inventory of All the Sacred Bodies and Relics That Are Located in Italy, France, Germany, Spain, and Other Kingdoms and Countries.*

One cannot gather from the title itself that the author is attacking the veneration of relics, but Calvin's name and the contents make that clear. Since that was the intention, the title was more or less satirical. The treatise was written in French so as to reach the common people. Those who think that the church is infallible will have to change their minds when they immerse themselves in the ludicrous matter of the veneration of relics.

Calvin writes that Augustine already was aware of this fraud that was foisted upon the common people and that since then had only become worse. The root of the evil is that people look for Jesus Christ not in the Word and the sacraments, but in all sorts of less important things. One can, of course, say that relics are worshiped with Christ in mind, but Paul says that worship that arises out of human reflection is foolishness. Besides, the veneration of relics is a superfluous practice that leads to idolatry. The honor of God is transferred to something else, and dead, vacuous things are worshiped instead of the living God.

A related evil is the fraud that relics perpetrate. It would take Calvin too much time to enumerate all the frauds committed with forgeries, so he limits himself to a number of examples to rouse people and bring them to their senses. He hopes that Christian monarchs will protect their subjects from this fraud.

Next Calvin gives a detailed summary of what has been happening in the area of relics in France, Germany, Spain, and other countries. He mentions various relics in connection with Jesus Christ, Mary, Saint Michael, John the Baptist, the apostles, martyrs, and saints. Finally, he calls upon all his readers to give up the pagan superstition surrounding relics, and he ends with a reference to what Paul writes in 2 Thessalonians 2:3–12.

As for the sources that Calvin drew from in writing this treatise, he himself mentions, among others, Ambrose and Eusebius. In her introduction to the treatise, Irena Backus points to late medieval criticism of the veneration of relics. Even if Calvin's critique is more fundamental, he cannot be viewed in isolation from the criticism that had preceded him.[16]

It should be mentioned that in 1549 the Roman Catholic polemicist Johannes Cochlaeus attacked the Latin edition of Calvin's treatise (from the hand of Nicolas Des Gallars) in his *De sacris reliquiis Christi et sanctorum eius, Brevis contra Ioannis Calvini calumnias et blasphemias responsio* (Mainz, 1549).

---

16. *La Vraie Piété*, ed. Backus and Chimelli, 160.

Debating with Albertus Pighius

In early 1543 Calvin's little book *Defensio sanae et orthodoxae doctrinae de servitute et liberatione humani arbitrii adversus calumnias Alberti Pighii Campensis* (*CO* 6:225–404) appeared,[17] which he dedicated to Melanchthon (see *CO* 11:515–17, a letter to Melanchthon on February 15, 1543). The dedication reveals that Calvin wanted to respond quickly to the treatise *De libero hominis arbitrio et divina gratia libri X,* published in Cologne by Pighius (who hailed from Kampen) in 1542. Pighius had dedicated his work, written for "my Germans," to Cardinal Sadoleto. In the dedication he says that he is responding to the heresies that are threatening the church, and he mentions in particular "the most pernicious Luther." Pighius disputes the view that we sin necessarily and that it is impossible for us to live good and just lives or to obey God's commandments. In his work Pighius examines what Luther and Calvin had said in their writings about free will.

In his *Defensio* Calvin refutes the first six books of Pighius's work. He begins by accusing Pighius of plagiarism, for the heading of book 1, chapter 1, reads: "The knowledge of God and knowledge of ourselves are mutually correlative and mutually dependent" (cf. the beginning of Calvin's *Institutes*). Calvin goes on to treat various church fathers, especially Augustine, whom Pighius had cited in support of free will, and he comes to the defense of Luther. But Scripture is the only real standard for faith.

Calvin continued the debate with Pighius in 1552. He had been planning for a long time to write something more to refute Pighius's ideas, but had been prevented by various circumstances. The proceedings against Jérôme Bolsec in 1551, in which the doctrine of predestination also played a role, contributed to Calvin's publication of a new treatise in Geneva in 1552, *De aeterna Dei praedestinatione* (*CO* 8:249–366). A French translation was published the same year.[18]

---

17. The French text is found in *Recueil des opuscules,* 257–438. See also Pierre Pidoux, "Albert Pighius de Kampen, adversaire de Calvin," thèse de licence, University of Lausanne, 1932; Gerard Melles, *Albertus Pighius en zijn strijd met Calvijn over het liberum arbitrium* (Kampen, 1973); L. F. Schulze, *Calvin's Reply to Pighius* (Potchefstroom, 1970); idem, "Calvin's Reply to Pighius—A Micro and Macro View," in *Calvinus ecclesiae Genevensis custos,* ed. Wilhelm H. Neuser (Frankfurt am Main, 1984), 171–85.

18. The complete title of the Latin edition reads: *De aeterna Dei praedestinatione, qua in salutem alios ex hominibus elegit, alios suo exitio reliquit; item de providentia qua res humanas gubernat, Consensus pastorum Genevensis ecclesiae, a Io. Calvino expositus.* The French translation was entitled *De la prédestination éternelle de Dieu, par laquelle les uns sont éleuz à salut, les autres laissez en leur condemnation . . . ,* and was published in Geneva in 1552 (*Recueil des opuscules,* 1219–1314). For an English translation see *Calvin's Calvinism: Treatises on the Eternal Predestination of God and the Secret Providence of God,* trans. Henry P. Cole (Grand Rapids, 1987); John Calvin, *Concerning the Eternal Predestination of God,* trans. J. K. S. Reid (London, 1961).

In this treatise Calvin refutes books 7 through 10 of Pighius's work mentioned earlier. He also takes on others, among them the Benedictine Georgius Siculus, who had argued against him by appealing to received revelation. Bolsec is not mentioned by name, but Calvin defends in particular the double-sided character of predestination, since Bolsec thought that he had refuted the absolute decree of reprobation with an appeal to Heinrich Bullinger, Philipp Melanchthon, and Johann Brenz.

Calvin's treatise served as a joint statement for all the Genevan ministers, as the full title indicates (. . . *Consensus pastorum Genevensis ecclesiae . . .*). On January 1, 1552, he composed the foreword, in which he dedicated the work to the syndics and the Council of Geneva. He had to attend a couple of meetings of the Council before he received permission to publish the work. Permission was eventually granted, which, along with the dedication, implied agreement with the treatise. As Calvin writes in the foreword, it is offered in the name of the Council to all pious people.

In the dedication Calvin writes that for our assurance of salvation we should not look to the hidden decree of God, for that is inaccessible to us. Rather, we should fix our gaze upon Christ, in whom eternal life is revealed and offered to us. Through faith in Christ we gain access to God's kingdom. Whoever is content with the clear promises of the gospel must also recognize that it is God who has opened our eyes, because he elected us to be faithful before we were conceived in the womb.[19]

Debating with the Sorbonne (1544)

In 1543, on the authority of Francis I, the theological faculty of the Sorbonne drew up and published twenty-five articles rejecting Reformation teaching. More than sixty doctors signed the articles and subsequently laid them before candidates and theological students, who were to pledge under oath to remain faithful to the Catholic faith. By royal decree Francis and the Parlement of Paris ratified the articles of the Sorbonne and thus gave them the status of official doctrine.

Calvin published and refuted these articles in 1544 in his *Articuli a facultate sacrae theologiae Parisiensi determinati super materiis fidei nostrae hodie controversis. Cum antidoto* (*CO* 7:1–44). There he provides the text of each article, fol-

---

19. The work on predestination caused quite a reaction in various quarters. In Basel, Celio Curione and Sebastian Castellio attacked Calvin (see p. 53), and the Council of Bern took certain measures (see pp. 58–59). For Theodore Beza's opinion on this treatise see his *Correspondance,* ed. Hippolyte Aubert et al., 12 vols. (Geneva, 1960–86), 1:81–83.

lowed by his commentary on it. He uses "their own jargon in order to expose their stupidity" (Beza, *Histoire ecclésiastique*, 1.50), thus ridiculing scholastic theology. He refutes the content of each article with biblical arguments. The first edition of the work was written in Latin, but a French edition also appeared in 1544 (*Recueil des opuscules*, 471–506).

A pamphlet from Calvin's pen also dates from 1544: *Advertissement sur la censure qu'ont faicte les bestes de Sorbonne, touchant les livres qu'ilz appellent hérétiques.*[20] In it he attacks the Sorbonne, which in 1544 had published a catalogue of censured books.

The Council of Trent and the Augsburg Interim

On October 25, 1543, Calvin received a letter from Martin Bucer (*CO* 11:634–35) asking him to explain the state of affairs between Roman Catholics and Protestants in connection with the upcoming diet in Speyer in February 1544. Calvin wrote his *Supplex exhortatio ad Caesarem*, which also appeared in French translation in 1544.[21]

The treatise is a humble exhortation to Emperor Charles V to undertake, along with the princes, the restoration of the church.[22] Although he is speaking of his own accord, Calvin asks the emperor to hear in his voice the echo of all who desire to restore the church to her former state. He mentions princes and governments that are engaged in that endeavor and a countless multitude of pious people who concur with him in his pleading. Everyone knows, he says, that the church is seriously ill. We have been forced by the greatest necessity to follow in the footsteps of Luther and others to introduce changes. It is these changes that Calvin wishes to defend. He goes on to state that he will discuss the infirmities of the church that have led to the search for remedies, then what

---

20. See Francis M. Higman, "Un Pamphlet de Calvin restitué à son auteur," *RHPhR* 60 (1980): 167–80, 327–37 (text of Calvin's response to the Sorbonne catalogue).

21. Full title: *Supplex exhortatio ad invictissimum Caesarem Carolum quintum et illustrissimos principes, aliosque ordines, Spirae nunc imperii conventum agentes. Ut restituendae ecclesiae curam serio velint suscipere. Eorum omnium nomine edita qui Christum regnare cupiunt* (Geneva, 1543—*CO* 6:453–534). The French edition is entitled *Supplication et remonstrance sur le faict de la chrestienté, et de la réformation de l'église faicte au nom de tous amateurs du regne de Jésus Christ, à l'empereur, et aux princes et estatz tenans maintenant journée impériale à Spire* (Geneva, 1544). For the text see *Recueil des opuscules*, 506–79. For an abridged English translation with an introduction see *Calvin: Theological Treatises*, ed. Reid, 183–216. See also J. N. Bakhuizen van den Brink, "Calvijn en Karel V," in *Protestantse pleidooien*, 2 vols. (Kampen, 1962), 2:97–122.

22. Joachim Staedtke, *Johannes Calvin: Erkenntnis und Gestaltung* (Göttingen, 1969), 56, calls this treatise "a detailed and brilliantly written justification of the Reformation, for which Calvin earned high praise."

the appropriate remedies are that have to be employed, and finally why there is no more time to wait, but help must be provided immediately.

In the last part of the work Calvin deals with the accusation that the correction of the church's defects has produced only discord. The last and most serious slander that people heap upon us, says Calvin, is that we have separated ourselves from the church. He disputes that by referring to the apostles and prophets. The true church and her unity have to do entirely with Christ, the head of the church. He is the highest authority in the church.

Finally, in view of the wretched condition of the church, Calvin calls upon the emperor and the princes to help her as the bride of Christ. He acknowledges that if it pleases Christ to do so, he will miraculously preserve his church apart from the actions of men. "But I tell you, if you hesitate any longer, we will find the visible church in Germany no more."

How difficult Calvin found it to write this treatise is evident from the letter he wrote to Farel on November 10, 1543 (*CO* 11:642–44). Needing advice and support in this matter, he urgently appeals to Farel to come to Geneva.

Calvin sent his *Supplex exhortatio ad Caesarem* to Melanchthon on April 21, 1544. Although he believed that his appeal to Charles V for reform would be to no avail, he wished to learn from Melanchthon what people in Wittenberg thought about the content of the *Supplex* (*CO* 11:696–98).

In a decision at the diet in Speyer on June 10, 1544, Charles V accommodated the Protestants by promising to convene a general, free, Christian council. Pope Paul III responded to that on August 24, 1544, with a "fatherly admonition" directed at the emperor. In it he reproaches the emperor for arbitrarily going ahead, reaching a temporary settlement with the Protestants, and planning a council without consulting him about it. It befits an emperor to listen, not to instruct, writes the pope.

Calvin published the admonition of the pope along with his own comments: *Admonitio paterna Pauli III. Romani pontificis ad invictissimum Caesarem Carolum V. Cum scholiis* (*CO* 7:249–88). In his comments Calvin sharply criticizes the pope, who in his "fatherly admonition" to the emperor has deprived the Protestants of any prospect for rapprochement. Calvin argues that Christian princes have an obligation with respect to the church when the ecclesiastical hierarchy is deficient in its task. As for the possibility of a council, Calvin thinks that the pope should not be the judge of that; rather, the matter should be decided according to the Word of God. Finally, he makes an indirect appeal to the emperor to keep the promise that he made at the diet in Speyer.

Pope Paul III determined in September 1544 that a council would convene in Trent on March 15, 1545. It opened, however, already in December 1544.

Calvin wrote to Antoine Fumée in January 1545 (*CO* 12:23–26) that he, unlike people in France, does not have much faith in the council. He also does not expect anything from the diet to be convened by Charles V in Worms in February 1545. He thinks that the emperor will look at the different ideas of the Protestants and Roman Catholics and then say that nothing can be decided without the consent of the pope. But Protestants and Roman Catholics will also disagree about a council, Calvin thinks. Even if it is possible to convene a council, the emperor will still prefer to focus the attention on the struggle against the Turks and will leave the ecclesiastical situation as it is. And then, he adds, the pope will probably postpone the council.

The Protestants refused to attend the council organized by the pope because it did not meet their conditions. After seven sessions the Council of Trent adjourned on March 3, 1547, until 1551. Farel, Viret, and others urged Calvin to refute the decrees of Trent, and in December 1547 he produced the *Acta Synodi Tridentinae cum antidoto* (*CO* 7:365–506), in which he provides the text of the decrees, of the canons, and of a speech delivered at Trent, followed by his own commentary.[23] With his antidote he wants to assist his fellow believers in disputing the ideas of Trent.

Because the Council of Trent was rejected by the Protestants, and because Emperor Charles V was not satisfied with the way things were going at the council, he issued the Interim in May 1548 at the diet in Augsburg. The Interim was drafted by Roman Catholics Julius Pflug and Michael Helding in cooperation with the Lutheran Johannes Agricola. It provisionally established the conditions necessary to restore unity between Roman Catholics and Protestants while they awaited the decisions of a general council.

Calvin responded to the Interim in the spring of 1549 with the treatise *Interim adultero-germanum, cui adiecta est Vera Christianae pacificationis et ecclesiae reformandae ratio* (*CO* 7:545–674), although permission for the publication was not easy to obtain.[24] The work, which also appeared in French translation in Geneva in 1549 (*L'Interim avec la vraye façon de réformer l'église*), consists of two parts: the text of the Interim, and Calvin's explanation of the true manner in which to achieve Christian peace and to reform the church. Protestants had reacted angrily to the Interim because the only temporary concessions they had won were the passing of the cup during the celebration of

23. For the French text see *Recueil des opuscules*, 880–1009. See also W. F. Dankbaar, "Calvijns oordeel over het concilie van Trente, inzonderheid inzake het rechtvaardigingsdecreet," *NAK* 14 (1962): 79–112 (this article is also found in idem, *Hervormers en humanisten: Een bundel opstellen* [Amsterdam, 1978], 67–99).

24. For the French text see *Recueil des opuscules*, 1009–1118.

the Lord's Supper and permission for priests to marry. Written protests were also making their appearance, even though Charles V had forbidden such a thing on pain of death. Both Heinrich Bullinger and Martin Bucer had urged Calvin to respond in print to the Interim.

In his criticism of the Interim, Calvin reviews the matter in some depth. He gives in "brief enumeration" an exposition of "the doctrines on which not the least bit of ground may be yielded," treating in order justification by faith, confession of guilt and penance, the service of God, the church, the sacraments, intercession of the saints and angels and prayers for the dead, and fasting, celibacy, and ceremonies.

This treatise was also translated into German, probably by the German theologian Flacius Illyricus. The peculiar thing about the German edition is that a section of the original work was left out, and in a critical note Calvin was accused of Pelagianism in connection with his conception of infant baptism. Moreover, Calvin had rejected the administration of baptism by women in the case of children who are near death, but this practice was defended in the German edition. The result was that in 1550 Calvin published a postscript, *Appendix Libelli adversus Interim adultero-germanum* (*CO* 7:675–86), along with the original work, defending himself in particular against the charge of Pelagianism and providing a further explanation of his view.[25]

In May 1551 Pope Julius III called the Council of Trent into session for its second round of deliberations. Calvin had written to Bullinger in April (*CO* 14:100–101) that he did not expect the council to continue because the king of France had called upon all the bishops to do a thorough visitation of their dioceses. That was supposed to take place during the next half year along with their reports to the archbishops, after which the king was planning to call a national council. In this letter Calvin makes the ironic observation that Bullinger and he would very likely not receive an invitation from the pope if by some chance the Council of Trent did in fact reconvene.

---

25. *Appendix Libelli adversus Interim adultero-germanum, in qua refutat Ioannes Calvinus censuram quandam typographi ignoti de parvulorum sanctificatione et muliebri baptismo* (Geneva, 1550).

6

Debating with Other Movements and Individuals

Anabaptists

Psychopannychia *(1542 and 1545)*

After leaving Paris, Calvin spent some time in 1534 in Orléans. It was there that he wrote his *Psychopannychia*, as the first foreword (addressed to a friend) indicates.[1] A second foreword, which he composed in Basel in 1536, was intended

---

1. John Calvin, *Psychopannychia,* ed. Walther Zimmerli (Leipzig, 1932). For a French translation see *Recueil des opuscules*, 1–56. See also Charles Dardier, "Un Problème biographique: Quelle est la date de la première édition de la Psychopannychia de Calvin?" *BSHPF* 19/20 (1870): 371–82; Jung-Uck Hwang, *Der junge Calvin und seine Psychopannychia* (Frankfurt, 1991).

for the readers of the work. It has become quite clear in the course of Calvin research that the treatise was first printed in Strasbourg in 1542.

When Calvin penned the first version of the *Psychopannychia* in 1534, he sent it to Wolfgang Capito in Strasbourg, who advised against its publication (see *CO* 10b:45–46). Apart from the fact that Calvin would be able to acquire a deeper knowledge of Scripture on the subject, Capito felt that it was not the right time for publication. There was already so much confusion, and in the difficult situation in which they found themselves, the churches needed the straightforward preaching of Christ.

Calvin took Capito's advice to heart. It is clear both from his letter to Christophe Fabri on September 11, 1535 (*CO* 10b:52), and from his second foreword from Basel in 1536 that he rewrote the first version.

Martin Bucer was also critical of the treatise at first, but later insisted that it be published (*CO* 10b:260). However, the *Psychopannychia* was not published until 1542 in Strasbourg under the title *Vivere apud Christum non dormire animis sanctos, qui in fide Christi decedunt* (*CO* 5:165–232). According to the title, this work, which is a treatment of the state of the soul after death, demonstrates that the saints, who die in faith in Christ, live with him, and their souls do not fall asleep.

Three years later there appeared in Strasbourg a reprint in which the title began with the word *Psychopannychia*.[2] This term literally has to do with staying awake all night, but it had acquired another meaning and was used to refer to soul sleep.

The doctrine of soul sleep had been condemned at the Fifth Lateran Council in 1513, but it continued to have its supporters, and not only among the Anabaptists (the name Ulrich Zwingli and Calvin used to refer to adherents of this doctrine). In the foreword of 1534 Calvin says that at the insistence of friends he had given in to the request to dispute the heresy of soul sleep. This heresy, he says, is not new, for it had appeared already in the third century in Arabia. Pope John XXII was also an adherent of the doctrine and had been forced into a retraction in 1333. In the second foreword of 1536 Calvin says that he has a pastoral goal in mind, namely, to reclaim those who have erred. Because of their lack of Bible knowledge, the sectarians, among whom Calvin mentions the Anabaptists in particular, are creating schisms in the church.[3]

---

2. The complete title reads: *Psychopannychia qua refellitur quorundam imperitorum error qui animas post mortem usque ad ultimum iudicium dormire putant. Libellus ante septem annos compositus nunc tamen primum in lucem aeditus.*

3. It is difficult to say whom exactly Calvin meant by the Anabaptists. See the introduction to John Calvin, *Treatises against the Anabaptists and against the Libertines,* trans. and ed. Benjamin Wirt Farley (Grand Rapids, 1982), 19–24.

In the first part of the *Psychopannychia*, Calvin seeks to demonstrate that the soul is a substance and that after the death of the body, it lives on in a state of consciousness (with feeling and rationality). For the sake of clarity, he begins this section by looking at what Scripture says about spirit and soul. Next he argues on the basis of the account of creation (in which we are told that humanity was created in the image of God) and of other texts that the soul is a different substance from the body. He then appeals to a number of Scripture passages to argue that after death the soul lives on with feeling and rationality.

In the second part of the work, Calvin turns immediately to those whom he is refuting and on the basis of Scripture tries to rebut the arguments that they adduce to prove that the soul also dies. He gives attention as well to a number of statements from the church fathers. It is noteworthy, however, that throughout the work there is a strong emphasis on texts from both the Old and New Testaments.

Finally, we note that Calvin's *Brìève instruction contre les anabaptistes* of 1544 concludes with an exposition on the life and condition of the soul between death and the final resurrection (*CO* 7:114–39). This exposition is an abridged, less technical French translation of his *Psychopannychia* (according to Benjamin Farley).

Calvin's Brève instruction *(1544) against the Anabaptists*

Calvin's little book *Brìève instruction pour armer tous bons fidèles contre les erreurs de la secte commune des anabaptistes* (*CO* 7:45–142) appeared in Geneva on June 1, 1544.[4] It was dedicated to the ministers of Neuchâtel. Guillaume Farel had grown concerned about the Anabaptist influence in Neuchâtel and its vicinity and had sent Calvin a letter on February 23, 1544 (*CO* 11:680–83), along with a copy of the *Confessio Schlattensis* (Schleitheim Confession) that a resident of Neuchâtel had translated from German into French.[5] This confes-

---

4. The text can also be found in *Recueil des opuscules*, 579–646. For an English translation (with notes!) see Calvin, *Treatises against the Anabaptists,* ed. and trans. Farley, 11–158. See also Willem Balke, *Calvin and the Anabaptist Radicals,* trans. William J. Heynen (Grand Rapids, 1981), 182–95; Richard Stauffer, "Zwingli et Calvin, critiques de la confession de Schleitheim," in *The Origins and Characteristics of Anabaptism,* ed. Marc Lienhard (The Hague, 1977), 126–47 (this article is also found in Richard Stauffer, *Interprètes de la Bible: Etudes sur les réformateurs du XVIe siècle* [Paris, 1980], 103–28); Carlos M. N. Eire, "Calvin and Nicodemism: A Reappraisal," *SCJ* 10 (1979): 45–69; David A. Haury, "English Anabaptism and Calvin's *Brìève Instruction,*" *Menn.QR* 57 (1983): 145–51.

5. For the text see Beatrice Jenny, *Das Schleitheimer Täuferbekenntnis 1527,* vol. 28 of *Schaffhäuser Beiträge zur vaterländischen Geschichte* (Thayngen, Switz., 1950). See also Doopsgezinde Historische Kring, *Broederlijke vereniging,* trans. H. W. Meihuizen (Amsterdam, 1974). Balke, *Anabaptist Radicals,* 175–76, n. 26, has demonstrated that the tractate sent to Calvin was the *Confessio Schlattensis* rather than Balthasar Hubmaier's *Von dem christlichen Tauf,* as, for example, both A.-L. Herminjard

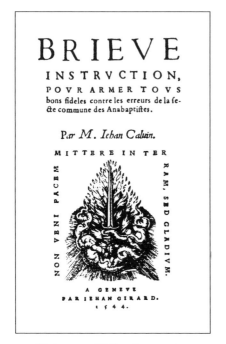

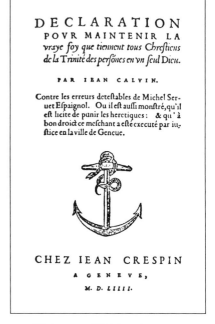

Title page of Brève Instruction

Title page of Déclaration pour maintenir la vraye foy . . . de la Trinité

sion contained seven articles that the Anabaptists, led by Michael Sattler, had adopted in February 1527 at their synodical meeting in Schleitheim and that had been published along with the account of Sattler's martyrdom. Farel appealed to Calvin on behalf of the ministers of Neuchâtel to write a refutation of the Anabaptist errors so that the ministers would have something to withstand Anabaptist propaganda. At the end of April, Farel also requested that Calvin add to the booklet in progress what he had already written against soul sleep.

In his *Brève instruction* Calvin examines the seven articles of the *Confessio Schlattensis* concerning baptism, discipline, the Lord's Supper, separation from the world, the office of the pastor, civil authority, and oaths. After reviewing and refuting the seven articles, Calvin goes on to treat two other subjects. The first concerns the incarnation; here he disputes particularly the notion of the "celestial flesh" of Christ that had been advocated and propa-

---

and, more recently, Rodolphe Peter and Jean-François Gilmont (*Bibliotheca Calviniana: Les Oeuvres de Jean Calvin publiées au XVIe siècle*, vol. 1, *Ecrits théologiques, littéraires et juridiques 1532–1554* [Geneva, 1991], 159–60) have thought.

gated by Melchior Hofmann.[6] According to this doctrine, which had found support already in the early church among the Manicheans and Marcionites, Christ did not derive from human seed—a denial of his true humanity (see also p. 181). The second additional topic that Calvin brings up in his *Brièwe instruction* is soul sleep. Here he provides the summary of *Psychopannychia* that we have already mentioned.

The Libertines

Contre la secte phantastique des libertins *(1545)*

In 1545 Calvin took on the Libertines in the treatise *Contre la secte phantastique et furieuse des libertins, qui se nomment spirituelz* (*CO* 7:145–248).[7] He indicates in the foreword why he wrote this work. The shepherds of the church must not only provide good food for the flock of Jesus Christ, but must also keep watch against wolves and thieves. He feels called to argue against the sect of the Libertines because he considers them to be more dangerous than thieves or wolves. He compares them to poisoners. Besides, he says, good believers have asked him to speak out against this sect in view of the havoc it is creating. Among these believers were Valérand Poullain and Guillaume Farel, who had sent letters to Calvin urging him to write.[8]

It is evident from the work itself that by Libertines Calvin has in mind particularly the followers of Quintin Thieffry, who were therefore also known as Quintinists. Calvin had met Thieffry in Paris sometime around 1535. During the period that Calvin was writing this treatise, Thieffry was at the court of Marguerite of Angoulême along with another member of the sect, Antoine Pocque, who had sought Calvin's support in Geneva in 1542.

Calvin finds this sect to be the most pernicious in all the world. In chapters 1–3 of the treatise he shows the affinity between the Libertines and such heretics of the early church as Cerdo, Marcion, and Valentinus. Next, in chapters

6. See Balke, *Anabaptist Radicals,* 301–4.

7. The text can also be found in *Recueil des opuscules,* 646–713. For an English translation with an introduction see Calvin, *Treatises against the Anabaptists,* ed. Farley, 159–326. In the introduction Farley provides an overview of the earlier studies of this work of Calvin's. An important question in the research has been who exactly the Libertines were. Farley discusses, among others, the views of Karl Müller, "Calvin und die Libertiner," *ZKG* 40 (1922): 83–129; Wilhelm Niesel, "Calvin und die Libertiner," *ZKG* 48 (1929): 58–74; and Robert G. Wilkie and Allen Verhey, "Calvin's Treatise 'Against the Libertines,'" *CTJ* 15 (1980): 190–219 (an introduction and English translation of a few important chapters from this work).

8. The letter from Poullain was dated May 26, 1544 (*CO* 11:711–14), and the letter from Farel was dated October 2, 1544 (*CO* 11:750–51).

4–6 he sketches the origin of the Libertine movement. There also it becomes clear that his primary targets will be Quintin Thieffry and Antoine Pocque. In chapters 7–10 he deals with their use of Scripture. Not only do they interpret Scripture allegorically, says Calvin, they even want us to go beyond it in search of new revelations. The word *spirit* that is constantly on their lips is misused in a number of ways. Chapters 11–22 form the heart of the treatise, for it is here that Calvin argues against the most important articles of their doctrine. They talk of a pantheistic spiritualism or mysticism, holding that there is only one spirit of God, which is and lives in all creatures. Because that one spirit directs everything, a person has no will, and all distinction between good and evil is eliminated. The devil and sin are fantasy and not something genuine. The reality of Jesus Christ and his saving work is minimized. Christ is more an example of saving insight. And the resurrection of the dead has already taken place (2 Timothy 2:17–18).

In the context of the argument in chapters 13–16 against the pantheistic determinism of the Libertines, Calvin gives a lucid explanation of the way in which God rules. He then also deals with the relation between the work of God and that of Satan and the ungodly, and describes how God leads his children by his Spirit.

In chapters 23–24 Calvin gives a critique of one of Antoine Pocque's writings and warns not just about this work, but also about other publications from the Libertine circle. Finally, in the last chapter Calvin calls upon his readers to adhere to what is revealed to us in Scripture.

When Marguerite of Angoulême got hold of Calvin's treatise, she indicated to him in a letter written for her by someone else that she was disappointed with the contents. She believed that the book had been directed against her and her ministers. Calvin replied to her in a letter on April 28, 1545 (*CO* 12:65–68), that he holds her in high esteem. He hopes that she will not let herself be persuaded by people who are inciting her against him. They are merely trying to see to it that she loses her loving disposition towards God's church, and they wish to deprive her of the courage to serve the Lord Jesus and his members, as she has done up to the present time. As for her ministers Quintin Thieffry and Antoine Pocque, he hopes they realize that he is justly rebuking them. He then turns to the sect of the Libertines to which Thieffry and Pocque belong. This sect wreaks nothing but havoc. Poor believers had asked him to write against the Libertines, but he had delayed for a time to see whether the evil would go away if he remained silent. Now he feels he must respond. "A dog barks if it sees someone attacking its master. I would be cowardly if I remained silent and did not make a single sound when I see the truth of God being attacked." Marguerite must not be offended if the duty of his office will not allow him to spare her ministers. In so doing it is not in any way his intention to turn against her. He is not out for a position at court or for worldly renown, but he is called to serve God in the place where he now holds his office. Furthermore, he has not, as Marguerite has reproached him, retracted his earlier conviction. He has always detested the cowardice of denying Jesus Christ in order to save one's life or possessions. What has been said about him is slander. Marguerite need only ask Gérard Roussel about that; he can confirm it for her.

Epistre contre un certain cordelier *(1547)*

On August 20, 1547, Calvin addressed the believers in Rouen by letter to warn them about a certain Franciscan monk: *Epistre contre un certain cordelier, suppost de la secte des libertins, lequel est prisonnier à Roan* (*CO* 7:341–64).[9] Calvin had received several writings from this monk, who made it appear that he was a martyr for his Christian faith. In the letter Calvin refutes the monk's ideas, which bear a strong resemblance to those of the Libertines. He reproaches the monk for toying with Scripture and transforming countless texts to support his own ideas. "And especially, like a pig with its snout, he has turned upside down the seventh chapter of the Epistle to the Romans." The crucial point, according to Calvin, is the accusation against God of having created man wicked, which obscures the difference between good and evil. The monk also has defended the ideas of Quintin, one of the leaders of the Libertines. Calvin's letter was appended in 1547 to a reprint of his *Contre la secte phantastique des libertins* of 1545.

Debating about Doctrinal Issues

In this section we deal with Calvin's debates with Pierre Caroli, Michael Servetus, and Sebastian Castellio. We have already treated Calvin's defense against the 1543 charge by Jean Courtois that he was not orthodox in his doctrines of the Trinity and Christ (see p. 61).

Debate with Pierre Caroli

In February 1537 Calvin and Guillaume Farel became involved in a conflict with Pierre Caroli, a doctor of theology and one of the first priests to decide for the Reformation. When his preaching in Paris created problems for him with the Sorbonne in 1524, he was forced to flee and obtained a pastoral posi-

9. The text can also be found in *Recueil des opuscules*, 714–26.

tion in Alençon with the help of Marguerite of Angoulême. Because his name was included in 1535 on the list of those suspected in the affair of the placards, he fled to Geneva, where he came into conflict with Farel and Pierre Viret. He then moved on to Basel, where he tried to defame them. He succeeded in finding a ministerial post in Neuchâtel in 1536, and a short time later became a minister and colleague of Viret in Lausanne, where he instigated more unrest. While Viret was in Geneva, Caroli created confusion with a sermon in which he defended the mass for the dead. Viret hastily returned to Lausanne with Calvin, and a discussion with Caroli took place on February 15–17, at which several representatives from Bern were also present. They encouraged Caroli to abandon his positions and to conduct himself peaceably. He seemed ready to comply, but then suddenly accused Farel and Calvin of Arianism. When Calvin defended himself by quoting from his catechism, Caroli came out in support of the old formulas: the Apostles', Nicene, and Athanasian creeds. One ought to subscribe to them and not to the modern confessions.[10]

The synod that Calvin had requested to deal with the problems with Caroli met in Lausanne on May 14 under the leadership of Kaspar Megander, minister in Bern. More than a hundred other ministers participated. Calvin delivered a major address on May 14, which appeared in print as *Confessio de Trinitate propter calumnias P. Caroli* (*CO* 9:703–10).

The most significant point raised in the treatise has to do with the confession of God's trinitarian nature. Caroli had based his charge of Arianism on the fact that Farel avoided words like "Trinity" and "person" in his *Summaire*. That was also the case in the confession of faith drafted in Geneva in 1537. Calvin declares that Farel and he have no objection to the use of these words (see, for example, what he says about the use of extrabiblical words in the section on the Trinity in the *Institutes* of 1536 [2.A.8]). What he is opposed to is the compulsory use of certain words.

In his address to the Lausanne synod Calvin also deals with subscription to confessions. He explains that he does not reject the three creeds mentioned earlier, but he is against obligatory subscription. He calls it tyranny if those who do not agree with subscribing to what another has dictated are regarded as heretics; he does not wish that kind of tyranny to be introduced.

The synod at Lausanne voted unanimously to depose Caroli, as did a large synod held in Bern from May 31 to June 5. Caroli fled to France, asked Pope Paul III in a letter for permission to return to the Roman Catholic Church,

10. See E. Baehler, "Petrus Caroli und Johann Calvin," *JSG* 29 (1904): 41–169; Willem Nijenhuis, "Calvin's Attitude towards the Symbols of the Early Church during the Conflict with Caroli," in idem, *Ecclesia Reformata: Studies on the Reformation* (Leiden, 1972), 73–96.

and then decided to become Protestant again, trying his best in 1539 to obtain a ministerial position in Strasbourg, among other places. In a letter to Calvin in 1540 he accused Calvin and Farel of obstructing his efforts to become a minister. Calvin responded with a letter on August 10, 1540 (see *CO* 11:72–75), in which he appealed to Caroli for reconciliation, but nothing came of it.

In 1543 Caroli found himself in Metz and clearly showed in the sermons he was preaching there that he would have nothing more to do with the Reformation movement. In a letter on May 14, 1543, he challenged Farel to a disputation in Rome, Trent, or a Spanish or French university. Caroli sent copies of this letter to, among others, the pope, Emperor Charles V, and Francis I. Farel, who answered Caroli in a letter on May 21, wanted Calvin to be involved in the disputation, which would have to be held in Metz. Calvin, meanwhile, had gone to Strasbourg (where Farel was) via Bern and Basel, where he delivered a letter from the Genevan Council to the Council of Basel. The Council of Strasbourg thought that it would be best for them to send a letter to Smalcald to try to get the princes to take charge of the matter (see the letter that Calvin sent from Strasbourg to the Council of Geneva on July 1—*CO* 11:587–89). Calvin and Farel waited around in Strasbourg, but about the middle of August they still did not know how things stood, for the Council of Metz had involved the emperor in the matter in an attempt to bring about a delay or even a cancelation of the disputation. Because they still did not know what was going to happen, Calvin and Farel decided not to wait around any longer but to return home. The correspondence between Caroli and Farel was published by Farel in Geneva in 1543. The foreword is from the hand of Calvin (*CO* 9:839–40).[11]

In 1545 a work by Calvin appeared in which he once again addressed Caroli: *Pro Farello et collegis eius adversus Petri Caroli calumnias defensio Nicolai Gallasii* (*CO* 7:289–340). Calvin had the treatise published in the name of Nicolas Des Gallars in order to create a greater impression of objectivity. He had corresponded about this with Viret, whom he had permitted to read the beginning of the treatise (see the letters written in July—*CO* 12:100–101, 107–8).

Debate with Michael Servetus and Sebastian Castellio

Michael Servetus and Calvin began an exchange of letters in 1546.[12] Through Jean Frellon, a bookdealer and printer in Lyons, Servetus first approached Calvin with three questions. These concerned Jesus as the Son of

---

11. For more information on this correspondence see *Guillaume Farel, 1489–1565* (Neuchâtel, 1930), 43, 497–503.

12. On the conflict between Servetus and Calvin see Roland H. Bainton, *Hunted Heretic* (Boston, 1953); Jerome Friedman, *Michael Servetus: A Case Study in Total Heresy* (Geneva, 1978).

God (whether the man Jesus was crucified as the Son of God and what that Sonship implies), belonging to the kingdom of Christ (how one belongs to it and how one is born again), and baptism (whether baptism, like the Lord's Supper, must take place in faith and what the significance of the two is in the new covenant).[13]

Calvin replied under the name Charles d'Espeville, and Servetus initiated a debate. He sent Calvin a copy of the section on infant baptism from a book he was writing (*Christianismi restitutio*). Calvin responded by sending a copy of a number of pages from the *Institutes* that dealt with the same subject. Servetus then returned these pages with critical notes that he had added in the margins. He also sent Calvin a tractate consisting of thirty letters addressed to Calvin.[14]

On February 13, 1546, at the beginning of his correspondence with Servetus, Calvin wrote to Frellon (*CO* 12:281–82) that he would answer Servetus, but that he did not think it would do much good because of the spirit in which Servetus wrote. The same day he reported to Farel in a letter (*CO* 12:282–84) that Servetus had written him and had also sent a thick volume "with his absurdities, in which I, according to his arrogant boasting, would find sensational and heretofore unheard of things." With Calvin's permission Servetus wanted to come to Geneva, but, Calvin wrote to Farel, if he himself had anything to say about it, Servetus would never leave there alive.

On August 13, 1553, Calvin heard after the morning service that he had conducted in the Madeleine Church that Servetus had been among those present. Servetus was the author of *Christianismi restitutio*, a book that had been printed anonymously (only the letters M. S. V. are mentioned at the end) in Vienne in January 1553. In it he disputes a number of Christian doctrines, especially the Trinity, but also original sin, infant baptism, and justification by faith.[15] He attacks Calvin in particular. Included in the book are the thirty letters to Calvin in 1546 mentioned earlier. The title of the book gives the impression that it is a counter to Calvin's *Institutes*. In any case, it is clear that Servetus wants to provide a new foundation for Christianity, for according to him, present-day Christianity has been mutilated by the Roman Catholic Church and the Reformation.

Servetus had gotten into difficulty in February 1553 when a resident of Lyons wrote a letter to his cousin Guillaume de Trie in Geneva. The letter spoke very

---

13. See *CO* 8:482–95 for Servetus's three questions, Calvin's response, and Servetus's refutation of that response.

14. Despite Servetus's request, Calvin never sent them back.

15. Servetus had written about the Trinity already in 1531 (*De Trinitatis erroribus libri septem*) and 1532 (*Dialogorum de Trinitate libri duo*). These works were included in revised form in *Christianismi restitutio*.

negatively about the reform in Geneva. De Trie wrote back that they were not heretics in Geneva, for they believed in the Triune God. At the same time he called attention to Servetus, who was staying in the vicinity of Lyons in Vienne. He had written a book full of heresies, yet he was left undisturbed.

When an investigation did not uncover enough evidence to incriminate Servetus, de Trie's cousin asked for further documentation. De Trie pleaded with Calvin to supply him with incriminating material, and Calvin finally gave him personal letters from Servetus and the section from the *Institutes* on infant baptism on which Servetus had made marginal notes. Servetus was imprisoned and examined by the Inquisition, but he managed to escape (on June 17 he was burned in effigy in Vienne) and next surfaced in Calvin's audience in Geneva on August 13.

In Geneva Servetus was arrested. An official complaint, consisting of thirty-nine points (see *CO* 8:727–31), was lodged by Calvin's secretary, Nicolas de La Fontaine. According to the custom of the time, he too was imprisoned until the proceedings began (on August 17).[16] During the proceedings, the uproar that Servetus had created with his false teaching during his sojourns in Basel and Strasbourg was also discussed. It was decided to send a messenger to Vienne with a letter (see *CO* 8:761) to find out why Servetus had been arrested there and how he had been able to escape. That was not very productive, however. Vienne requested the extradition of Servetus (see *CO* 8:783–84), but Geneva refused (see *CO* 8:790).

In connection with the decision of the Council to ask the churches (i.e., the councils and ministers) of other Swiss cities for their opinion, Servetus had to respond in writing to thirty-eight points on which he, according to Calvin and the other ministers, had departed from the Word of God and generally accepted doctrine (see *CO* 8:501–8). This Servetus did (see *CO* 8:507–18). That was followed by a *brevis refutatio* by the ministers (see *CO* 8:519–53), to which Servetus then vehemently responded with marginal notations (see *CO* 8:799–801).

The Council finally sent out letters on September 21 asking for advice from Zurich, Bern, Basel, and Schaffhausen (see *CO* 8:802–3). All of them condemned Servetus's teaching, but left it up to the Council of Geneva to decide what punishment he deserved.[17]

16. See *CO* 8:721–872 ("Actes du procès de Michel Servet. 1553").
17. See *CO* 8:808 (*Réponse du Conseil de Zurich*); *CO* 8:555–58 (the reply of the ministers of Zurich, included in Calvin's *Defensio* of 1554); *CO* 8:809 (*Réponse du Conseil de Schaffhouse*); *CO* 8:810 (*Réponse des ministres de Schaffhouse*); *CO* 8:818 (*Réponse du Conseil de Berne*); *CO* 8:818–19 (*Réponse des ministres de Berne*; see also *CO* 8:811–17 [*Consultation des ministres de Berne touchant la doctrine de Servet*]); *CO* 8:820 (*Réponse du Conseil de Bâle*); and *CO* 8:820–23 (*Réponse des ministres de Bâle*).

Probably encouraged by the struggle taking place in Geneva between the church and civil government over the right of excommunication, Servetus vehemently attacked Calvin in a letter to the Council on September 22. He was of the opinion that Calvin ought to be taken prisoner until it was decided who deserved the death penalty, Calvin or he. He added that Calvin ought to be condemned as a sorcerer and banished (see *CO* 8:804–6).

On October 26 Servetus was sentenced to burn at the stake. Calvin tried to get the sentence changed to the less inhumane punishment of beheading, but did not succeed. On October 27, the day of the execution, both Farel and Calvin visited Servetus in his cell. Servetus begged for mercy and asked Calvin's forgiveness. Calvin said that he had not become involved in the prosecution of Servetus because of any offenses against him personally. They then made a final attempt to get Servetus to change his mind about the Trinity, but without success.

Just before Servetus was brought to the stake, one of the syndics read out the sentence, which consisted of fourteen points. In the sentence the book *Christianismi restitutio* was the first item mentioned. Also cited were his heresies concerning the Trinity and infant baptism (see *CO* 8:827–30). Right before Servetus died at the stake, he cried out, "Jesus, Son of the eternal God, take pity on me."[18]

Following the execution of Servetus, Calvin felt compelled by criticism of the case to write about Servetus and his condemnation. The criticism came mainly from Basel, where the work *Historia de morte Serveti* appeared in 1553, probably composed by Sebastian Castellio.[19] Others too, including Heinrich Bullinger (see the letter to Calvin dated November 28, 1553—*CO* 14:684), had urged him to publish a justification.

Calvin's *Defensio orthodoxae fidei de sacra Trinitate, contra prodigiosos errores Michaelis Serveti Hispani . . .* (*CO* 8:453–644) appeared in February 1554 along with a French translation.[20] In this writing, with which the other ministers in

---

18. In this way Servetus held firmly to his conviction. He spoke of Jesus, Son of the eternal God, and not of Jesus, the eternal Son of God.

19. On February 10, 1554, the chancellor of Bern, Nikolaus Zurkinden, had written Calvin a critical letter (*CO* 15:19–22), which he did not further publicize. For more on the criticism in Basel, see Uwe Plath, *Calvin und Basel in den Jahren 1552–1556* (Zurich, 1974), 88–93. For more on the debate between Calvin and Castellio, see Uwe Plath, "Calvin und Castellio und die Frage der Religionsfreiheit," in *Calvinus ecclesiae Genevensis custos*, ed. Wilhelm H. Neuser (Frankfurt am Main, 1984), 191–95.

20. The full title reads: *Defensio orthodoxae fidei de sacra Trinitate, contra prodigiosos errores Michaelis Serveti Hispani, ubi ostenditur haereticos iure gladii coercendos esse, et nominatim de homine hoc tam impio iuste et merito sumptum Genevae fuisse supplicium.* The French translation was entitled *Déclaration pour maintenir la vraye foy que tiennent tous chrestiens de la Trinité des personnes en un seul Dieu. Contre les erreurs détestables de Michel Servet Espaignol. Où il est aussi monstré qu'il est licite de punir les hérétiques, et qu'à bon droict ce meschant a esté exécuté par iustice en la ville de Genève* (Geneva, 1554; text in *Recueil des opuscules*, 1315–1469).

Geneva expressed their agreement, Calvin defends the orthodox doctrine of the Trinity against the errors of Servetus in particular, and justifies magisterial action against heresy with an appeal to various texts from Scripture. He also frequently cites Augustine, who had supported the church's call for state assistance in acting against the Donatists. At the same time Calvin explains his own attitude toward the arrest and prosecution of Servetus.[21]

In March, almost immediately after the appearance of Calvin's *Defensio*, the treatise *De haereticis an sint persequendi* came out in Basel under the name of Martinus Bellius, which many believe Castellio was using as a pseudonym.[22] In the foreword to Christoph von Württemberg, Castellio gives his own opinion about the execution of heretics, advocating instead religious liberty and tolerance. Next follows a collection of texts from individuals like Martin Luther, Johann Brenz, Erasmus, Chrysostom, Augustine, and even Calvin, which are adduced as proof that they had opposed the killing of heretics. In the case of Calvin, Castellio refers to statements in the first edition of the *Institutes* (*CO* 1:77) and in the foreword to Calvin's commentary on Acts (*CO* 14:294).

The treatise concludes with contributions by Georg Kleinberg (*Quantum orbi noceant persecutiones, sententia Georgii Kleinbergii*) and Basilius Montfort (*Basilii Montfortii refutatio eorum, quae pro persecutione dici solent*), also probably pseudonyms for Castellio. A French translation of *De haereticis* appeared in Rouen in 1554.[23]

Because Calvin was so busy working on his Genesis commentary, Theodore Beza responded to Castellio's treatise with *De haereticis a civili magistratu puniendis* in September 1554.[24] Castellio retorted in 1555 with the treatise *De haereticis non puniendis* (printed in Geneva in 1971), penned under the name Basilius Montfort.[25] He also replied to Calvin's *Defensio orthodoxae fidei de sacra Trinitate* in his *Contra libellum Calvini in quo ostendere conatur haereticos iure gladii coercendos esse*, which was published in Holland in 1612.

---

21. See Plath, *Calvin und Basel*, 93, 120–27.

22. A facsimile edition was published in Geneva in 1954 by Sape van der Woude; Roland H. Bainton produced an English edition, *Concerning Heretics* (New York, 1935). See also Plath, *Calvin und Basel*, 128–36.

23. *Traicté des hérétiques, à savoir, si on les doit persécuter, et comment on se doit conduire avec eux, selon l'advis, opinion, et sentence de plusieurs autheurs, tant anciens, que modernes* (Rouen, 1554).

24. Complete title: *De haereticis a civili magistratu puniendis libellus, adversus Martini Bellii farraginem, et novorum academicorum sectam, Theodore Beza Vezelio auctore* (Geneva, 1554). Six years later Nicolas Colladon produced a French translation of this work: *Traité de l'authorité du magistrat en la punition des hérétiques et du moyen d'y procéder, fait en latin par Théodore de Besze . . .* (Geneva, 1560). See also Plath, *Calvin und Basel*, 221–30.

25. Complete title: *De haereticis a civili magistratu non puniendis pro Martini Bellii farragine, adversus libellum Theodori Bezae libellus, authore Basilio Montfortio*. See also Plath, *Calvin und Basel*, 231–44.

In an anonymous writing in early 1557, Castellio attacked Calvin's view of predestination. Calvin responded the same year with the publication of his *Responses à certaines calomnies et blasphèmes.* Both treatises have been lost, but the revised Latin translation of Calvin's piece, which appeared a few weeks after the French edition, has survived: *Brevis responsio Io. Calvini ad diluendas nebulonis cuiusdam calumnias quibus doctrinam de aeterna Dei praedestinatione foedare conatus est* (CO 9:257–66).[26] In 1558 Calvin published the work *Calumniae nebulonis cuiusdam, quibus odio et invidia gravare conatus est doctrinam Ioh. Calvini de occulta Dei providentia. Ioannis Calvini ad easdem responsio* (CO 9:269–318).[27] The first part contains fourteen articles in which Castellio challenges Calvin's ideas (*Calumniae nebulonis cuiusdam adversus doctrinam Iohannis Calvini de occulta Dei providentia*), and the second part is Calvin's reply. That was Calvin's last response to Castellio; he left any further disputing with Castellio to Beza.

Debating with the Antitrinitarians Gribaldi, Blandrata, and Gentilis

In May of 1558 confusion was growing in the Italian refugee congregation in Geneva, which had already been experiencing problems for some time.[28] At first they had been caused primarily by Matteo Gribaldi, a lawyer from Padua, who spent his vacations on the Farges estate near Gex (in Bernese territory) in the vicinity of Geneva. He had thrown the congregation into disorder in September 1554 with his criticism of the doctrine of the Trinity, and a short time later had explained his views in a letter to the congregation (see CO 15:246–48). At Calvin's invitation he appeared before the Consistory on June 29, 1555, in connection with the ideas he was propagating, but the meeting was unproductive. Next Gribaldi had to appear before the Council to defend his position, but no measures were taken there because he lived in Bern's territory.

Gribaldi's aberrant ideas had to do with the relation between Christ and God the Father. For him Christ was God, but because Gribaldi never talked

---

26. The earlier French edition was entitled *Responses à certaines calomnies et blasphèmes, dont quelsques malins s'efforcent de rendre la doctrine de la prédestination de Dieu odieuse.* This edition has been lost, but the reply to Castellio was appended to the *Traité de la prédestination éternelle de Dieu . . .* of 1560 (see p. 114, n. 48), which is identical to the *Treze sermons traitans de l'élection . . .* of 1562. The French text can be found in *Recueil des opuscules,* 1767–75.

27. For a French translation see *Recueil des opuscules,* 1776–1822; for an English translation and introduction see *Calvin: Theological Treatises,* ed. J. K. S. Reid (London and Philadelphia, 1954), 331–43.

28. On the subject of Calvin, the antitrinitarians, and their relation to Servetus see Antonio Rotondò, *Calvin and the Italian Anti-Trinitarians,* trans. John and Anne Tedeschi (St. Louis, 1969). See also the review of this book by E. David Willis in *ARG* 62 (1971): 279–82.

about one essence, he was really, according to Calvin (*CO* 15:644), speaking of two gods.[29]

In May 1558 Giorgio Blandrata, an Italian physician, brought about great confusion in the Italian congregation with his antitrinitarian ideas.[30] Calvin wrote to Nikolaus Zurkinden in Bern on July 4 (*CO* 17:235–39) that in their conversations together Blandrata, who had fled to Bern and whom Zurkinden had more or less defended in a letter to Calvin (see *CO* 17:204–8), had plagued him with his ideas for a year already. Calvin had listened to him time and again, but eventually the situation in the Italian congregation had become unbearable (see also the letter from Calvin to Galeazzo Caraccioli di Vico on July 19—*CO* 17:255–59). Although Calvin had tried to restore calm, Blandrata did not know when to stop and finally fled to Bern. From there he went to Poland by way of Zurich.[31] Calvin wrote down his views on the questions Blandrata had put to him in his *Responsum ad quaestiones Georgii Blandratae* (*CO* 9:321–32).[32]

Trouble also arose in the Italian refugee congregation with Giovanni Valentino Gentilis. After first refusing, he subscribed in May 1558 to the confession of faith that had been drawn up to put an end to the disorder in the congregation, but a short time later he was once again voicing his antitrinitarian ideas. He was imprisoned in July, abandoned his false teaching, and asked forgiveness of the Council and Calvin for what he had said and done. On the advice of a committee of five lawyers, Gentilis was condemned to death. When others interceded, however, the punishment was postponed and finally commuted to public penance. Gentilis had to throw his writings into the fire with

29. See also Calvin's letter to Melchior Wolmar in June of 1555 (*CO* 15:644), and his letter to Count Georg von Württemberg on May 2, 1557 (*CO* 16:463–66). The count had inquired of Calvin about a possible appointment of Gribaldi to the University of Tübingen.

30. See *TRE*, s.v. "Biandrata"; Joseph N. Tylenda, "The Warning That Went Unheeded: John Calvin on Giorgio Biandrata," *CTJ* 12 (1977): 24–62.

31. In Poland Blandrata obtained a leadership position in the church. On several occasions Calvin received letters from Poland appealing to him to reconcile with Blandrata. Pierre Statorius, rector of the gymnasium in Pińczów, wrote Calvin a letter in 1559 (*CO* 17:600–603) in which he called upon Calvin, in view of his prestige in Poland, to reconcile with Blandrata. Calvin replied on November 15 (*CO* 17:676–77) that he felt offended that Statorius would without a knowledge of the facts prescribe to him what he ought to do. Statorius later offered Calvin his apologies, and Calvin responded (see *CO* 18:101–2). Francesco Lismanino (who had come under the influence of unitarianism) and the ministers of Vilnius likewise made an attempt to bring about reconciliation between Calvin and Blandrata. On October 9, 1561, Calvin wrote about the matter in letters to the ministers in Vilnius and to Lismanino (*CO* 19:38–39, 41–43). With the letter to Vilnius he included a summary of what had taken place during Blandrata's stay in Geneva (*CO* 19:39–40).

32. For an English translation of a letter from Blandrata to Calvin (*CO* 17:169–71) and of Calvin's *Responsum ad quaestiones Georgii Blandratae,* see Tylenda, "Warning," 52–62.

his own hands. He was released on September 16, and then left to join Matteo Gribaldi in spite of a promise that he would remain in the city.

In 1559 Gentilis broke another promise he had made and in his *Antidoto* challenged what Calvin had written about the Trinity in the *Institutes* (1.13.20–29). This was followed in 1561 with the appearance of Calvin's *Impietas Valentini Gentilis detecta et palam traducta, qui Christum non sine sacrilega blasphemia Deum essentiatum esse fingit* (*CO* 9:361–420), which described the entire course of events in 1558 and supplied the relevant documents.[33] Gentilis worked in Poland beginning in 1563, but had to leave in 1566 on account of his views. That same year he was condemned to death (under Bern's jurisdiction) and was beheaded on September 10.

Debating with the Unitarians in Poland

With the concurrence of the other ministers in Geneva, Calvin wrote two treatises against the views of Francesco Stancaro: *Responsum ad fratres Polonos, quomodo mediator sit Christus, ad refutandum Stancaro errorem* (*CO* 9:333–42), which he composed in June 1560, and *Ministrorum ecclesiae Genevensis responsio ad nobiles Polonos et Franciscum Stancarum Mantuanum de controversia mediatoris* (*CO* 9:345–58), dated March 1561.[34]

Stancaro was a monk from Mantua who had become a Lutheran. In Poland he created confusion and conflict with his attempt to gain supporters for the view that Christ was mediator only according to his human nature. He also argued against Philipp Melanchthon, as can be seen from a personal letter from Calvin to Stancaro on February 26, 1561 (*CO* 19:230–31). On that same date, Calvin also addressed himself to Stanislaus Stadnitzki about the internal discord in Poland and warned about Stancaro, who was stirring up unrest (see *CO* 18:378–80).

In 1563 Calvin again became involved with the unitarianism in Poland. He responded in April (*CO* 19:729–30) to a letter from Jakob Sylvius (dated October 20, 1562—*CO* 19:558–61) urging him to write against the unitarianism that was gaining so much influence in Poland. Calvin produced both *Brevis admonitio Ioannis Calvini ad fratres Polonos, ne triplicem in Deo essentiam pro tribus personis imaginando, tres sibi deos fabricent* (Geneva, 1563—*CO* 9:629–38)[35]

---

33. For the French text see *Recueil des opuscules*, 1921–64. See also *Procès de Valentin Gentilis et de Nicolas Gallo (1558)*, ed. Henri Fazy (Geneva, 1879); *OS* 3:139–40; Wilhelm Niesel, "Zum Genfer Prozess gegen Valentin Gentilis," *ARG* 26 (1929): 270–73.

34. For the French text of *Responsum ad fratres Polonos* . . . see *Recueil des opuscules*, 1755–59. See also Joseph N. Tylenda, "Christ the Mediator: Calvin versus Stancaro," *CTJ* 8 (1973): 5–16; and idem, "The Controversy on Christ the Mediator: Calvin's Second Reply to Stancaro," *CTJ* 8 (1973): 131–57.

35. For the French text see *Recueil des opuscules*, 1964–70.

and *Epistola Ioannis Calvini qua fidem admonitionis ab eo nuper editae apud Polonos confirmat* (Geneva, 1563—*CO* 9:641–50).[36]

Debating with Menno about Christology

Although Calvin never made personal contact with Menno Simons, he did become involved with Menno's ideas, particularly through Martin Micron. Micron had entered into debate with Menno's conception of the incarnation of Christ and had asked Calvin, among others, to help him refute Menno. Menno was claiming that Christ became human by taking celestial flesh along with him in his coming to earth, stressing therefore that Christ was born *in* Mary and not *of* Mary.

In a letter to Micron in 1558 (*Contra Mennonem*—*CO* 10a:167–76), Calvin disputed this view, about which he was well informed from the written debate between Menno and Micron.[37] Calvin closely followed the arguments advanced by Menno and emphasized the true humanity of Christ. The connection between Adam and Christ was not severed, as it was in Menno's view. Hence Christ brought about genuine reconciliation in the course of his suffering and dying.[38]

36. For the French text see *Recueil des opuscules*, 1970–74.

37. In 1556 Micron published *Een waerachtigh verhaal der t'zamensprekinghe tusschen Menno Simons en Martinus Mikron van der menschwerdinghe Jesu Christi.* Menno responded with *Een gantsch duidlyck ende bescheyden antwoordt* and *Een seer hertgrondelycke (doch scherpe) sendt-brief aan Martinus Micron.*

38. See Balke, *Anabaptist Radicals*, 202–8, and the secondary sources mentioned there.

7

Striving for Unity and the Ensuing Debate

Confessio fidei de eucharistia (1537)
Agreement with Bullinger and Zurich (*Consensus Tigurinus* of 1549)
Debate with the Lutherans Westphal and Heshusius about the *Consensus Tigurinus*

Confessio fidei de eucharistia (1537)

In September 1537 Calvin and Guillaume Farel took part in a synod held in Bern. At the request of the Bernese Council, the Council of Geneva had delegated them to the meeting, in which theologians from Strasbourg and Basel also participated. There they met Wolfgang Capito, Martin Bucer, Oswald Myconius, Simon Grynaeus, and Pierre Viret. The discussion centered on the doctrines of the Trinity and the Lord's Supper. This exchange of ideas was crucial in the quest for unity, for in May 1536 Bucer and Capito had represented Strasbourg in discussions in Wittenberg concerning the Lord's Supper, and along with the others present (Martin Luther among them) had signed a *Formula concordiae* (see *WAB* 12, no. 4261) drawn up by Philipp Melanchthon.

At the synod in Bern, Bucer and Capito defended their rapprochement with Luther expressed in the signing of the Wittenberg Concord. A confession written by Calvin concerning the Lord's Supper, the *Confessio fidei de eucharistia* (*CO* 9:711–12; *OS* 1:435), was also accepted by the Strasbourgers Bucer and Capito.[1] In this confession Calvin highlights the fellowship that believers

---

1. For an English translation (with an introduction) see *Calvin: Theological Treatises*, ed. J. K. S. Reid (London and Philadelphia, 1954), 167–69. For secondary sources on Calvin and the Lord's Supper see p. 134, n. 24.

HENRICVS BVLLINGERVS.

Heinrich Bullinger

have with Christ through the Spirit, both with the body and blood of Christ and with his spirit. Calvin rejects the presence of Christ in the elements of bread and wine, since Christ is in heaven. Nonetheless, through the Spirit the fellowship with Christ is a real fellowship.

Agreement with Bullinger and Zurich (*Consensus Tigurinus* of 1549)

In September 1544 Luther published his *Kurzes Bekenntnis vom heiligen Sakrament wider Schwenckfeld und die Schweizer* (*WA* 54:141–67), which renewed the old conflict between Luther and the followers of Ulrich Zwingli. Calvin, too, dealt with the eucharistic conflict between Luther and Zurich (Heinrich Bullinger and his supporters) in a letter to Farel on October 10, 1544 (*CO* 11:755). Farel had requested that Calvin go to Zurich to appeal to the brothers there for peace, but Calvin wrote back that he did not have at his disposal all the written materials from this debate. Besides, he felt that it would not be of much help to ask the Zurichers to cease debating about this issue; Luther is the one who should be called upon to stop the fighting.

The relationship between Luther and Zurich also came up for discussion in a letter from Calvin to Bullinger on November 25, 1544 (*CO* 11:772–75). According to Calvin, Luther should, of course, have made a greater effort to hold himself in check. It would be better if from now on he would direct his innate passion against the enemies of the truth instead of letting it erupt against the servants of Christ. If only he would try harder to see his faults. Nevertheless, writes Calvin, in rebuking what is wrong with him, we must also take into consideration his brilliant gifts. Bullinger and his colleagues should especially remember that we are dealing here with one of the first among the servants of Christ, someone to whom we owe a great debt. A fight with Luther accomplishes nothing except to bring delight to unbelievers. Even though Luther has irritated us somewhat, it is better to give up the fight than to do further damage, which could only be to the detriment of the entire church. Calvin does not go into the eucharistic issues themselves, preferring instead to discuss them orally.

In spite of Calvin's appeal in his November 25 letter to Bullinger, the Zurichers did respond to Luther's *Kurzes Bekenntnis vom heiligen Sakrament* in the treatise *Wahrhaftes Bekenntnis der Diener der Kirche zu Zürich* (see *BSRK* 153–59). On June 28, 1545, Calvin wrote to Melanchthon (*CO* 12:98–100) about the conflict between Luther and the Zurichers over the Lord's Supper. The Zurichers had reason to respond, he says, at least if their version of the matter is correct. It is also his opinion, however, that they should either have written something different or written nothing at all. As for the central point in their disagreement about the Lord's Supper, he feels that they have handled the issue in an unfortunate way. But he cannot speak well of Luther either, about whom he is very ashamed. The worst thing, in his judgment, is that Luther thunders about like Pericles, and no one tries to bring him under control. We must have the boldness to complain about that, he feels. Furthermore, he hopes that Melanchthon will reveal his view of the Lord's Supper, for there are many doubters who are awaiting it.

On January 24, 1547, by order of the Council, Calvin began a journey through a number of Swiss cities in order to encourage the inhabitants. Charles V had been successful in his struggle with the German Protestant princes, and the south of Germany was now under his control because Johann Friedrich of Saxony and Philip of Hesse, under threat by Maurice of Saxony, had retreated to their own territories. The German Protestants were in a difficult position, and the Swiss felt threatened.

When Calvin stopped in Zurich on this journey, Bullinger presented him with a treatise he had written on the Lord's Supper, *Absoluta de Christi Domini et catholicae ecclesiae sacramentis tractatio* (printed in 1551). Calvin read the treatise as soon as he got home and, at Bullinger's request, wrote him (see the letter dated February 25, 1547—*CO* 12:480–89) what did not entirely please him in the exposition. One of the things Calvin deals with is the presence of Christ in the Lord's Supper. Christ is not present before the eyes, for his body is in heaven and the Lord's Supper is celebrated on earth. But for the believing heart this spatial gulf is bridged by the power of the Spirit. The bread and wine are indeed signs, but not empty signs. "For the bread signifies not only that the body was once sacrificed for me, but also that it is offered to me today as the food by which I live."

As far as ecclesiastical office is concerned, Calvin objects to Bullinger's idea that God's work of regeneration is not tied to the office. By himself, apart from God, a minister of the Word can do nothing, but on the other hand human effort is to be highly regarded if the work of the Spirit is joined with it.

Calvin's journey through the Swiss cities also took him to Bern, where he ascertained that there were large differences between the Zwinglian and Lutheran ministers. He was greatly concerned about the growing differences between these ministers, and he later wrote a letter to them (*CO* 12:675–79) in the hope that they would be able to bridge their differences through discussions in which both sides were open to his position. In the letter (of which, unfortunately, we have only a part of the text) he brings up three points for discussion: the purpose and functions of spiritual office, what the sacraments offer to us, and how the body of Christ is offered to us in the Lord's Supper.

Meanwhile, Bullinger responded to Calvin's comments on his treatise on the Lord's Supper. Unfortunately, that letter has been lost, but the next letter from Calvin to Bullinger (March 1, 1548—*CO* 12:665–67) makes it clear that Bullinger had tried to refute everything Calvin had written. Calvin replies that he does not wish to argue with Bullinger. In his answer he had only been fulfilling at Bullinger's request a friend's obligation, and he would like to come to some agreement with Bullinger. Calvin writes that his understanding of fellowship with Christ in the Lord's Supper is more profound than Bullinger has expressed it, but he hopes that they can reach a fuller agreement.

The conflict in Bern between the Zwinglian-minded ministers led by Kilchmeier and the Lutheran ministers Sulzer, Gerung, and Schmidt was becoming more serious. Viret and a colleague in Lausanne had been accused of Lutheran ideas and had to defend themselves in Bern in April. They asked Calvin to accompany them, but Calvin thought it better to keep out of it (see the letter of April 29—*CO* 12:687–89). Sulzer and the two other Lutheran-minded ministers in Bern were deposed from office. Because Viret and his col-

Ulrich Zwingli at age 48

league accomplished nothing positive in Bern, Calvin decided, at Viret's request, to go with Farel to Zurich after Pentecost in the hope that Zurich would exert a favorable influence on Bern. Calvin and the others were not successful in Zurich, however, in engaging their colleagues in a real discussion about the Lord's Supper, so Calvin did not expect a positive effort from them with respect to Bern (see Calvin's letter to Sulzer, who became a professor in Basel after he was forced to leave Bern—*CO* 12:720–21). Calvin's group was, however, given an audience with the Council of Zurich.

In a letter to Bullinger on June 26 (*CO* 12:727–31) after returning to Geneva, Calvin regrets that he and Farel were not able to talk with Bullinger and his colleagues about the Lord's Supper. They were looking for agreement, not a quarrel. Calvin also expresses the hope that Bullinger will cooperate in developing better relations with Bern. Furthermore, he tries to convince Bullinger that he does not equate signs with what they signify. The sacraments, he says, are of no benefit whatsoever if they do not lead us by the hand to Christ, so that we seek all that is good in him. I really do not see, he continues, what more you can rightly demand of this doctrine, which holds that salvation must be sought in Christ alone, makes God the sole author of salvation, and assures that it can be received only through the secret work of the Spirit.

Calvin also deals in the letter with his relation to Bucer, who was viewed with suspicion in Zurich. What right does he have to distance himself from Bucer if Bucer subscribes to the confession that he has just composed?

Bullinger responded to Calvin's letter of June 26 in November 1548. He arranged what Calvin had written him about the Lord's Supper into twenty-four points, which he sent to Calvin with his own notes added (*CO* 7:693–700). On January 21, 1549, Calvin replied by letter (*CO* 13:164–66) to Bullinger's notes on the twenty-four points, trying to clear up any misunderstandings. If there has been no basic distrust between them up to now, he says, then they have had nothing or very little to argue about for a long time already.

Bullinger answered (probably in March) in a letter (*CO* 13:221–23) in which he asked forgiveness for his clumsiness and expressed his affection for Bucer. Unity in confession concerning the Lord's Supper could now be reached. With that in mind, the ministers in Geneva drew up a confession consisting of twenty articles on the Lord's Supper (*CO* 7:723–26). They sent the confession to Bern, where a synod was meeting. The confession was not presented to the synod, however.

On May 20 Calvin went with Farel to Zurich. He had not yet received Bullinger's letter of May 11 (*CO* 13:278–80) suggesting that the matter could be settled in writing. For Calvin the trip bore an official stamp, since he was going with the permission of the Council to Bern and Zurich to try to convince them of the need for an alliance with France (see Calvin's letter to Bullinger dated May 7 [*CO* 13:266–69], in which he urges Bullinger to ask the civil government of Zurich to please think about their persecuted brethren in France). Calvin and Farel went straight to Zurich and in a few hours reached agreement on the Lord's Supper. The Genevan confession served as the basis for the discussion, and seventeen of its twenty points were adopted almost word for word. The agreement was recorded in the *Consensio mutua in re sacramentaria ministrorum Tigurinae ecclesiae, et D. Ioannis Calvini ministri Genevensis ecclesiae, iam nunc ab ipsis authoribus edita* (*CO* 7:735–44; *OS* 2:247–53).[2] The *Consensus Tigurinus* consists of twenty-six articles, divided into three parts: a christological introduction (1–6); an explanation of the sacraments (7–20), in

---

2. An English translation by Ian D. Bunting can be found in *JPH* 44 (1966): 45–61.

which Roman Catholic and Lutheran views are rejected; and a concluding section (21–26) devoted entirely to the refutation of other views.[3]

Calvin returned to Geneva on June 5. He urged speedy publication of the *Consensus* because he considered the agreement to be significant for the churches in Germany, which would now be able to tell that the Swiss were not Sacramentarians. But the *Consensus* was not published until 1551, when the churches in Switzerland officially adopted the agreement. The foreword and afterword were left out of the official edition because Bern objected to them. Instead, a letter that Calvin had written on August 1, 1549, in which he had asked for clarification of a few points, now introduced the document, and at the end of the twenty-six articles was a letter with which the Zurich theologians had responded on August 30, 1549.

The Latin text of the *Consensus* appeared at about the same time (February/March) in both Zurich and Geneva. Calvin published a French translation a short time later: *L'Accord passé et conclud touchant la matière des sacremens, entre les ministres de l'église de Zurich, et Maistre Iehan Calvin ministre de l'église de Genève* (Geneva, 1551—*Recueil des opuscules*, 1137–45). Bullinger produced a German translation: *Einhälligkeit der Dienern der Kilchen zu Zürich und herren Joannis Calvini Dieners der Kilchen zu Genff deren sy sich im Handel der heyligen Sacramenten gägen andern erklärt und vereinbared habend* (Zurich, 1551).

On June 28, 1549, Calvin sent Bucer a copy of the *Consensus* along with a letter (*CO* 20:393–95). Perhaps, he writes, Bucer will find that the *Consensus* leaves something to be desired, but he regards it as a positive achievement. He is curious to know what Bucer thinks. Bucer responded with some critical observations in a letter on August 14 (see *CO* 13:350–58). He believed that the *Consensus* did not do justice to Luther. It also spoke too cautiously and not biblically enough about communion with Christ. And the significance of the ascension was not clearly enough confessed.

Calvin replied (*CO* 13:437–40) that as far as the effect of the sacrament is concerned, it was not his fault that some things were not discussed more extensively. He does consider it good, however, that both sides are one in the truth and adhere to the main point.

Calvin also wrote to Oswald Myconius in Basel about the *Consensus*, for he had heard from Theodore Beza that Myconius was piqued at not being asked for his advice. Calvin explained to Myconius in a letter on November 13 how the *Consensus* came about (*CO* 13:456–57). When the *Consensus* was unexpectedly reached after an exchange of personal letters between him and Bullinger,

3. See *TRE*, s.v. "Consensus Tigurinus."

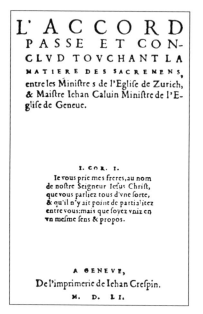
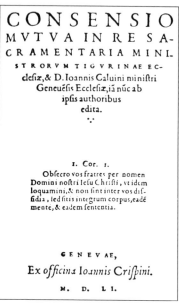

Title page of the Consensus Tigurinus *(French and Latin editions)*

it was the brothers in Zurich in particular who judged that consultation with Basel was unnecessary. This was not out of contempt for Myconius, Calvin believes, for nothing but positive things had been said about him.

Debate with the Lutherans Westphal and Heshusius about the *Consensus Tigurinus*

In 1554 Calvin responded to some writings by Joachim Westphal, minister in Hamburg, in which he had attacked the *Consensus Tigurinus* that had been reached in 1549 and published in 1551.[4] Westphal was a follower of Luther in his view of the Lord's Supper, and he considered the increasingly popular view of Calvin and others as a serious threat that he should warn about. His *Farrago confusanearum et inter se dissidentium opinionum de coena Domini ex sacramentariorum libris congesta* appeared in Magdeburg in 1552. In it he labels a number of individuals as Sacramentarians on the basis of citations from their writings, including Zwingli, Oecolampadius, Bucer, Bullinger, Calvin, and Johannes a Lasco. A predominantly exegetical-dogmatic work, *Recta fides de coena Domini*

4. See Joseph N. Tylenda, "The Calvin-Westphal Exchange: The Genesis of Calvin's Treatises against Westphal," *CTJ* 9 (1974): 182–209.

ex verbis apostoli Pauli et evangelistarum demonstrata ac communita, also published in Magdeburg, followed in 1553.

Bullinger's insistence notwithstanding, Calvin refused at first to respond (*CO* 15:95), but when he saw, for example, that Westphal's attacks were having an adverse influence on Lutheran-Reformed relations in various places (such as Frankfurt and Wesel) and that, much to his disappointment, Melanchthon was staying out of the matter, he finally decided to answer Westphal. On October 6, 1554, Calvin sent Bullinger his *Defensio sanae et orthodoxae doctrinae de sacramentis,* in which he argued not against Lutherans as such, but against fanatics like Westphal. The intent was that the work appear as a communal answer of the Swiss churches to Westphal's publications. Calvin would send it to Bern and Basel only when Zurich agreed to it (see Calvin's letter to Bullinger of October 6—*CO* 15:255–56).

From Zurich Calvin learned that he had been too harsh with Westphal and too gentle with Luther (*CO* 15:272–90); in response he suggested a few changes. He showed more restraint towards Westphal, but as far as Luther was concerned, he had no desire to emphasize again the agreement between the Swiss and Luther, according to which the sacraments are not bare signs because in them God certifies what he portrays there.

Bullinger wrote back that Zurich was in agreement, and he insisted on a speedy publication in Geneva and later in Zurich. He also felt that for the sake of time they ought to forgo agreement from the other churches (*CO* 15:349–52). Publication of *Defensio sanae et orthodoxae doctrinae de sacramentis* (*CO* 9:5–36; *OS* 2:263–87) followed in January 1555 in both Geneva and Zurich.[5]

The publication in Geneva did not proceed without problems, however, for the Council wanted to censor the treatise first.[6] This made Calvin so angry that he almost burned the manuscript. "Even if I should live another hundred

5. Full title: *Defensio sanae et orthodoxae doctrinae de sacramentis eorumque natura vi fine usu et fructu, quam pastores et ministri Tigurinae ecclesiae et Genevensis antehac brevi consensionis mutuae formula complexi sunt una cum refutatione probrorum quibus eam indocti et clamosi homines infamant.* There was also a French translation by Calvin in 1555: *La Brève Résolution sur les disputes qui ont été de nostre temps quant aux sacrements, contenant l'approbation de l'accord fait par ci-devant entre les ministres et pasteurs des églises de Zurich et Genève, touchant la nature, fin, usage et fruit des sacrements, pour montrer que ceux qui en médisent sont gens écervelés qui ne cherchent qu'à obscurir ou pervertir la bonne et saine doctrine* (for the text see *Recueil des opuscules,* 1469–97, and *Calvin, homme d'église: Oeuvres choisies du réformateur et documents sur les églises réformées du XVIe siècle* [2d ed., Geneva, 1971]). See also Bernard Cottret, "Pour une sémiotique de la Réforme: Le *Consensus Tigurinus* (1549) et La *Brève Résolution* . . . (1555) de Calvin," *AESC* 39 (1984): 265–85.

6. For the whole course of events surrounding the publication of Calvin's treatise see Uwe Plath, *Calvin und Basel in den Jahren 1552–1556* (Zurich, 1974), 174–92.

years," he wrote to Farel, "I will not have another thing published in their city" (*CO* 15:356).

The treatise consisted of three parts: a letter of dedication to the other churches, a defense of the *Consensus Tigurinus*, and the text of the consensus.

In January 1556 Calvin wrote a second treatise against Westphal, *Secunda defensio piae et orthodoxae de sacramentis fidei contra Ioachimi Westphali calumnias* (Geneva, 1556—*CO* 9:41–120).[7] In this work he responds to Westphal's *Adversus cuiusdam sacramentarii falsam criminationem iusta defensio* (Frankfurt, 1555), which was a reply to Calvin's *Defensio*. As Westphal's title indicates, he continued to regard the Swiss as Sacramentarians. Furthermore, he thought that Calvin's reading of Luther's position was erroneous and that the *Consensus Tigurinus* and the *Confessio Augustana* did not, as Calvin claimed in his *Defensio*, agree with each other.

At the request of others—among them Bullinger, who wanted Calvin to explain the entire doctrine of the Swiss churches in his answer (*CO* 15:854, a letter dated November 2, 1555)—Calvin finally responded to Westphal's latest publication with his *Secunda defensio* of 1556. Just before it came out, he wrote to Bullinger (on December 25, 1555—*CO* 15:358–59) that he had accomplished the feat of only slightly attacking his opponent. In reading it, Bullinger will notice how hard he has tried both to avoid the animosity of those who can still be healed and to pacify their anger.

Calvin dedicated the treatise to the ministers of Saxony. In the dedication he explains how the dispute with Westphal originated. When the *Consensus Tigurinus* had finally been reached after more than twenty years of debate about the Lord's Supper, Westphal had rekindled the controversy with his attacks on the Swiss. Calvin makes it clear that he does not favor this fighting. The discord should have been quelled long ago. It has been inflamed again for no other reason than the haughty recklessness of the other side. With an appeal to unity in Christ, he calls upon the Lutheran ministers to fight against this divisiveness.

Following Calvin's second treatise against Westphal, however, the literary battle increased in intensity. Bullinger published an apologia, and various Lutheran ministers, rallying behind Westphal, launched attacks on the Swiss.

The dispute between Calvin and Westphal resumed in 1557 after Westphal, using Melanchthon as support, wrote three new pamphlets in reply to Calvin's *Secunda defensio*. Calvin responded with his *Ultima admonitio ad Westphalum*

---

7. For the French translation see *Recueil des opuscules*, 1498–1577.

(Geneva, 1557—*CO* 9:137–252).[8] What is striking about this response is Calvin's repeated references to Augustine, which were the result of Westphal's charge that Calvin had hardly read the church father, if he had done so at all. In the second section of the work Calvin treats the confession of faith of the Saxon ministers (*Confessio fidei ministrorum Saxoniae inferioris*), to whom he had dedicated his previous work against Westphal, for Westphal had castigated him for not being fair to this confession and had appended it to his last treatise as evidence. Westphal published his *Refutatio* yet in 1557. Calvin did not respond with a separate work, but we do find the debate with Westphal once again in the *Institutes* of 1559 (4.17.20–34).

After all the debate with Westphal, Calvin did in 1561 devote one more piece to the issue of the Lord's Supper because of a fierce debate on the matter that had been carried on in Heidelberg since 1559. When the strict Lutheran Tilemann Heshusius (Calvin counted him among the apes of Luther—*CO* 18:84), who taught at the university in Heidelberg, was called to account before the elector of the Palatinate, he asserted that he could not celebrate the Lord's Supper with Calvin and Bullinger. Chancellor Georg von Erbach then asked him whether he would also not want to go to heaven if Calvin and Bullinger were there (see Calvin's letter dated October 5, 1559—*CO* 17:655–56). Heshusius published the treatise *De praesentia corporis Christi in coena Domini contra sacramentarios* in Jena in 1560. Calvin got hold of it through Bullinger and answered with his *Dilucida explicatio sanae doctrinae de vera participatione carnis et sanguinis Christi in sacra coena ad discutiendas Heshusii nebulas* (Geneva, 1561—*CO* 9:457–524; see also *OS* 2:289–95).[9] In this work Calvin discusses in great detail the way in which we participate in the body and blood of Christ when we celebrate the Lord's Supper. He gives considerable attention to the ideas of the church fathers.

Calvin turned over further debate with Heshusius to Beza, who in 1559 had also resumed the debate with Westphal.

8. Complete title: *Ultima admonitio Ioannis Calvini ad Ioachimum Westphalum, cui nisi obtemperet, eo loco posthac habendus erit, quo pertinaces haereticos haberi iubet Paulus. Refutantur etiam hoc scripto superbae Magdeburgensium et aliorum censurae, quibus coelum et terram obruere conati sunt.* For the French translation see *Recueil des opuscules*, 1578–1694.
9. For the French translation see *Recueil des opuscules*, 1694–1751; for an English translation see *Calvin: Theological Treatises*, ed. Reid, 258–324.

8

The Institutes

Institutes (1536)

At the end of 1533 or beginning of 1534 Calvin was staying in the south of France, where, under the pseudonym Charles d'Espeville, he spent considerable time at the home of Louis Du Tillet, pastor in Claix and a canon of the cathedral in Angoulême. There he was able to use Du Tillet's unusually large library in complete peace and quiet and had the opportunity both to do further study and to work on the first edition of the *Institutes*.

Calvin completed the first edition in 1535. It begins with a letter dated August 23, 1535, and addressed to King Francis I.[1] The letter indicates that in this book he wishes to provide instruction in the Christian faith in order to equip those with only limited knowledge. Many of his own countrymen, he

---

1. Calvin himself translated this letter for the 1541 French edition of the *Institutes*. The letter was also published separately in 1541 under the title *Epistre au tr̀eschrétien Roy de France, Françoys premier de ce nom, en laquelle sont démonstrées les causes dont procedent les troubles qui sont auiourdh'huy en l'église.* Jacques Pannier published the text of the letter with an introduction and notes: *Jean Calvin, Epître au Roi . . .* (Paris, 1927). For the character of the *Institutes* see Harmannus Obendiek, "Die Institutio Calvins als 'Confessio' und 'Apologie,'" in *Theologische Aufsätze: Karl Barth zum 50. Geburtstag,* ed. Ernst Wolf (Munich, 1936), 417–31.

writes, are hungering and thirsting after Jesus Christ, yet only a very few have a right knowledge of him.

By including such a letter Calvin was following the lead of two earlier books that had appeared in France, namely, Guillaume Farel's *Summaire et briefve déclaration d'aucuns lieux fort nécessaires à ung chascun chrestien pour mettre sa confiance en Dieu et ayder son prochain,* which had been published in Basel in 1525 and dedicated to King Francis I, and the 1529 *Somme chrestienne* by François Lambert of Avignon. Lambert had written the latter book when he was a professor in Marburg. He had it delivered to Emperor Charles V by order of Philip of Hesse in order to convince the emperor of the truth of evangelical teaching.

It is striking that although Calvin wrote the 1536 *Institutes* for the instruction of the common people, we know of no French translation of the work. Calvin also intended that the *Institutes* serve as a confessional defense to the king for the evangelicals in France, who were being identified with Anabaptist rebels and were being severely persecuted. In their writings, traditional Roman Catholics (Johannes Cochlaeus and Robert Ceneau) and Christian humanists (Guillaume Budé and Cardinal Sadoleto) alike had equated the evangelicals with Anabaptist agitators. The king had also signed a manifesto to the German Protestant princes on February 1 in which he tried to gloss over the persecution of evangelicals after the *affaire de placards.* According to the king, the evangelicals were not on the same level with the German Protestants, for the evangelicals were Anabaptist rebels against whom the authorities had to take action. By means of the *Institutes* Calvin wished to inform the king about the motivation of those disposed to reformation. In his letter to the king, he distances himself from the Anabaptists and refutes the accusations brought against the evangelicals, showing himself especially sensitive to the Roman Catholic charge of sectarianism. What is involved here for Calvin is the one, holy, catholic church, and he proceeds to outline its true form.

The first (Latin) edition of the *Christianae religionis institutio* (*CO* 1:1–252; *OS* 1:11–283) was published in Basel in March 1536 by Thomas Platter and Balthasar Lasius. The full title reads: *Christianae religionis institutio, totam fere pietatis summam, et quidquid est in doctrina salutis cognitu necessarium, complectens; omnibus pietatis studiosis lectu dignissimum opus, ac recens editum.*[2]

2. John Calvin, *Institutes of the Christian Religion* (1536 edition), ed. Ford Lewis Battles, rev. ed. (Grand Rapids, 1986); Walter G. Hards, *A Collation of the Latin Texts of the First Edition of Calvin's Institutes* (Baltimore, 1958); H. W. Simpson, "The *Editio Princeps* of the *Institutio Christianae Religionis* by John Calvin," in *Calvinus Reformator: His Contribution to Theology, Church and Society* (Potchefstroom, 1982), 26–32; Peter Barth, "Die Erwählungslehre in Calvins Institutio von 1536," in *Theologische Aufsätze,* ed. Wolf, 432–42.

Such an extensive title was very common in that time, for the intention was that the title clearly describe and recommend a book. The title of the *Institutes* indicates that the book provides almost the whole sum of piety and describes whatever is absolutely necessary to know about the doctrine of salvation. It also says that the newly published work is very well worth reading by all who are eager to achieve piety.

Calvin begins the *Institutes* by stating that the sum of almost the whole of sacred doctrine consists of two parts: the knowledge of God and of ourselves, an opening that he says he himself devised (see *CO* 1:27). It was indeed original in the sense that the entire *Institutes* is written in the light of these opening lines, but the statement itself is not wholly original, for Martin Luther, Ulrich Zwingli, and Martin Bucer had also expressed themselves in this way.

In a letter to François Daniel in Orléans on October 13, 1536 (*CO* 10b:63–64), Calvin indicated his plan to translate the *Institutes* into French, but no such French edition is known.[3] The Latin edition quickly sold out.

Calvin research has devoted a lot of attention to the question of the sources that influenced him in the writing of the *Institutes*.[4] Formally, the *Institutes* resembles a catechism. Calvin follows Luther's *Der kleine Catechismus* of 1529 in the design of the book, particularly in the sequence of the first four chapters. In these chapters Calvin gives, as indeed was customary in the Middle Ages, an explanation of the law, the Apostles' Creed, the Lord's Prayer, and the sacraments (baptism and the Lord's Supper—it is noteworthy that he believes the Lord's Supper should be celebrated at least weekly, and he provides an order of worship for such a church service—*CO* 1:139–40; *OS* 1:161). The apologetic character of the book can be seen in the next two chapters, one on the remaining five (false) sacraments, and the other on Christian freedom, the Christian doctrine of church and state, and spiritual and temporal government.

We notice the influence of Luther not only in the form of the *Institutes* but also in the content. Calvin was clearly influenced by several of Luther's most important writings of 1520 (for example, *Von der Freiheit eines Christenmenschen* and *Vorspiel von der babylonischen Gefangenschaft der Kirche*), but he also

---

3. Wilhelm Niesel and Peter Barth, "Eine französische Ausgabe der ersten Institutio Calvins," *ThBl* 7 (1928): 2–10; Jacques Pannier, "Une Première «Institution» française dès 1537," *RHPhR* 8 (1928): 513–34.

4. August Lang, "The Sources of Calvin's Institutes of 1536," *EvQ* 8 (1936): 130–41; François Wendel, *Calvin: The Origins and Development of His Religious Thought,* trans. Philip Mairet (New York, 1963; reprint, Durham, N.C., 1987), 122–44; Alexandre Ganoczy, *The Young Calvin,* trans. David Foxgrover and Wade Provo (Philadelphia, 1987), 133–81. See also the notes in Calvin, *Institutes,* ed. Battles.

made use of other publications by Luther.[5] In addition, he was influenced by Philipp Melanchthon,[6] Bucer,[7] and Zwingli.[8]

Institutes (1539)

When Calvin settled in Basel in 1538 after his banishment from Geneva, he found the opportunity to write the second Latin edition of the *Institutes*. On August 1, 1539, he composed the foreword to the new edition, which was three times as large as the 1536 edition and published in Strasbourg.[9] A number of

5. See Wendel, *Calvin*, 131–34; Ganoczy, *Young Calvin*, 137–45. Wilhelm Diehl, "Calvins Auslegung des Dekalogs in der ersten Ausgabe seiner *Institutio* und Luthers Katechismen," *ThStKr* 71 (1898): 141–62, points out the influence of Luther on Calvin's interpretation of the Ten Commandments. See also Willem van 't Spijker, *Luther en Calvijn: De invloed van Luther op Calvijn blijkens de Institutie* (Kampen, 1985), 16–21; and idem, "The Influence of Luther on Calvin according to the *Institutes*," in *John Calvin's Institutes: His Opus Magnum* (Potchefstroom, 1986), 83–105. For the connection between Calvin and Luther in general, see Willem Balke, "Calvijn en Luther," in idem, *Luther en het gereformeerd protestantisme* (The Hague, 1982), 99–117, and the secondary literature mentioned there; see also Joachim Rogge, "Themen Luthers im Denken Calvins," in *Calvinus servus Christi*, ed. Wilhelm H. Neuser (Budapest, 1988), 53–72.

6. See Wendel, *Calvin*, 134–35; Ganoczy, *Young Calvin*, 146–51, which deals with the relationship between Melanchthon's *Loci communes* (1521) and the *Institutes*. For more on the connection between Calvin and Melanchthon, see August Lang, "Melanchthon und Calvin," in idem, *Reformation und Gegenwart* (Detmold, 1918), 88–135.

7. The second printing of Bucer's commentary on the Gospels appeared in 1530. Bucer's influence is noticeable in Calvin's doctrine of repentance, and Calvin was also guided by Bucer's explanation of the Lord's Prayer. See Wendel, *Calvin*, 137–44; Ganoczy, *Young Calvin*, 158–68; and Willem van 't Spijker, "The Influence of Bucer on Calvin as Becomes Evident from the *Institutes*," in *John Calvin's Institutes: His Opus Magnum*, 106–32. On the connection between Calvin and Bucer in general, see Wilhelm Pauck, "Calvin and Butzer," *JR* 9 (1929): 237–56 (this article also appears in idem, *The Heritage of the Reformation* [Glencoe, Ill., 1961], 85–99); Jaques Courvoisier, "Bucer et Calvin," in Jean-Daniel Benoit et al., *Calvin à Strasbourg, 1538–1541* (Strasbourg, 1938), 37–66; and H. Strohl, "Bucer et Calvin," *BSHPF* 87 (1938): 354–60.

8. As far as Zwingli is concerned, Calvin must have been acquainted with his *Commentarius de vera et falsa religione* (1525). See Ganoczy, *Young Calvin*, 151–58. For the connection between Calvin and Zwingli in general, see Fritz Blanke, "Calvins Urteile über Zwingli," *Zwingliana* 11 (1959): 66–92 (this article is also found in idem, *Aus der Welt der Reformation: Fünf Aufsätze* [Zurich, 1960], 18–47).

9. On the various editions of the *Institutes*, see Wilhelm Niesel, "Descriptio et historia editionum Institutionis latinarum et gallicarum Calvino vivo emissarum," in *OS* 3:vi–l. For the relationship between the various editions of the *Institutes* and the development of Calvin's thought, see J. Köstlin, "Calvins Institutio nach Form und Inhalt in ihrer geschichtlichen Entwicklung," *ThStKr* 41 (1868): 7–62, 410–86; B. B. Warfield, "On the Literary History of Calvin's 'Institutes,'" *Presbyterian and Reformed Review* 10 (1899): 193–219; Jean-Daniel Benoit, "The History and Development of the *Institutio*: How Calvin Worked," in *Courtenay Studies in Reformation Theology*, vol. 1, *John Calvin*, ed. Gervase E. Duffield (Grand Rapids, 1966), 102–17; Pierre Imbart de La Tour, *Calvin et l'Institution de la religion chrétienne* (Paris, 1935); Wendel, *Calvin*, 111–49; Ford Lewis Battles, "Calculus fidei," in *Calvinus ecclesiae doctor*, ed. Wilhelm H. Neuser (Kampen, 1980), 85–110;

CHRISTIA

NAE RELIGIONIS INSTI-
tutio,totam ferè pietatis summã,& quic
quid est in doctrina salutis cognitu necessarium, complectens : omnibus pietatis studiosis lectu dignissimum opus,ac re
cens edi-
tum.

PRAEFATIO AD CHRI
stianißimum REGEM FRANCIAE, *qua*
hic ei liber pro confeßione fidei
offertur.

IOANNE CALVINO
Noniodunensi autore.

BASILEAE,
M. D. XXXVI.

Title page of the Institutes *(1536)*

copies were printed under Calvin's pseudonym Alcuinus because they were to
be distributed in Roman Catholic territories. The title was now *Institutio christianae religionis*. The opening was slightly changed to read, "Almost the whole
sum of our wisdom, that is to say, true and sound wisdom, consists of two
parts: the knowledge of God and of ourselves." The new edition was to serve
as a dogmatic handbook to familiarize students with the main points of biblical doctrine.

The work now comprised seventeen chapters, the expansion consisting
largely of supplements to the first edition. It appears, especially from a chapter
on the relationship between the Old and New Testaments, a section on infant
baptism, and what he now writes about the church, that Calvin had quite a bit
of contact with Anabaptists in Strasbourg. In order to become a citizen of the
city, he had joined the tailors' guild, to which a good number of Anabaptists
belonged.

---

and Wilhelm H. Neuser, "The Development of the *Institutes* 1536 to 1559," in *John Calvin's Institutes:
His Opus Magnum*, 33–54.

In this edition of the *Institutes*, one detects the influence of Bucer, whose commentary on the Epistle to the Romans had come out in 1536. This influence can be seen particularly in what Calvin writes about predestination.[10] The doctrines of predestination and providence, which he discusses together in a single chapter, are not separated from practical questions about salvation: why is it that one person hears a sermon and wishes to know nothing of the gospel, whereas someone else thanks God for the riches of his grace and prays to him for the power of faith?

Calvin translated the *Institutes* of 1539 into French for the benefit of those who could not read Latin. That edition, entitled *Institution de la religion chrestienne*, appeared in 1541, not long after his return to Geneva.[11] Both the Latin and French editions were condemned in France, and an edict issued by the Parlement of Paris on July 1, 1542, ordered that anyone possessing the *Institutes* had to be reported.

Institutes (1543 and 1545)

A new Latin edition of the *Institutes* appeared in 1543 and was reprinted in 1545. The number of chapters had grown by four to a total of twenty-one. The new material included a chapter on monasticism, expansion of the discussion of the Apostles' Creed to four chapters, a more detailed treatment of the creed's article on the church, and an extensive section on the theological foundation of the offices. The French translation of this edition came out in 1545 in Geneva with an endorsement by Jean Sturm on the title page. In 1551 a section of this edition was published anonymously in Geneva as *Exposition sur l'oraison de nostre Seigneur Iésus Christ* (*CO* 3:424–50).

Institutes (1550)

In the spring of 1550 the fourth Latin edition of the *Institutes* appeared in Geneva, followed by reprints in 1553 and 1554. The 1550 edition was again somewhat larger in size than the previous one, adding, among other things, an

---

10. See Willem van 't Spijker, "Prädestination bei Bucer und Calvin: Ihre gegenseitige Beeinflussung und Abhängigkeit," in *Calvinus theologus*, ed. Wilhelm H. Neuser (Neukirchen, 1976), 85–111. Van 't Spijker concludes the article with these words: "In the second edition of the *Institutes,* what Calvin added to his discussions of predestination was for the most part a defense, in which the doctrine of double predestination was strongly emphasized because it was on this point that the opposition was the greatest. Nevertheless, these expansions did not adversely affect the practical-religious dimension of the doctrine and his faithfulness to Scripture. In this respect Calvin remained true to Bucer."

11. Jean Calvin, *Institution de la religion chrestienne*, ed. Jacques Pannier (Paris, 1936–39).

exposition on the conscience (see *Institutes* 3.19.15–16). Calvin also divided the material into chapters with numbered paragraphs. A few sections of this edition were published separately.[12]

The French translation of this edition came out in 1551, followed by identical reprints in 1553, 1554, and 1557. The translation of 1551 includes some supplements to the Latin edition of 1550, in particular an exposition on the bodily resurrection (for that text see *OS* 4:443–45); this addition had resulted from correspondence between Calvin and Lelio Sozzini in 1549 (see pp. 211–12). The supplementary material was finally included also in the Latin edition of 1559 (see *Institutes* 3.25.7–8).

Institutes (1559)

On August 1, 1559, Calvin wrote the foreword for the last edition of the *Institutes*, which appeared the same year. He also produced a French translation, which came off the press in 1560.[13] In the foreword he informs us that during the winter of 1558–59 he had been seriously ill and had thought he would die. He had then put forth a lot of effort to publish one more new edition of the *Institutes*, since he was not yet completely satisfied with the previous editions. He further writes in the foreword that it is his intention to help students in theology understand the Scriptures by means of his book, for the *Institutes* should be regarded as a summary of piety which makes clear both what we ought to look for in Scripture and to what end the content of Scripture is directed.

The differences in form between the last edition of 1559 and its predecessors are striking.[14] The 1559 *Institutes* consists of four books subdivided into a total of eighty chapters. The first book deals with the knowledge of God the Creator, and the second with the knowledge of God the Redeemer in Christ, first disclosed to the fathers under the law and then also to us in the gospel. The third book treats the way in which the grace of Christ is received, the benefits

12. Published as a booklet were *De praedestinatione et providentia Dei* (*CO* 1:861–902) and *De libertate Christiana* (*CO* 1:830–40). Another section was published as *De vita hominis Christiani* (Geneva, 1550— *CO* 1:1123–54), and also appeared in Geneva that year in French translation: *Traicté de la vie chrestienne*. In 1552 *Disputatio de cognitione hominis* (*CO* 1:305–72) was published in Geneva, with Augustine's *De praedestinatione sanctorum* added as a second chapter.

13. Jean Calvin, *Institution de la religion chrestienne*, critical edition by Jean-Daniel Benoit (Paris, 1957–63). At first there was a lot of uncertainty about Calvin's authorship of this French edition. See Wendel, *Calvin*, 118–19. Jean Cadier produced a modern French translation, *Institution de la religion chrétienne* (Geneva, 1955–58).

14. The editions that appeared during Calvin's lifetime after the Latin edition of 1559 and the French edition of 1560 were all reprints.

that come to us from it, and the effects that follow. The fourth book is about the external means or aids by which God invites us into the society of Christ and keeps us in it.

The content of the last edition of the *Institutes* has again been expanded beyond that of the previous edition. That is evident already in the title, where not only is mention made of the division into books and chapters, but it is also stated that the material has increased to such an extent that it can almost be spoken of as a new work. As far as the expansion of the material is concerned, we can detect first of all the influence of the doctrinal debates that Calvin had been engaged in with others, such as the conflict with the Lutherans, especially Joachim Westphal, over the Lord's Supper; the debate with Andreas Osiander about the image of God, the work of Christ, and justification; and the debate with Lelio Sozzini about the merits of Christ and the bodily resurrection from the dead. But Calvin also enlarged the material on certain topics like the fall of humanity into sin and the loss of free will.

9

Miscellaneous Publications

Calvin as Jurist
    Defense for Guillaume de Fürstenberg (1539–40)
    Apology for Jacques de Bourgogne, Lord of Falais (1548)
Document about Ecclesiastical Goods (1545)
Two Forewords by Calvin
    Foreword for Melanchthon's *Loci communes* (1546)
    Foreword for a Book about Francesco Spiera (1550)
Congratulation to Gabriel de Saconay (1561)
Debating with François Baudouin (1561–63)

In this chapter we shall focus our attention on a few publications that could not be placed in any of the previous chapters. We mention first a few works that Calvin wrote for other people, specifically Guillaume de Fürstenberg and Jacques de Bourgogne, to help them defend their cases. For this category we have chosen the heading "Calvin as Jurist." He is also probably the author of a manuscript that presents his view of ecclesiastical goods. In addition, he wrote the forewords to two publications, Philipp Melanchthon's *Loci communes* and a book about Francesco Spiera. Finally, we take note of both an ironical congratulation that Calvin wrote to Gabriel de Saconay and those writings associated with a debate carried on with François Baudouin.

Calvin as Jurist

Defense for Guillaume de Fürstenberg (1539–40)

In 1539 Calvin came into contact in Strasbourg with Guillaume de Fürstenberg, a count from South Germany who often resided in Strasbourg. Since 1535 the count had supported King Francis I, who had appointed him governor of Vaud. When at the beginning of 1538 Francis I needed several divisions of soldiers for his struggle against Charles V, he called upon de Fürstenberg for help. To assist in the recruitment of soldiers, de Fürstenberg enlisted Sébastien Vogelsperger, a former assistant of his who had recently been discharged by the king. It appears that at some point Vogelsperger along with his men chose to leave de Fürstenberg's service, an action that led to a loss of prestige for de Fürstenberg. Not only that, but the French king was intent upon reducing de Fürstenberg's power at the very time that the cities of Strasbourg, Basel, Geneva, and Bern were hoping that he could use his influence with the king to benefit the French evangelicals.

Calvin helped de Fürstenberg with the writing of two defenses. The first, *Déclaration faicte par Monsieur Guillaulme, conte de Fürstenberg*, is dated September 15, 1539; and the second, *Seconde déclaration faicte par Monsieur Guillaulme*, bears the date February 9, 1540. Both writings also appeared in German translation.[1]

Apology for Jacques de Bourgogne, Lord of Falais (1548)

In February 1548 the Council gave Calvin permission to go to Basel, where he visited Jacques de Bourgogne, lord of Falais and Breda, and his wife Yolande. De Falais had grown up in the court of Charles V and had joined the Reformation already in his youth. He no longer felt safe in his homeland, however, and Calvin, using the name Charles d'Espeville, wrote him a letter on October 14, 1543 (*CO* 11:628–31), advising him to emigrate. De Falais and his wife set out for Geneva in 1545, but got no farther than Strasbourg because de Falais fell ill. On account of the Smalcald War, they moved on in January 1547 to Basel, where Calvin paid them a visit. Calvin tried hard to find a place for them to live in Geneva and even consulted with Ami Perrin, who traveled to Paris via Basel at the end of May 1547 with a letter from Calvin to de Falais (*CO* 12:529–30). The move was still being held up in February 1548 when Calvin discussed it with de Falais and his wife in person. That summer, however, de Falais and his wife settled on the Veigy estate, which lay in Bernese territory outside the city of Geneva.

In consultation with de Falais, Calvin wrote in his behalf an apology intended for the emperor. The treatise appeared in March 1548 with no mention either of the place of publication or of Calvin's name. The title reads:

---

1. Rodolphe Peter, "Jean Calvin, avocat du comte Guillaume de Fürstenberg," *RHPhR* 51 (1971): 63–78.

Excuse de noble Seigneur Jaques de Bourgoigne, S. de Fallez et Bredam, pour se purger vers la M. Imperiale, des calomnies à luy imposées, en matière de sa foy, dont il rend confession.[2]

Document about Ecclesiastical Goods (1545)

One matter that occupied the churches' attention was the ecclesiastical property obtained by the civil government, for example, after the closing of a monastery. Guillaume Farel sought Calvin's support in a debate with the civil authorities in Neuchâtel in 1545. But, Calvin writes to Farel on October 13 (*CO* 12:189–90), it would seem better to him not to turn to the Council in Neuchâtel, for holding forth on the use of ecclesiastical property could be counterproductive. He himself has not been successful in Geneva so far in accomplishing what he would like on that score (see also the letter to Farel that is dated November 2—*CO* 12:205–6). Nevertheless, if Farel continues to insist, he will respond.

That is perhaps what happened. For in the ministers' library in Neuchâtel there is a handwritten exposition of the legal ownership and use of ecclesiastical goods that were once dedicated to God (for the text see *CO* 10a:249–51); a note at the top explains, in another handwriting, that the document presents Calvin's view.

Two Forewords by Calvin

Foreword for Melanchthon's Loci communes *(1546)*

In 1546 a French translation of Melanchthon's 1545 edition of the *Loci communes* appeared in Geneva under the title *La Somme de théologie, ou Lieux communs, reveuz et augmentez pour la dernière foys, par M. Philippe Melancthon.* Calvin wrote a foreword for this translation (*CO* 9:847–50), stating first that God had adorned Melanchthon with special gifts, and then introducing the book to the reader. Calvin is not critical of Melanchthon, not even of his material on free will and predestination. That is surprising because later (1552) in a debate with Jean Trolliet about predestination, it is very clear that Calvin and Melanchthon did not agree in every respect. Trolliet made references to

---

2. For the text of François Baudouin's 1548 Latin translation, see *CO* 10a:273–94. A. Cartier produced a reprint (with an introduction) in 1896 (2d ed., Geneva, 1911) of the rediscovered original French edition: *L'Excuse de noble Seigneur Jacques de Bourgogne, Seigneur de Falais et de Bredam, par Jean Calvin, réimprimée pour la première fois sur l'unique exemplaire de l'édition de Genève 1548, avec une introduction.*

Philipp Melanchthon
(painting by Lucas Cranach the Elder)

Melanchthon in accusing Calvin of tracing sin back to God himself (see *CO* 14:334–35). Calvin composed a written response that he presented to the Council on October 6, 1552 (*CO* 14:371–77). According to Calvin, it ought to be clear that the whole church is done a grave injustice by those who pit Melanchthon and him against each other. He does admit, however, that he and Melanchthon differ in their manner of instruction. Melanchthon has been too willing to accommodate to human understanding, taking care not to give the curious any opportunity to probe too deeply the secrets of God. Thus Melanchthon has spoken on the matter of predestination more as a philosopher (he even mentions Plato) than as a theologian.[3]

Foreword for a book about Francesco Spiera (1550)

Henri Scrimger published a book in Geneva in 1550 about the Italian Francesco Spiera, who had renounced his evangelical faith and died in despair. The book was entitled *Exemplum memorabile desperationis in Francisco Spera, propter abiuratam fidei confessionem* and contained a foreword by Calvin (*CO* 9:855–58).[4]

---

3. See Calvin's letter to Melanchthon that is dated November 27, 1552 (*CO* 14:415–18).

4. See *De verschrickelijcke historie van Franciscus Spira . . .* (Utrecht, 1669). Calvin's foreword can be found on pp. 189–94.

Congratulation to Gabriel de Saconay (1561)

In 1561 Calvin penned an ironical congratulation to Gabriel de Saconay, *Gratulatio ad venerabilem presbyterum dominum Gabrielem de Saconay, praecentorem ecclesiae Lugdunensis, de pulchra et eleganti praefatione quam libro regis Angliae inscripsit* (*CO* 9:421–56).[5] De Saconay was a priest in Lyons who had republished and added a foreword to Henry VIII's 1521 *Assertio septem sacramentorum*, in which the king had attacked Luther's *De captivitate Babylonica ecclesiae*. Calvin responded to this with his "congratulations."

Debating with François Baudouin (1561–63)

Calvin wrote a letter to Jeanne d'Albret on December 24, 1561 (*CO* 19:196–98), after he learned that François Baudouin (Latin name: Balduinus) had been allured by Antoine de Bourbon to take charge of the education of his bastard son. Calvin warns Jeanne about Baudouin, who is an apostate and is intent upon winning the favor of those in high places in order to work against the servants of God. In 1561 Calvin also criticized Baudouin in his *Responsio ad versipellem quendam mediatorem, qui pacificandi specie rectum evangelii cursum in Gallia abrumpere molitus est* (*CO* 9:525–60), which was published in Geneva the same year.[6]

François Baudouin was a well-known lawyer who had been friendly with Calvin for some time and had also served as his secretary. Baudouin had abused the trust placed in him, however, by stealing several of Calvin's letters. Good relations were restored in 1556, but Baudouin left for France in 1561 and offered his services to Cardinal Charles van Lotharingen. When Calvin heard that Baudouin had advised the cardinal to arrest the participants at the Colloquy of Poissy who supported reform, the relationship came to a definite end. In addition, Baudouin was suspected of being the author of the little book *De officio pii ac publicae tranquillitatis vere amantis viri, in hoc religionis dissidio*, published anonymously in Basel in 1561. The book was in fact from the hand of George Cassander, but was disseminated throughout France by Baudouin. Calvin replied to the "unreliable mediator" in the work mentioned above.[7]

---

5. For a French translation see *Recueil des opuscules*, 1822–50. For an English translation by Douglas Floyd Kelly see *Calvin Studies II*, ed. John H. Leith and Charles Raynal (Davidson, N.C., 1985), 109–18 ("Congratulations to the Venerable Presbyter, Lord Gabriel of Saconay, Precentor of the Church at Lyon for the Beautiful and Elegant Preface That He Wrote for the Book of the King of England").

6. For a French translation see *Recueil des opuscules*, 1885–1918.

7. See Richard Stauffer, "Autour du colloque de Poissy: Calvin et le De officio pii ac publicae tranquillitatis vere amantis viri," in *L'Amiral de Coligny et son temps* (Paris, 1974), 135–53 (this article is also found in idem, *Interprètes de la Bible: Etudes sur les réformateurs du XVIe siècle* [Paris, 1980], 249–67).

The battle in print between Calvin and Baudouin continued in 1562. In his *Ad leges de famosis libellis et de calumniatoribus commentarius*, which appeared in Paris in 1562, Baudouin expressed resentment toward Calvin for considering him to be the author of *De officio . . .* and attacked him viciously.

Calvin answered with his *Responsio ad Balduini convicia* (Geneva, 1562— *CO* 9:561–80), in which he addressed the charges brought against him.[8] This reply forms part of a work containing fourteen letters that Baudouin had written to Calvin earlier, when he still fully backed Calvin; also included were a few pieces against Baudouin by others. Baudouin reacted with his *Responsio altera ad Ioan. Calvinum*, published in Paris in 1562, to which Calvin replied only briefly in a letter that also served as the foreword to a little book by Theodore Beza that was published in Geneva in 1563: *Ad Francisci Balduini apostatae Ecebolii convicia, Theodori Bezae Vezelii Responsio, et Joannis Calvini brevis Epistola* (*CO* 9:859–62).[9] Calvin then left any further disputation to Beza. Baudouin did answer again with *Pro Fr. Balduino Responsio ad Calvinum et Bezam cum refutatione Calvini de scriptura et traditione* (1564), but Beza never again responded.

8. For a French translation see *Recueil des opuscules*, 1974–91.
9. For a French translation see *Recueil des opuscules*, 1918–20.

10

Letters

Correspondence with Lelio Sozzini
Correspondence with Poland
Letter to Menso Poppius
Correspondence with the Ministers in Montbéliard
Correspondence with England

Calvin's letters constitute an important part of his literary output, as one can readily see by consulting the *Opera Calvini*. In Parts 10b–20, Johann Wilhelm Baum, August Eduard Cunitz, and Eduard Reuss included not only a large number of letters by Calvin, but also letters written to him.[1] These letters, however, were not first published in the *Opera Calvini*. Just before his death, Calvin had entrusted his letters to Theodore Beza for possible publication if the church could make use of them; and with the help of Charles de Jonvillers, Beza produced the first publication of letters in 1575.[2] Various other editions followed,[3] among them Jules Bonnet's two-part edition in French translation, *Lettres de Jean Calvin, recueillies pour la première fois et publiées d'après les manuscripts origineaux* (Paris, 1854),[4] and A.-L. Herminjard's nine-part edition, *Cor-*

---

1. Parts 10b–20 of *Ioannis Calvini Opera* (Brunswick, 1872–79) make up the *Thesaurus epistolicus Calvinianus*.

2. *Ioannis Calvini epistolae et responsa, quibus interiectae sunt insignium in ecclesia Dei virorum aliquot etiam epistolae. Eiusdem I. Calvini vita a Theodoro Beza Genevensis ecclesiae ministro accurate descripta* (Geneva, 1575).

3. Douglas Kelly, "The Transmission and Translation of the Collected Letters of John Calvin," *SJTh* 30 (1977): 429–37.

4. This edition, which, incidentally, contains quite a few errors, was translated into English by David Constable and Marcus Robert Gilchrist: *Letters of John Calvin,* ed. Jules Bonnet, 4 vols. (New York, 1972 reprint [vols. 1–2, Edinburgh, 1855, 1857; vols. 3–4, New York and Philadelphia, 1858]).

respondance des réformateurs dans les pays de la langue française recueillie et publiée avec d'autres lettres relatives à la Réforme et des notes historiques et bibliographiques (Geneva, 1866–97).[5] Herminjard did not get beyond the year 1544 in his publication of the letters, but his edition is important because of the explanatory notes that accompany the letters. Every now and then a letter of Calvin's is discovered that has not yet been published.[6]

Calvin's letters are significant in a number of respects. First of all, they give us the opportunity to get to know him personally in his interaction with others and in his analysis of a variety of situations. He corresponded especially often with his colleagues Guillaume Farel in Neuchâtel, Pierre Viret in Lausanne, and Heinrich Bullinger in Zurich.[7] He also wrote many pastoral letters to people in one sort of crisis or another to provide them with spiritual support in their particular circumstances. He often urged those in high positions who were trying to serve the Lord to stay on the course that they had adopted. We have already seen such encouragement in various letters dedicating his books to prominent persons. There are also quite a few letters in which he deals with questions posed to him, for example, the correspondence with Lelio Sozzini and the letter to Menso Poppius, which are treated in this chapter. The correspondence with the ministers in Montbéliard (also covered in this chapter) is an example of the way in which Calvin provides advice that has been requested of him. Letters like this contain a great deal of significant information.

In the first chapter, but also subsequently, we made frequent use of data from Calvin's letters. In this chapter we deal with several of the contacts that he had with other people by letter. We have already mentioned the correspon-

5. A reprint was published in Nieuwkoop in 1965. See also note 3 and Jacques Pannier, *Calvin écrivain: Sa place et son rôle dans l'histoire de la langue et de la littérature française* (Paris, 1930); Hedwig Ruff, *Die französischen Briefe Calvins: Versuch einer stilistischen Analyse* (Glarus, Switz., 1937); Jean-Daniel Benoit, "Calvin the Letter-Writer," in *Courtenay Studies in Reformation Theology*, vol. 1, *John Calvin,* ed. Gervase E. Duffield (Grand Rapids, 1966), 67–101; Paul Gerhard Chee, "Johannes Calvin—ein Bild nach seinen Briefen," *RKZ* 21 (1980): 159–61; and J. Swanepoel, "Calvin as Letter-Writer," in *Our Reformational Tradition: A Rich Heritage and Lasting Vocation* (Potchefstroom, 1984), 279–99. Willem Nijenhuis, *Calvinus oecumenicus: Calvijn en de eenheid der kerk in het licht van zijn briefwisseling* (The Hague, 1959), devotes a lot of attention to Calvin's correspondence.

6. Uwe Plath gives several examples in his article "Ein unbekannter Brief Calvins vom Vorabend der Religionskriege in Frankreich," *ARG* 62 (1971): 244–66 (see pp. 244–45, note 2). See also the letters from the Sarrau collection: *Les Lettres à Jean Calvin de la collection Sarrau*, ed. Rodolphe Peter and Jean Rott, *CRHPhR* 43 (Paris, 1972).

7. For the correspondence between Calvin and Bullinger, see André Bouvier, *Henri Bullinger, réformateur et conseiller oecuménique, le successeur de Zwingli, d'après sa correspondance avec les réformés et les humanistes de langue française* (Neuchâtel/Paris, 1940); W. Kolfhaus, "Der Verkehr Calvins mit Bullinger," in *Calvinstudien: Festschrift zum 400. Geburtstage Johann Calvins,* ed. Josef Bohatec (Leipzig, 1909), 27–125; F. Büsser, "Calvin und Bullinger," in *Calvinus servus Christi*, ed. Wilhelm H. Neuser (Budapest, 1988), 107–26.

dence with Lelio Sozzini, the letter to Menso Poppius, and the correspondence with the ministers in Montbéliard. We shall also look at some of his contacts with Poland and at his correspondence with England (Edward Seymour, Thomas Cranmer, and John Knox). In this way we hope to convey some sense of the significance of Calvin's letters.

Correspondence with Lelio Sozzini

In 1549 Calvin began his correspondence with Lelio Sozzini, an Italian refugee (from Siena) who had originally resettled in Zurich but later moved to Poland.[8] Sozzini had written Calvin a letter asking for his opinion of mixed marriages, of having children baptized in the Roman Catholic Church, and of the bodily resurrection. In Calvin's first letter (end of June—*CO* 13:307–11) he was compelled by circumstances, as he himself says, to deal with the questions only briefly. He answers the question about the resurrection in the most detail, citing various texts from Scripture and representing the opinion of the church fathers with citations from Tertullian to underscore the fact that the resurrection does involve the body. If the Lord God does not raise our bodies, one cannot speak of a resurrection from the dead (see *Institutes* 3.25.7–8). Sozzini, however, was not fully satisfied with these answers.

In a second letter (dated December 7, 1549—*CO* 13:484–87) Calvin writes that he cannot go any further into the bodily resurrection of the dead because he wishes to limit himself to what Scripture says about it. He does, however, further explain his views of mixed marriage and the baptism of children in the Roman Catholic Church. As far as marriage is concerned, Calvin believes that a Christian ought to marry a woman who is prepared to follow Christ with him. As for Sozzini's question whether or not the church should recognize a mixed marriage, Calvin says that the promise made when the marriage is contracted remains in effect. With respect to baptism, whoever does not have his children baptized in the Roman Catholic Church does more wrong than if he does have them baptized there. But in the latter case, Christian duty does require public condemnation of that part of the baptism that is in conflict with the command of Christ. The efficacy of the baptism does not depend on the one who administers it. Even though there is much that is wrong in the administration of the baptism, it is done by the command of Christ in the name of the Father, the Son, and the Holy Spirit as a testimony to regeneration. When

---

8. See Ralph Lazzaro, trans. and ed., "Four Letters from the Socinus-Calvin Correspondence 1549," in *Italian Reformation Studies in Honor of Laelius Socinus*, ed. J. A. Tedeschi (Florence, 1965), 215–30.

Calvin talks about certain vestiges of the church that can be found among the Roman Catholics, he is alluding not to the elect, but to the ruins of a devastated church that exists under the papacy.

The correspondence continued on January 1, 1552, when Calvin wrote Sozzini again (*CO* 14:229–30) and appealed to him for moderation (no paradoxes; no quibbling; in the school of the Word one is taught only what is useful). Calvin hopes that he will no longer be bothered with the kind of speculative questions that Sozzini has been posing.

In 1555 Calvin's *Responsio ad aliquot Laelii Socini senensis quaestiones* (*CO* 10a:160–65) appeared, in which he responds to four questions that Sozzini had put to him. We do not know exactly what the questions were, so we have to rely on Calvin's answers. The first had to do with the word *merit*, which Sozzini wished to avoid (see *Institutes* 2.17.1), the second with predestination, the third with faith, and the fourth with the experience of God's anger and love.

Sozzini's *Brevis explicatio in primum Johannis caput* appeared in 1561, which marks the beginning of the Socinian phase among the Italian antitrinitarians.

Correspondence with Poland

On December 29, 1555, Calvin sent nine letters to Poland (*CO* 15:900–914) at the request of Francesco Lismanino, who in 1546 had accompanied the Italian queen Bona Sforza to Poland as her confessor. There Lismanino came under the influence of Calvin and even read from the *Institutes* to King Sigismund August twice a week. When he had the opportunity to visit Calvin in Geneva in 1553, he laid aside his monk's habit and entered into marriage. He returned to Poland in early 1556, but before he left, he gave Calvin a letter with a list of the names of a number of Polish nobles to whom Calvin could write (*CO* 15:868–71).

In the nine letters mentioned above, Calvin challenges these Poles to stand fast in the faith and calls upon them to vigorously promote the introduction of the Reformation. By that he has in mind also the translation of the Bible into the vernacular and the establishment of a school where future ministers can be trained.

A letter signed on May 2, 1556, by seven ministers and ten nobles at a synod meeting in Pińczów requested Calvin to come to Poland (*CO* 16:129). The ministers supported this request with a letter to the Council of Geneva (*CO* 16:131–32), in which they asked that Calvin be given a few months' leave for a trip to Poland.

Johannes a Lasco

Calvin informed the Polish ministers and nobles on March 8, 1557 (there had been no earlier opportunity to send a letter along with someone) that he could not grant their request to spend some time in Poland because he could not be spared from Geneva (*CO* 16:420–21). Furthermore, since in the meantime Johannes a Lasco had arrived in Poland, Calvin's presence was not so urgently needed.

On November 19, 1558, Calvin wrote several letters to prominent Poles, among them Jan Tarnowski, who had responded on June 26, 1556 (*CO* 16:215), to Calvin's letter of December 29, 1555. Tarnowski felt that introducing the Reformation would lead to unrest. Calvin states in his 1558 letter (see *CO* 17:382–83) that he appreciates Tarnowski's honest response. He then points out the great importance of religion for peace in a state, quoting a passage from Xenophon in which Apollo speaks through an oracle about the great significance of religion. Calvin thinks that those who give leadership must do their duty and be guided by God. The Lord, he says, referring to Psalm 46, can cope with any unrest that cannot be avoided.

Tarnowski responded in May 1559 (see *CO* 17:517–20), and Calvin answered on November 15 (*CO* 17:673–76) with a further examination of the relation between service to God and political responsibility. Tarnowski claims that men of state must seek after peace and calm above everything else, but, says Calvin, that is not their only duty. Paul talks in 1 Timothy 2:2 about a peaceful and quiet life *in all godliness and holiness*. We must not separate what God in that passage has joined together with a sacred bond. It is also not correct, says Calvin, to designate religion as the source of all kinds of confusion. In political activity it is a good thing to proceed prudently by making allowances for time and place. But cunning ought never to take the place of prudence. If Tarnowski considers it advisable to do nothing to abolish superstition and introduce the true service of God, does he then think he is wiser than God?

In a subsequent letter (June 9, 1560—*CO* 18:102–3) Calvin explains that he wants nothing other than that Tarnowski crown all the good that he is doing with a warm interest in the reformation of the church.

Another one of those whom Calvin wrote on November 19, 1558, was Jacob Uchanski, the bishop of Kujawy, who wanted to introduce a number of innovations into his diocese, such as the celebration of the Lord's Supper with bread and wine, an end to the prohibition on marriage for priests, and the introduction of Polish into the church service. In his letter (*CO* 17:380–82) Calvin offers encouragement to the bishop, who is sure to encounter all kinds of problems. The bishop, however, later changed his plans, reconciled with Rome, and became an archbishop.[9]

Letter to Menso Poppius

On February 26, 1559, Calvin answered a letter that he had received from Menso Poppius, a minister in Manslagt (East Friesland), who had turned to him for advice on a large number of questions related to the life of the church, such as the training of ministers, the education of children, emergency baptism, and discipline. Calvin writes that he is sorry about the brevity of his response to the questions, but he is weighed down with all sorts of official duties and with both public and private matters in which he is deeply involved. Furthermore, he has been largely confined to his home for five months because of illness. He is doing somewhat better now, but, weakened by his illness, he cannot yet cope with all the work. Nevertheless, he did address the questions and also provided Poppius with some financial support (see *CO* 17:451–54; for Poppius's response see the letter dated September 10—*CO* 17:629–32).

Correspondence with the Ministers in Montbéliard

On October 14, 1543, Calvin wrote a letter to the ministers in Montbéliard, including Pierre Toussaint, because they were not sure what they should do now that the duke had introduced the Lutheran practice of the sacraments (*CO* 11:624–26). Calvin approves of the fact that those who wish to participate in the Lord's Supper do present themselves for an examination, but in order

9. For more on Calvin's contacts with Poland see pp. 180–81.

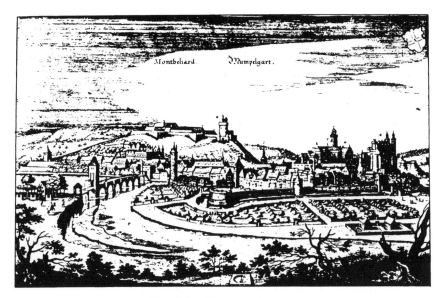

Montbéliard in the 17th century

to prevent abuse, he lays down what such an examination should strive for: private instruction of the ignorant, admonition of those who in their daily lives fall short of their obligations as Christians, and the comforting of troubled consciences. Celebrating the Lord's Supper with the sick is good if it is necessary and appropriate.[10] The same is true for criminals facing execution—if they desire to have communion and are prepared for it. The celebration, however, must take place in a fellowship of believers. It is not good for a celebration of communion to follow a regular church service at the request of just one member of the congregation. It ought to be announced beforehand, so that all know about it and can prepare themselves for it. If some wish to have communion more often, that should not be refused.

Calvin strongly opposes emergency baptism. With respect to funerals, it seems better to him not to bring the casket into the church, but to go directly to the cemetery and deliver the funeral address there. He advises against bell ringing, but does not rigidly oppose it because he does not consider it something worth fighting about. He does, however, wish to stand by his rejection of those feast days which tend not to edify and which have a superstitious character. Moreover, he advises the ministers not to be troublesome and opinion-

---

10. It was not the custom in Geneva to celebrate communion in the homes of the sick. For Calvin's stance on this see also his letter of December 1, 1563, to Kaspar Olevianus (*CO* 20:200–201).

ated in their behavior toward the prince. He will be indulgent for sure if he notices that they have reason to turn to him.

On May 8, 1544, after deliberating with his colleagues, Calvin again wrote to the ministers in Montbéliard (*CO* 11:705–8) because he had received further information from them about how things had been going with the initiation of Lutheran practices. He feels that those who are carrying this out are wrong when they point to the church in Wittenberg. Luther would not agree with that any more than we do, he writes. As far as emergency baptism is concerned, he points out that salvation is not based on baptism. Baptism is a sealing of the covenant, in which we are included and elected as God's people. The children of believers also belong to that covenant on the basis of God's promise. If baptism, by which the promise is sealed, cannot be administered, the promise is sufficient in and of itself. Baptism belongs to the domain of the church, not of midwives, and it ought to be joined with the service of the Word. Although Augustine did not speak clearly and plainly about the custom of lay baptism in the early church, he nonetheless did not approve of it. According to Calvin, it was decided at the (Fourth) Council of Carthage that women ought not to presume to baptize.

As to the question of what the ministers should do, Calvin answers that they should explain to their prince what it is that prevents them from obeying him. If that is of no concern to the prince, then they must follow the instruction of Peter to obey God rather than men.

With regard to bell ringing and the keeping of feast days, Calvin calls upon the ministers to bear with such things rather than leave the positions God has given them. That does not mean, however, that they should not make their objections known.

What Calvin identifies as truly intolerable is that the prince forbids the ministers to meet together. What will become of the church if the ministers can no longer deliberate together? It would be preferable to die a hundred deaths than to consent to such an annihilation of the church, he feels.

On October 10, 1544, Calvin called on Erhard Schnepf (*CO* 11:751–54), a minister in Württemberg, to assist the brethren in Montbéliard by restraining Engelmann, one of the ministers in Montbéliard, who had made an appeal to Schnepf. Engelmann had created a problem by bringing to the fore the question whether unbelievers receive the body of Christ in the celebration of the Lord's Supper. Calvin does feel that a couple of things ought to be clear, namely, that the wickedness of unbelievers has no effect on the essence or efficacy of the sacrament, and that unbelievers do not receive Christ in the sacrament in such a way that they have fellowship with him. But Calvin is also of the opinion that it is better to drop such a line of questioning than to quarrel over it. After all, what good is such questioning to the congregation as long as the two points mentioned above are maintained?

Correspondence with England

Sometime in 1549 or 1550,[11] Calvin wrote a detailed letter to Edward Seymour (*CO* 13:65–77), who in 1547 had become head of the Regency Council because King Edward VI was still underage. Calvin had already on July 15, 1548, dedicated to Seymour the commentary on the Epistles to Timothy (see p. 97), and was now writing him again (unaware that Seymour was in prison) to encourage him to carry on with the Reformation in England. He warns Seymour both about the spiritualists, who under the guise of the gospel throw everything into disorder, and about those who persist in the superstitions of the antichrist in Rome. Those in authority must submit to Christ. Calvin names three specific things that are of great importance for the reforming of the church: the right manner of instructing the people, the abolition of abuses, and the fight against sin, things that give offense, and indiscipline.

In discussing the first matter, Calvin points out the importance of good preaching (2 Timothy 3:16), of a confession that summarizes what must be preached, and of a catechism to pass on sound doctrine to children and those lacking in knowledge, so that they can distinguish sound doctrine from lies and distortions.

In his discussion of the abolition of abuses, Calvin mentions prayers for the dead in the celebration of the Eucharist as a concrete example. It also seems better to him to do away with the anointing of oil at baptism and extreme unction, and to stick to the Word and to that which serves to build up the church. Whoever gives guidance in spiritual matters ought indeed to make allowances for the weak, but always for the purpose of strengthening them and bringing them to wholeness. Obliging someone for the sake of peace, as is done in non-ecclesiastical matters, is not appropriate; we must be led by the Word of God.

As for the third point, discipline, Calvin calls upon the bishops and ministers to see to it that the Lord's Supper is not desecrated by people who lead offensive lives. "Just as doctrine is, as it were, the soul that gives life to the church, so discipline and the punishment of sin are the sinews that hold the body together and give it strength."

---

11. There is some uncertainty about the exact date. See Rodolphe Peter and Jean-François Gilmont, *Bibliotheca Calviniana: Les Oeuvres de Jean Calvin publiées au XVIe siècle*, vol. 1, *Ecrits théologiques, littéraires et juridiques 1532–1554* (Geneva, 1991), 365.

There was also an exchange of letters between Thomas Cranmer, archbishop of Canterbury, and Calvin in 1552. In March, Cranmer proposed to Calvin (*CO* 14:306) that an evangelical council be held not only to discuss all their doctrines, but also to draw up a collective formulation that they could pass on to posterity as a work of great authority. Cranmer also wrote to Philipp Melanchthon and Heinrich Bullinger. Calvin answered Cranmer in April (*CO* 14:312–14). He likes Cranmer's plan, but thinks that it will be difficult to implement. As for Calvin himself, "if I could be of any use, I would not, if need be, object to crossing even ten seas for such a purpose." He charges Cranmer to persist until something is accomplished, even if it does not all go as he would like.

Cranmer wrote Calvin another letter in October 1552 (*CO* 14:370). He had heard nothing from Melanchthon (which Calvin had predicted, since Melanchthon lived in a place far away and difficult to reach by mail), and Bullinger did not consider it a propitious time for either him or Melanchthon because of the war between Charles V and the king of France. Cranmer realizes that nothing can be done about his plan for the time being. Meanwhile, he assures Calvin, he will vigorously carry on the Reformation in England.

Calvin also corresponded with John Knox (see the letters of November 8, 1559 [*CO* 17:665–68], and April 23, 1561 [*CO* 18:434–35]), who had returned to Scotland and was asking Calvin for advice on a variety of issues. For example, may children of excommunicated parents be baptized if the parents have shown no repentance? The correspondence did not proceed without a hitch, for a letter got lost and Calvin had to write again. He hopes that Knox moderates his strictness somewhat. Baptism must be kept holy. One must pay attention first and foremost to what God is saying there. If God has upheld his covenant for so many years, it is not suddenly broken if grandparents and parents fall away. God's promise not only applies to the first generation, but extends over a thousand generations. Others can answer besides the parents. The parents must, of course, be made aware of their obligation, but if someone else wishes to make the baptismal promise and provide for a good education, baptism may not be refused.

Bibliography of Primary Sources

In volume 59 of the *Calvini Opera,* pages 461–586, we find a *Bibliographia Calviniana,* which contains both a chronological catalog of Calvin's works and a systematic catalog of works about Calvin together with an alphabetical index of authors. This bibliography was published in Berlin by Alfred Erichson in 1900 and reprinted in Nieuwkoop in 1961.

Wilhelm Niesel, Dionysius Kempff, Joseph Tylenda, and Peter de Klerk have continued this work: Wilhelm Niesel, *Calvin-Bibliographie 1901–1959* (Munich, 1961); Pierre Fraenkel et al. produced a supplement to Niesel's work, "Petit supplément aux bibliographies calviniennes 1901–1963," *BHR* 33 (1971): 385–413 (pp. 387–89: "Corrigenda et addenda à W. Niesel: Calvin-Bibliographie"; pp. 392–413: "Supplément bibliographique 1901–1963"); Dionysius Kempff, *A Bibliography of Calviniana 1959–1974* (Potchefstroom, 1975; 2d ed., 1983); *Calvin Bibliography 1960–1970,* compiled by Joseph N. Tylenda, ed. Peter de Klerk, *CTJ* 6 (1971): 156–93; supplements: *CTJ* 7 (1972): 221–50; 9 (1974): 38–73, 210–40; 10 (1975): 175–207; 11 (1976): 199–243; 12 (1977): 164–87; 13 (1978): 166–94; 14 (1979): 187–212; 15 (1980): 244–60; 16 (1981): 206–21; 17 (1982): 231–47; 18 (1983): 206–24; 19 (1984): 192–212; 20 (1985): 268–80; 21 (1986): 194–221; 22 (1987): 275–94; 23 (1988): 195–221; 24 (1989): 278–99; 25 (1990): 225–48; 26 (1991): 389–411; 27 (1992): 326–52; 28 (1993): 393–419.

See also the supplements to the *Archiv für Reformationsgeschichte* that have appeared annually since 1972 and include, among other things, secondary literature on Calvin: *ARG.B* 1 (1972): 35–38; 2 (1973): 30–33; 3 (1974): 31–34; 4 (1975): 24–26; 5 (1976): 21–23; 6 (1977): 23–25; 7 (1978): 28–31; 8 (1979): 21–23; 9 (1980): 26–27; 10 (1981): 22–23; 11 (1982): 24–27; 12 (1983): 40–41; 13 (1984): 45–46; 14 (1985): 36–38; 15 (1986): 32–34; 16 (1987): 28–30; 17 (1988): 23–24; 18 (1989): 22–25; 19 (1990): 19–23; 20 (1991): 20–24; 21 (1992): 23–25.

Finally, mention should be made of Lester De Koster's *Living Themes in the Thought of John Calvin* (Ann Arbor, 1964; microfilm); and of Rodolphe Peter and Jean-François Gilmont, *Bibliotheca Calviniana: Les Oeuvres de Jean Calvin publiées au XVIe siècle,* vol. 1, *Ecrits théologiques, littéraires et juridiques 1532–1554* (Geneva, 1991).

Collections of Calvin's Works

In 1552 a one-volume collection of a number of Calvin's writings appeared in Geneva, the *Opuscula J. Calvini in unum volumen collecta.* These writings were all in Latin. Those originally written in French had been translated into Latin by Nicolas Des Gallars.

In 1566 a book of Calvin's writings appeared in French, the *Recueil des opuscules, c'est à dire, Petits traictez de M. Iean Calvin. Les uns revues et corrigez sur le latin, les autres translatez nouvellement de latin en françois* (Geneva, 1566). The book was dedicated to Renée of France by Theodore Beza. A second printing came out in 1611.

A Latin edition of all theological works by Calvin along with a foreword by Beza was published in Geneva in 1576: *Tractatus theologici omnes, nunc primum in unum volumen, certis classibus congesti.*

Johann Wilhelm Baum, August Eduard Cunitz, and Eduard Reuss produced an edition of Calvin's works entitled *Ioannis Calvini opera quae supersunt omnia,* consisting of fifty-nine volumes (1863–1900). In most scholarly works this edition is referred to with the abbreviation *CO.* Because, however, this edition also comprises volumes 29–87 of the *Corpus Reformatorum,* which contains as well the works of Philipp Melanchthon and Ulrich Zwingli, references to Calvin's works are sometimes designated with the abbreviation *CR* (thus *CR* 29 is *CO* 1). A revised edition of the *Calvini Opera,* with a critical apparatus and notes, is being published by Librairie Droz in Geneva under the direction of the praesidium of the International Congress on Calvin Research. The first volume (volume 16 in the *Opera Exegetica*) appeared in 1992: *Commentarii in Pauli Epistolas ad Galatas, ad Ephesios, ad Philippenses, ad Colossenses,* ed. Helmut Feld (Geneva, 1992).

There is also a so-called Schipper edition of the works of Calvin, named after Johannes Jacob Schipper, who published it in Amsterdam in 1667. In the nineteenth century August Tholuck used this edition when he published Calvin's commentaries on the New Testament, Genesis, and the Psalms. Scholarly publications usually cite the *Calvini Opera,* however, and not this edition.

Peter Barth, Wilhelm Niesel, and Dora Scheuner produced a selection of Calvin's works in five volumes, *Johannis Calvini Opera Selecta* (Munich, 1926–52), which has been reprinted several times (cited as *OS*).

Many of Calvin's sermons can be found in the *Calvini Opera.* An important additional source is the *Supplementa Calviniana: Sermons inédits,* of which five volumes have appeared since 1936: vol. 1, *Predigten über das 2. Buch Samuelis,* ed. Hanns Rückert (Neukirchen, 1936, 1961); vol. 2, *Sermons sur le Livre d'Isaïe chapitres 13–19,* ed. Georges Barrois (Neukirchen, 1961, 1964); vol. 5, *Sermons sur le Livre de Michée,* ed. Jean-Daniel Benoit (Neukirchen-Vluyn, 1964); vol. 6, *Sermons sur les livres de Jérémie et des Lamentations,* ed. Rodolphe Peter (Neukirchen-Vluyn, 1971); and vol. 7, *Psalmenpredigten, Passions-, Oster-, und Pfingstpredigten,* ed. Erwin Mülhaupt (Neukirchen-Vluyn, 1981). For a summary of the material that has not yet been published see page 116.

Other Important Editions

Institutes

1541 (French): *Institution de la religion chrestienne,* ed. Jacques Pannier (Paris, 1936–39).
1560 (French): *Institution de la religion chrestienne,* ed. Jean-Daniel Benoit (Paris, 1957–63).

Commentaries

Iohannis Calvini Commentarius in Epistolam Pauli ad Romanos, ed. T. H. L. Parker (Leiden, 1981).

Other Writings

Pseaumes octantetrois de David, mis en rime françoise par Clément Marot et Théodore de Bèze (Geneva, 1551).
Le Catéchisme français de Calvin publié en 1537, réimprimé pour la première fois d'après un exemplaire nouvellement retrouvé, et suivi de la plus ancienne Confession de foi de l'église de Genève, avec deux notices, ed. Albert Rilliet and Théophile Dufour (Geneva, 1878).
Psychopannychia, ed. Walther Zimmerli (Leipzig, 1932).
Calvin's First Psalter, ed. Richard R. Terry (London, 1932).
La Forme des prières et chantz ecclésiastiques, avec la manière d'administrer les sacremens, et consacrer le mariage, selon la coustume de l'église ancienne, ed. Pierre Pidoux (Kassel and Basel, 1959).
Deux congrégations et Exposition du catéchisme, ed. Rodolphe Peter (Paris, 1964).
L'Abécédaire genevois ou catéchisme élémentaire, ed. Rodolphe Peter (Paris, 1965).
Calvin's Commentary on Seneca's De Clementia, trans. and ed. Ford Lewis Battles and André Malan Hugo (Leiden, 1969).
Three French Treatises, ed. Francis M. Higman (London, 1970).
La Forme des prières ecclésiastiques et Catéchisme par Jean Calvin (Geneva, 1552; New Brunswick, N.J., 1973).

"Die Genferkirchenordnung (1561)," in *Die Kirche im Zeitalter der Reformation*, ed. Heiko A. Oberman (Neukirchen, 1981), 246–49.

Des Scandales, ed. Olivier Fatio and C. Rapin (Geneva, 1984).

Advertissement contre l'astrologie judiciaire, ed. Olivier Millet (Geneva, 1985).

Letters

A.-L. Herminjard, *Correspondance des réformateurs dans les pays de langue française recueillie et publiée avec d'autres lettres relatives à la Réforme et des notes historiques et bibliographiques*, 9 vols. (Geneva, 1866–97; reprint, Nieuwkoop, 1965).

Lettres anglaises 1548–1561, ed. Albert-Marie Schmidt (Paris, 1959).

Les Lettres à Jean Calvin de la collection Sarrau, ed. Rodolphe Peter and Jean Rott, CRHPhR 43 (Paris, 1972).

Lettres à Monsieur et Madame de Falais, ed. Françoise Bonali-Fiquet (Geneva, 1991).

Important Modern-Language Editions and Translations

Institutes

Institution of the Christian Religion (1536 edition), ed. Ford Lewis Battles (Atlanta, 1975).

Institutes of the Christian Religion (1536 edition), ed. Ford Lewis Battles, rev. ed. (Grand Rapids, 1986).

Institutes of the Christian Religion, ed. John T. McNeill, trans. Ford Lewis Battles, 2 vols., *LCC* 20–21 (Philadelphia and London, 1960).

Institution de la religion chrétienne, ed. Jean Cadier and Pierre Marcel, 4 vols. (Geneva, 1955–58).

Unterricht in der christlichen Religion, trans. and ed. Otto Weber, 4th ed. (Neukirchen, 1986).

Institutie of onderwijzing in den christelijken godsdienst, trans. Alexander Sizoo (Delft, 1931).

Institutie 1536, trans. Willem van 't Spijker (Kampen, 1992).

Commentaries

Calvin's Commentaries (Edinburgh, 1843–55; reprint, Grand Rapids, 1981).

Calvin's New Testament Commentaries, ed. David W. Torrance and Thomas F. Torrance, 12 vols. (Edinburgh, 1972).

Other Writings

Calvin: Theological Treatises, ed. J. K. S. Reid (London and Philadelphia, 1954).

Sermons on Isaiah's Prophecy of the Death and Passion of Christ, trans. and ed. T. H. L. Parker (London, 1956).

Petit traité de la sainte cène, ed. H. Châtelain and P. Marcel (Paris, 1959).

Concerning the Eternal Predestination of God, trans. and ed. J. K. S. Reid (London, 1961).

Catechism 1538, trans. and ed. Ford Lewis Battles (Pittsburgh, 1976).

Concerning Scandals, trans. John W. Fraser (Grand Rapids, 1978).

Treatises against the Anabaptists and against the Libertines, trans. and ed. Benjamin Wirt Farley (Grand Rapids, 1982).

"Congratulations to the Venerable Presbyter, Lord Gabriel of Saconay, Precentor of the Church at Lyon for the Beautiful and Elegant Preface That He Wrote for the Book of the King of England," trans. Douglas Floyd Kelly, in *Calvin Studies II*, ed. John H. Leith and Charles Raynal (Davidson, N.C., 1985), 109–18.

La Vraie Piété: Divers traités de Jean Calvin et Confession de foi de Guillaume Farel, ed. Irena Backus and Claire Chimelli (Geneva, 1986).

Calvin's Calvinism: Treatises on the Eternal Predestination of God and the Secret Providence of God, trans. Henry P. Cole (Grand Rapids, 1987).

John Calvin and Jacopo Sadoleto, *A Reformation Debate,* ed. John C. Olin (New York, 1966; reprint, Grand Rapids, 1976).

Calvin's Ecclesiastical Advice, trans. Mary D. Beaty and Benjamin Wirt Farley (Louisville, 1991).

Instruction in Faith (1537), trans. and ed. Paul T. Fuhrmann (Philadelphia, 1949; reprint, Louisville, 1992).

Letters

Lettres de Jean Calvin, recueillies pour la première fois et publiées d'après les manuscrits origineaux, ed. Jules Bonnet, 2 vols. (Paris, 1854).

Letters of John Calvin, ed. Jules Bonnet, 4 vols., trans. David Constable and Marcus Robert Gilchrist (New York, 1972 reprint [vols. 1–2, Edinburgh, 1855, 1857; vols. 3–4, New York and Philadelphia, 1858]).

Johannes Calvins Lebenswerk in seinen Briefen: Eine Auswahl von Briefen Calvins in deutscher Übersetzung, ed. Rudolf Schwarz, 2 vols. (Neukirchen, 1961–62).

Bibliography of Secondary Literature

Actes du colloque Guillaume Farel. Edited by Pierre Barthel et al. 2 vols. *Cahiers de la revue de théologie et de philosophie* 9.1–2. Lausanne, 1983.

Augustijn, C. *De godsdienstgesprekken tussen Rooms-Katholieken en Protestanten van 1538 tot 1541.* Haarlem, 1967.

Autin, Albert. *L'Echec de la Réforme en France.* Paris, 1918.

———. *Un Episode de la vie de Calvin: La Crise du nicodémisme, 1535–1545.* Toulon, 1917.

Babelotzky, Gerd. *Platonische Bilder und Gedankengänge in Calvins Lehre vom Menschen.* Wiesbaden, 1977.

Baehler, E. "Petrus Caroli und Johann Calvin." *JSG* 29 (1904): 41–169.

Bainton, Roland H. *Hunted Heretic.* Boston, 1953.

Bakhuizen van den Brink, J. N. *La Confession de foi des églises réformées de France de 1559, et la Confession des Pays-Bas de 1561.* Vol. 5.6 of *Bulletin des Eglises Wallones.* Leiden, 1959.

———. *Protestantse pleidooien.* Vol. 2. Section 3, "Frankrijk en Calvijn." Kampen, 1962.

Balke, Willem. "Calvijn en Luther." In idem, *Luther en het gereformeerd protestantisme,* 99–117. The Hague, 1982.

———. "Calvijn over de geschapen werkelijkheid in zijn *Psalmencommentaar.*" In Willem Balke et al., eds., *Wegen en gestalten in het gereformeerd protestantisme: Een bundel studies over de geschiedenis van het gereformeerd protestantisme aangeboden aan Prof. Dr. S. van der Linde,* 89–103. Amsterdam, 1976.

———. *Calvin and the Anabaptist Radicals.* Translated by William J. Heynen. Grand Rapids, 1981.

———. "Het avondmaal bij Calvijn." In *Bij brood en beker: Leer en gebruik van het heilig avondmaal in het Nieuwe Testament en in de geschiedenis van de westerse kerk,* edited by Willem van 't Spijker et al., 178–225. Goudriaan, 1980.

Bartel, Oscar. "Calvin und Polen." In *Regards contemporains sur Jean Calvin: Actes du colloque Strasbourg 1964,* 253–68. Paris, 1965.

Barth, Peter. "Die Erwählungslehre in Calvins Institutio von 1536." In *Theologische Aufsätze: Karl Barth zum 50. Geburtstag,* edited by Ernst Wolf, 432–42. Munich, 1936.

Barthélemy, Dominique; Meylan, Henri; and Roussel, Bernard. *Olivétan: Celui qui fit passer la Bible d'hébreu en français.* Textes de Calvin et d'Olivétan. Biel, 1986.

Battles, Ford Lewis. "Calculus fidei." In *Calvinus ecclesiae doctor*, edited by Wilhelm H. Neuser, 85–110. Kampen, 1980.

Bauer, Karl. *Die Beziehungen Calvins zu Frankfurt a. M.* SVRG 38. Leipzig, 1920.

Bavaud, Georges. *La Dispute de Lausanne (1536): Une Etape de l'évolution doctrinale des réformateurs romands.* Fribourg, 1956.

Beekenkamp, W. H. "Calvijn en Sadoleto." *Veritatem in Caritate* 4 (1959): 21–27.

Benoit, Jean-Daniel. *Calvin, directeur d'âmes.* Strasbourg, 1947.

———. "Calvin the Letter-Writer." In *Courtenay Studies in Reformation Theology.* Vol. 1, *John Calvin*, edited by Gervase E. Duffield, 67–101. Grand Rapids, 1966.

———. "The History and Development of the *Institutio:* How Calvin Worked." In *Courtenay Studies in Reformation Theology.* Vol. 1, *John Calvin*, edited by Gervase E. Duffield, 102–17. Grand Rapids, 1966.

———, et al. *Calvin à Strasbourg, 1538–1541.* Strasbourg, 1938.

Berriot, M. François. "Un Procès d'athéisme à Genève: L'Affaire Gruet (1547–1550)." *BSHPF* 125 (1979): 577–92.

Berthoud, Gabrielle. *Antoine Marcourt, réformateur et pamphlétaire du "Livre des Marchans" aux placards de 1534.* Geneva, 1973.

Beza, Theodore. *Correspondance.* Edited by Hippolyte Aubert et al. 12 vols. Geneva, 1960–86.

Blanke, Fritz. "Calvins Urteile über Zwingli." *Zwingliana* 11 (1959): 66–92. (This article also appears in idem, *Aus der Welt der Reformation: Fünf Aufsätze* [Zurich, 1960], 18–47.)

Blaser, Emil. "Vom Gesetz in Calvins Predigten über den 119. Psalm." In *Das Wort sie sollen lassen stehn: Festschrift für D. Albert Schädelin*, 67–78. Bern, 1950.

Bohatec, Josef. *Budé und Calvin: Studien zur Gedankenwelt des französischen Frühhumanismus.* Graz, 1950.

———, ed. *Calvinstudien: Festschrift zum 400. Geburtstage Johann Calvins.* Leipzig, 1909.

Borgeaud, Charles. *Histoire de l'Université de Genève.* Vol. 1, *L'Académie de Calvin, 1559–1798.* Geneva, 1900.

Bouvier, André. *Henri Bullinger, réformateur et conseiller oecuménique, le successeur de Zwingli, d'après sa correspondance avec les réformés et les humanistes de langue française.* Neuchâtel/Paris, 1940.

Breen, Quirinus. *John Calvin: A Study in French Humanism.* Grand Rapids, 1931.

Brienen, T. *De liturgie bij Johannes Calvijn.* Kampen, 1987.

Buisson, Ferdinand. *Sébastien Castellion, sa vie et son oeuvre.* 2 vols. Paris, 1892; reprint, Nieuwkoop, 1964.

Bürki, Bruno. "Jean Calvin avait-il le sens liturgique?" In *Communio sanctorum: Mélanges offerts à Jean-Jacques von Allmen*, 157–72. Geneva, 1982.

Büsser, F. "Calvin und Bullinger." In *Calvinus servus Christi*, edited by Wilhelm H. Neuser, 107–26. Budapest, 1988.

Cadier, Jean. "Sadolet et Calvin." *RHPhR* 45 (1965): 72–92.

Calvin, homme d'église: Oeuvres choisies du réformateur et documents sur les églises réformées du XVIe siècle. 2d ed. Geneva, 1971.

Calvinus ecclesiae doctor. Edited by Wilhelm H. Neuser. Kampen, 1980.

Calvinus ecclesiae Genevensis custos. Edited by Wilhelm H. Neuser. Frankfurt am Main, 1984.

Calvinus Reformator: His Contribution to Theology, Church and Society. Potchefstroom, 1982.

Calvinus servus Christi. Edited by Wilhelm H. Neuser. Budapest, 1988.

Calvinus theologus. Edited by Wilhelm H. Neuser. Neukirchen, 1976.

Cambridge History of the Bible. Vol. 3. *The West from the Reformation to the Present Day*. Edited by S. L. Greenslade. New York, 1978.

Chaix, Paul; Dufour, Alain; and Moeckli, Gustave. *Les Livres imprimés à Genève de 1550 à 1600*. Rev. ed. Geneva, 1966.

Chee, Paul Gerhard. "Johannes Calvin—ein Bild nach seinen Briefen." *RKZ* 21 (1980): 159–61.

Chenevière, Marc-Edouard. *La Pensée politique de Calvin*. Geneva, 1937; reprint, 1970.

Cornelius, C. A. *Der Besuch Calvins bei der Herzogin Renata von Ferrara im Jahr 1536*. N.p., 1893.

Cottret, Bernard. "Pour une sémiotique de la Réforme: Le *Consensus Tigurinus* (1549) et La *Brève Résolution . . .* (1555) de Calvin." *AESC* 39 (1984): 265–85.

Courvoisier, Jaques. "Bucer et Calvin." In Jean-Daniel Benoit et al., *Calvin à Strasbourg, 1538–1541*, 37–66. Strasbourg, 1938.

———. "Les Catéchismes de Genève et de Strasbourg." *BSHPF* 85 (1935): 105–21.

Crottet, Alexandre. *Correspondance française de Calvin avec Louis Du Tillet, 1537–1538*. Lausanne/Paris, 1850.

Dankbaar, W. F. *Calvijn: Zijn weg en werk*. Nijkerk, 1957; 3d ed., 1986.

———. "Calvijns oordeel over het concilie van Trente, inzonderheid inzake het rechtvaardigingsdecreet." *NAK* 14 (1962): 79–112. (This article is also found in idem, *Hervormers en humanisten: Een bundel opstellen* [Amsterdam, 1978], 67–99.)

———. "Het apostolaat bij Calvijn." *NTT* 4 (1949–50): 177–92. (This article is also found in idem, *Hervormers en humanisten: Een bundel opstellen* [Amsterdam, 1978], 185–99.)

———. "Het doctorenambt bij Calvijn." In idem, *Hervormers en humanisten: Een bundel opstellen*, 153–83. Amsterdam, 1978. (This article originally appeared as "L'Office des docteurs chez Calvin," *RHPhR* 44 [1964]: 364–88.)

Dardier, Charles. "Un Problème biographique: Quelle est la date de la première édition de la Psychopannychia de Calvin?" *BSHPF* 19/20 (1870): 371–82.

de Boer, E. A. *Loflied en hekeldicht: De geschiedenis van Calvijn's enige gedicht. Het Epinicion Christo cantatum van 1 januari 1541*. Haarlem, 1986.

de Greef, Wulfert. *Calvijn en het Oude Testament*. Amsterdam, 1984.

———. "Das Verhältnis von Predigt und Kommentar bei Calvin, dargestellt an dem Deuteronomium Kommentar und den -Predigten." In *Calvinus servus Christi*, edited by Wilhelm H. Neuser, 195–204. Budapest, 1988.

de Groot, D.-J. "Melchior Volmar, ses rapports avec les réformateurs français et suisses." *BSHPF* 83 (1934): 416–39.

Diehl, Wilhelm. "Calvins Auslegung des Dekalogs in der ersten Ausgabe seiner *Institutio* und Luthers Katechismen." *ThStKr* 71 (1898): 141–62.

Dörries, Hermann. "Calvin und Lefèvre." *ZKG* 44 (1925): 544–81.

Douglas, Richard M. *Jacopo Sadoleto, 1477–1547: Humanist and Reformer*. Cambridge, 1959.

Doumergue, Emile. *Jean Calvin: Les Hommes et les choses de son temps.* 7 vols. Lausanne, 1899–1927.

Droz, Eugénie. "Calvin collaborateur de la Bible de Neuchâtel." In *Chemins de l'hérésie: Textes et documents,* 1:102–17. Geneva, 1970.

———. "Calvin et les nicodémites." In *Chemins de l'hérésie: Textes et documents,* 1:131–71. Geneva, 1970.

———. *Chemins de l'hérésie: Textes et documents.* 4 vols. Geneva, 1970–76.

Dubois, Claude-Gilbert. "Jean Calvin, commentaires sur le premier livre de Moyse." In idem, *La Conception de l'histoire en France au XVIe siècle (1560–1610),* 307–15. Paris, 1977.

Dufour, Théophile. *Notice bibliographique sur le Catéchisme et la Confession de foi de Calvin (1537) et sur les autres livres imprimés à Genève et à Neuchâtel dans les premiers temps de la Réforme (1533–1540).* Geneva, 1970. Reprint of 1878 edition.

Dumont, Eugène-Louis. "Histoires des traités." In *Genève 26–27 mai 1976, commémoration des traités de combourgeoisie avec Fribourg, Berne 1526 et Zürich 1584,* 49–59. Geneva, 1976.

Dunant, Emile. *Les Relations politiques de Genève avec Berne et les Suisses de 1536 à 1564.* Geneva, 1894.

Eire, Carlos M. N. "Calvin and Nicodemism: A Reappraisal." *SCJ* 10 (1979): 45–69.

———. *War against the Idols: The Reformation of Worship from Erasmus to Calvin.* Cambridge, 1986.

Erichson, Alfred. *L'Eglise française de Strasbourg au XVIe siècle.* Strasbourg, 1886.

Fazy, Henri. "Procès de Jacques Gruet, 1547." *Mémoires de l'Institut national genevois* 16 (1886).

Feld, Helmut. "Um die reine Lehre des Evangeliums: Calvins Kontroverse mit Sadoleto 1539." *Catholica* 36 (1982): 150–80.

Fischer, Danielle. "Michel Cop: Congrégation sur Josué 1/6–11 du 11 juin 1563, avec ce qui a été ajouté par Jean Calvin" (première impression du manuscrit original, avec une introduction et des notes). *FZPhTh* 34 (1987): 205–29.

Friedman, Jerome. *Michael Servetus: A Case Study in Total Heresy.* Geneva, 1978.

Gäbler, Ulrich. *Huldrych Zwingli: His Life and Work.* Translated by Ruth C. L. Gritsch. Philadelphia, 1986.

Gagnebin, Bernard. "L'Histoire des manuscrits des sermons de Calvin." In *SC* 2:xiv–xxviii.

Ganoczy, Alexandre. *The Young Calvin.* Translated by David Foxgrover and Wade Provo. Philadelphia, 1987.

———, and Müller, Klaus. *Calvins handschriftliche Annotationen zu Chrysostomus: Ein Beitrag zur Hermeneutik Calvins.* Wiesbaden, 1981.

Garside, Charles, Jr. *The Origins of Calvin's Theology of Music, 1536–1543.* Philadelphia, 1979.

Gautier, Jean-Antoine. *Histoire de Genève des origines à l'année 1691.* 9 vols. Geneva, 1896–1914.

Geering, Arnold. "Calvin und die Musik." In *Calvin-Studien 1959,* edited by Jürgen Moltmann, 16–25. Neukirchen, 1960.

Geisendorf, Paul F. *Théodore de Bèze.* Geneva, 1949.

Gilmont, Jean-François. *Bibliographie des éditions de Jean Crespin.* 2 vols. Verviers, Belgium, 1981.

————, et al. "Bibliotheca Gebennensis: Les Livres imprimés à Genève de 1535 à 1549." *Geneva* 28 (1980): 229–51.

Giran, Etienne. *Sébastien Castellion et la Réforme calviniste.* Paris, 1914.

Girardin, Benoit. *Rhétorique et théologique: Calvin, le commentaire de l'Epître aux Romains.* Paris, 1979.

Goeters, J. F. G. "Thomas von Kempen und Johannes Calvin." In *Thomas von Kempen: Beiträge zum 500. Todesjahr 1471–1971*, 87–92. Kampen, 1971.

Greengrass, Mark. *The French Reformation.* Oxford and New York, 1987.

Guggisberg, Kurt. "Calvin und Bern." In *Festgabe Leonhard von Muralt*, 266–85. Zurich, 1970.

Guillaume Farel, 1489–1565. Neuchâtel, 1930.

Halaski, Karl, ed. *Der Prediger Johannes Calvin: Beiträge und Nachrichten zur Ausgabe der Supplementa Calviniana.* Neukirchen, 1966.

Hards, Walter G. *A Collation of the Latin Texts of the First Edition of Calvin's Institutes.* Baltimore, 1958.

Hasper, H. *Calvijns beginsel voor den zang in den eredienst.* The Hague, 1955.

Haury, David A. "English Anabaptism and Calvin's *Brière Instruction.*" *Menn.QR* 57 (1983): 145–51.

Herminjard, A.-L. *Correspondance des réformateurs dans les pays de langue française recueillie et publiée avec d'autres lettres relatives à la Réforme et des notes historiques et bibliographiques.* Geneva, 1866–97; reprint, Nieuwkoop, 1965.

Heyer, Henri. *L'Eglise de Genève, 1535–1909.* Geneva, 1909.

Higman, Francis M. "The Question of Nicodemism." In *Calvinus ecclesiae Genevensis custos*, edited by Wilhelm H. Neuser, 165–70. Frankfurt am Main, 1984.

————. "Un Pamphlet de Calvin restitué à son auteur." *RHPhR* 60 (1980): 167–80, 327–37.

Höpfl, Harro. *The Christian Polity of John Calvin.* Cambridge, 1982; reprint, 1985.

Hugo, André Malan. *Calvijn en Seneca.* Groningen, 1957.

Hunt, R. N. Carew. *Calvin.* London, 1933.

Hwang, Jung-Uck. *Der junge Calvin und seine Psychopannychia.* Frankfurt, 1991.

Imbart de La Tour, Pierre. *Calvin et l'Institution de la religion chrétienne.* Paris, 1935.

Jenny, Beatrice. *Das Schleitheimer Täuferbekenntnis 1527.* Vol. 28 of *Schaffhäuser Beiträge zur vaterländischen Geschichte.* Thayngen, Switz., 1950.

Jenny, Markus. *Luther, Zwingli, Calvin in ihren Liedern.* Zurich, 1983.

John Calvin's Institutes: His Opus Magnum. Proceedings of the Second South African Congress for Calvin Research, July 31–August 3, 1984. Potchefstroom, 1986.

Junod, Eric, ed. *La Dispute de Lausanne (1536): La Théologie réformée après Zwingli et avant Calvin.* Lausanne, 1988.

Kelly, Douglas. "The Transmission and Translation of the Collected Letters of John Calvin." *SJTh* 30 (1977): 429–37.

Kingdon, Robert M. "Calvin and the Government of Geneva." In *Calvinus ecclesiae Genevensis custos*, edited by Wilhelm H. Neuser, 49–67. Frankfurt am Main, 1984.

————. *Geneva and the Coming of the Wars of Religion in France, 1555–1563.* Geneva, 1956.

————, and Linder, Robert D., eds. *Calvin and Calvinism: Sources of Democracy?* Lexington, Mass., 1970.

Koch, Ernst. "Erwägungen zum Bekehrungsbericht Calvins." *NAK* 61 (1981): 185–97.

Köhler, Walther. *Das Ehe- und Sittengericht in den Süddeutschen Reichsstädten, den Herzogtum Württemberg und in Genf.* Vol. 2, *Zürcher Ehegericht und Genfer Konsistorium.* Leipzig, 1942.

Kolfhaus, W. "Der Verkehr Calvins mit Bullinger." In *Calvinstudien: Festschrift zum 400. Geburtstage Johann Calvins,* edited by Josef Bohatec, 27–125. Leipzig, 1909.

Köstlin, J. "Calvins Institutio nach Form und Inhalt in ihrer geschichtlichen Entwicklung." *ThStKr* 41 (1868): 7–62, 410–86.

Kraus, Hans-Joachim. "Calvin's Exegetical Principles." *Interpretation* 31 (1977): 8–18.

———. "Vom Leben und Tod in den Psalmen: Eine Studie zu Calvins Psalmenkommentar." In idem, *Biblisch-theologische Aufsätze,* 258–77. Neukirchen, 1972.

Labarthe, Olivier. "La Relation entre le premier catéchisme de Calvin et la première confession de foi de Genève." Thèse de licence, University of Geneva, 1967.

Lane, A. N. S. "Calvin's Use of the Fathers and the Medievals." *CTJ* 16 (1981): 149–205.

Lang, August. *Die Bekehrung Johannes Calvins.* Leipzig, 1897; reprint, Aalen, 1972.

———. "Melanchthon und Calvin." In idem, *Reformation und Gegenwart,* 88–135. Detmold, 1918.

———. "The Sources of Calvin's Institutes of 1536." *EvQ* 8 (1936): 130–41.

Lange van Ravenswaay, J. M. "Calvin und Farel—Aspekte ihres Verhältnisses." In *Actes du colloque Guillaume Farel,* edited by Pierre Barthel et al., 2 vols., 1:63–72. Lausanne, 1983.

Lazzaro, Ralph, trans. and ed. "Four Letters from the Socinus-Calvin Correspondence 1549." In *Italian Reformation Studies in Honor of Laelius Socinus,* edited by J. A. Tedeschi, 215–30. Florence, 1965.

Lecoultre, H. "Calvin d'après son commentaire sur le De Clementia de Sénèque." *RThPh* 24 (1891): 51–77.

———. "Le Séjour de Calvin en Italie d'après des documents inédits." *RThPh* 19 (1886): 168–92.

Lecoultre, J. *Maturin Cordier et les origines de la pédagogie protestante.* Neuchâtel, 1926.

Léry, Jean de. *Histoire d'un voyage faict en la terre du Brésil autrement dit Amérique.* N.p., 1577. Republished as *Le Voyage au Brésil.* Paris, 1927.

Lohse, Bernhard. "Wiedervereinigungsversuche zwischen Katholiken und Protestanten." In *Handbuch der Dogmen- und Theologiegeschichte,* edited by Carl Andresen, 3 vols., 2:102–8. Göttingen, 1980–84.

Lupton, Lewis F. "Calvin's Commentary on Genesis." In idem, *A History of the Geneva Bible.* Vol. 5, *Vision of God,* 107–17. London, 1973.

McDonnel, Kilian. "Conception de la liturgie selon Calvin et l'avenir de la liturgie catholique." *Concilium* 42 (1969): 75–84.

McGrath, Alister E. "John Calvin and Late Mediaeval Thought: A Study in Late Mediaeval Influences upon Calvin's Theological Development." *ARG* 77 (1986): 58–78.

———. *A Life of John Calvin.* Oxford, 1990.

McKee, Elsie Anne. *Elders and the Plural Ministry: The Role of Exegetical History in Illuminating John Calvin's Theology.* Geneva, 1988.

———. *John Calvin: On the Diaconate and Liturgical Almsgiving.* Geneva, 1984.

McNeill, John T. "John Calvin: Doctor Ecclesiae." In *The Heritage of John Calvin,* edited by John H. Bratt, 9–22. Grand Rapids, 1973. (This article is also found in

Readings in Calvin's Theology, ed. Donald K. McKim [Grand Rapids, 1984], 11–20.)

Mansson, Nicolaus. *Calvin och gudstjästen* (Calvin and worship). Stockholm, 1970.

Melles, Gerard. *Albertus Pighius en zijn strijd met Calvijn over het liberum arbitrium.* Kampen, 1973.

Meylan, Henri, and Deluz, R. *La Dispute de Lausanne.* Lausanne, 1936.

Moltmann, Jürgen, ed. *Calvin-Studien 1959.* Neukirchen, 1960.

Monter, E. William. *Calvin's Geneva.* New York, 1967.

Mooi, Remko J. *Het kerk- en dogmahistorisch element in de werken van Johannes Calvijn.* Wageningen, 1965.

Müller, Karl. "Calvin und die Libertiner." *ZKG* 40 (1922): 83–129.

Naef, Henri. *La Conjuration d'Amboise et Genève.* Geneva, 1922.

———. *Les Origines de la Réforme à Genève.* 2 vols. Geneva, 1936; reprint, 1968.

Nauta, Doede. "Calvijns afkeer van een schisma." In *Ex auditu verbi: Theologische opstellen aangeboden aan Prof. Dr. G. C. Berkouwer,* 131–56. Kampen, 1965.

———. *Guillaume Farel: In leven en werken geschetst.* Amsterdam, 1978.

Neuser, Wilhelm H. "Calvins Beitrag zu den Religionsgesprächen von Hagenau, Worms und Regensburg (1540/41)." In *Studien zur Geschichte und Theologie der Reformation: Festschrift für Ernst Bizer,* edited by Luise Abramowski et al., 213–37. Neukirchen, 1969.

———. "Calvins Stellung zu den Apokryphen des Alten Testaments." In *Text-Wort-Glaube: Studien zur Überlieferung, Interpretation und Autorisierung biblischer Texte,* edited by Martin Brecht, 298–323. New York, 1980.

———. "Calvins Urteil über den Rechtfertigungsartikel des Regensb. Buches." In *Reformation und Humanismus: Robert Stupperich zum 65. Geburtstag,* edited by Martin Greschat et al., 176–94. Witten, 1969.

———. "The Development of the *Institutes* 1536 to 1559." In *John Calvin's Institutes: His Opus Magnum,* 33–54. Potchefstroom, 1986.

———, ed. *Die Vorbereitung der Religionsgespräche von Worms und Regensburg 1540/41.* Vol. 4 of *Texte zur Geschichte der evangelischen Theologie.* Neukirchen, 1974.

Niesel, Wilhelm. "Calvin und die Libertiner." *ZKG* 48 (1929): 58–74.

———. "Descriptio et historia editionum Institutionis latinarum et gallicarum Calvino vivo emissarum." In *OS* 3:vi–l.

———. "Zum Genfer Prozess gegen Valentin Gentilis." *ARG* 26 (1929): 270–73.

———, and Barth, Peter. "Eine französische Ausgabe der ersten Institutio Calvins." *ThBl* 7 (1928): 2–10.

Nijenhuis, Willem. "Calvijns 'subita conversio': Notities bij een hypothese." *NTT* 26 (1972): 248–69.

———. "Calvin's Attitude towards the Symbols of the Early Church during the Conflict with Caroli." In idem, *Ecclesia Reformata: Studies on the Reformation,* 73–96. Leiden, 1972.

———. *Calvinus oecumenicus: Calvijn en de eenheid der kerk in het licht van zijn briefwisseling.* The Hague, 1959.

Obendiek, Harmannus. "Die Institutio Calvins als 'Confessio' und 'Apologie.'" In *Theologische Aufsätze: Karl Barth zum 50. Geburtstag,* edited by Ernst Wolf, 417–31. Munich, 1936.

Our Reformational Tradition: A Rich Heritage and Lasting Vocation. Potchefstroom, 1984.

Pannier, Jacques. *Calvin à Strasbourg.* Strasbourg, 1925.

————. *Calvin écrivain: Sa place et son rôle dans l'histoire de la langue et de la littérature française.* Paris, 1930.

————. *Les Origines de la Confession de foi et la Discipline des églises réformées de France.* Paris, 1936.

————. "Une Première «Institution» française dès 1537." *RHPhR* 8 (1928): 513–34.

Parker, T. H. L. *Calvin's New Testament Commentaries.* London, 1971.

————. *Calvin's Old Testament Commentaries.* Edinburgh, 1986.

————. *Calvin's Preaching.* Edinburgh, 1992.

————. "Calvin the Exegete: Change and Development." In *Calvinus ecclesiae doctor,* edited by Wilhelm H. Neuser, 33–46. Kampen, 1980.

————. *John Calvin.* Philadelphia, 1975.

————. *The Oracles of God: An Introduction to the Preaching of John Calvin.* London, 1947.

Partee, Charles B. *Calvin and Classical Philosophy.* Leiden, 1977.

————. "Farel's Influence on Calvin: A 'Prolusion.'" In *Actes du colloque Guillaume Farel,* edited by Pierre Barthel et al., 2 vols., 1:173–86. Lausanne, 1983.

Pauck, Wilhelm. "Calvin and Butzer." *JR* 9 (1929): 237–56. (This article also appears in idem, *The Heritage of the Reformation* [Glencoe, Ill., 1961], 85–99.)

Peter, Rodolphe. "Calvin and Liturgy, according to the *Institutes.*" In *John Calvin's Institutes: His Opus Magnum,* 239–65. Potchefstroom, 1986.

————. "Calvin and Louis Budé's Translation of the Psalms." In *Courtenay Studies in Reformation Theology.* Vol. 1, *John Calvin,* edited by Gervase E. Duffield, 190–209. Grand Rapids, 1966.

————. "Calviniana et alia: Nouveaux compléments au répertoire des imprimés genevois de 1550 à 1600." *BHR* 34 (1972): 115–23.

————. "Etudes critiques: Notes de bibliographie calvinienne à propos de deux ouvrages récents." *RHPhR* 51 (1971): 79–87.

————. "The Geneva Primer or Calvin's Elementary Catechism." In *Calvin Studies V: Papers Presented at a Colloquium on Calvin Studies at Davidson College . . . ,* edited by John H. Leith, 135–61. Davidson, N.C., 1990.

————. "Jean Calvin, avocat du comte Guillaume de Fürstenberg." *RHPhR* 51 (1971): 63–78.

————. "Oeuvres de Calvin publiées à Genève entre 1550 et 1600." *BHR* 31 (1969): 181–83.

————. "Un Imprimeur de Calvin: Michel Du Bois." *BSHAG* 16 (1978): 285–335.

Peter, Rodolphe, and Gilmont, Jean-François. *Bibliotheca Calviniana: Les Oeuvres de Jean Calvin publiées au XVIe siècle.* Vol. 1, *Ecrits théologiques, littéraires et juridiques 1532–1554.* Geneva, 1991.

Piaget, Arthur, ed. "Les Actes de la dispute de Lausanne, 1536, publiés intégralement d'après le manuscrit de Berne." In *Mémoires de l'Université de Neuchâtel* 6 (1928).

Pidoux, Pierre. "Albert Pighius de Kampen, adversaire de Calvin." Thèse de licence, University of Lausanne, 1932.

Pin, Jean-Pierre. "Pour une analyse textuelle du catéchisme (1542) de Jean Calvin." In *Calvinus ecclesiae doctor,* edited by Wilhelm H. Neuser, 159–70. Kampen, 1980.

Plath, Uwe. *Calvin und Basel in den Jahren 1552–1556*. Zurich, 1974.

————. "Calvin und Castellio und die Frage der Religionsfreiheit." In *Calvinus ecclesiae Genevensis custos*, edited by Wilhelm H. Neuser, 191–95. Frankfurt am Main, 1984.

————. "Ein unbekannter Brief Calvins vom Vorabend der Religionskriege in Frankreich." *ARG* 62 (1971): 244–66.

Plomp, Johannes. *De kerkelijke tucht bij Calvijn*. Kampen, 1969.

Posthumus Meyjes, G. H. M. "Het doctorenambt in Middeleeuwen en Reformatie." *Rondom het Woord* 15.3 (Sept. 1973): 21–45.

Quack, Jürgen. "Calvins Bibelvorreden (1535–1546)." In idem, *Evangelische Bibelvorreden von der Reformation bis zur Aufklärung*, 89–116. Gütersloh, 1975.

Regards contemporains sur Jean Calvin: Actes du colloque Calvin Strasbourg 1964. Paris, 1965.

Rieser, Ewald. *Calvin—Franzose, Genfer oder Fremdling? Untersuchung zum Problem der Heimatliebe bei Calvin*. Zurich, 1968.

Rilliet, Jean. *Le Vrai Visage de Calvin*. Toulouse, 1982.

Roget, Amédée. *Histoire du peuple de Genève depuis la Réforme jusqu'à l'Escalade*. 7 vols. Geneva, 1870–83.

Rogge, Joachim. "Themen Luthers im Denken Calvins." In *Calvinus servus Christi*, edited by Wilhelm H. Neuser, 53–72. Budapest, 1988.

Roset, Michel. *Les Chroniques de Genève*. Geneva, 1894. Republished by Henri Fazy.

Rotondò, Antonio. *Calvin and the Italian Anti-Trinitarians*. Translated by John and Anne Tedeschi. St. Louis, 1969.

Rott, Jean. "Documents strasbourgeois concernant Calvin. I. Un Manuscrit autographe: La Harangue du recteur Nicolas Cop." *RHPhR* 44 (1964): 290–311. (This material is also found in *Regards contemporains sur Jean Calvin: Actes du colloque Calvin Strasbourg 1964* [Paris, 1965], 28–49.)

Ruff, Hedwig. *Die französischen Briefe Calvins: Versuch einer stilistischen Analyse*. Glarus, Switz., 1937.

Russell, S. H. "Calvin and the Messianic Interpretation of the Psalms." *SJTh* 21 (1968): 37–47.

Rutgers, Frederik L. *Calvijns invloed op de Reformatie in de Nederlanden, voor zooveel die door hemzelven is uitgeoefend*. Leiden, 1899; reprint, Leeuwarden, 1980.

Schellong, Dieter. *Calvins Auslegung der synoptischen Evangelien*. Munich, 1969.

Scholl, Hans. *Reformation und Politik: Politische Ethik bei Luther, Calvin und Frühhugenotten*. Stuttgart, 1976.

Schreiner, Susan E. "'Through a Mirror Dimly': Calvin's Sermons on Job." *CTJ* 21 (1986): 175–93.

Schultesz-Rechberg, G. von. *Der Kardinal Jacobo Sadoleto: Ein Beitrag zur Geschichte des Humanismus*. Zurich, 1909.

Schulze, L. F. *Calvin's Reply to Pighius*. Potchefstroom, 1970.

————. "Calvin's Reply to Pighius—A Micro and Macro View." In *Calvinus ecclesiae Genevensis custos*, edited by Wilhelm H. Neuser, 171–85. Frankfurt am Main, 1984.

Simpson, H. W. "The *Editio Princeps* of the *Institutio Christianae Religionis* by John Calvin." In *Calvinus Reformator: His Contribution to Theology, Church and Society*, 26–32. Potchefstroom, 1982.

Sprenger, Paul. *Das Rätsel um die Bekehrung Calvins*. Neukirchen, 1960.

Staedtke, Joachim. *Johannes Calvin: Erkenntnis und Gestaltung.* Göttingen, 1969.

Stauffer, Richard. "Autour du colloque de Poissy: Calvin et le De officio pii ac publicae tranquillitatis vere amantis viri." In *L'Amiral de Coligny et son temps,* 135–53. Paris, 1974. (This article is also found in idem, *Interprètes de la Bible: Etudes sur les réformateurs du XVIe siècle* [Paris, 1980], 249–67.)

————. *Dieu, la création et la Providence dans la prédication de Calvin.* Bern, 1978.

————. "Eine englische Sammlung von Calvinpredigten." In *Der Prediger Johannes Calvin: Beiträge und Nachrichten zur Ausgabe der Supplementa Calviniana,* edited by Karl Halaski, 47–80. Neukirchen, 1966.

————. "L'Apport de Strasbourg à la Réforme française par l'intermédiaire de Calvin." In idem, *Interprètes de la Bible: Etudes sur les réformateurs du XVIe siècle,* 153–65. Paris, 1980.

————. "Lefèvre d'Etaples, artisan ou spectateur de la Réforme?" *BSHPF* 113 (1967): 405–23. (This article is also found in *Positions luthériennes* 15 [1967]: 247–62; and in Stauffer, *Interprètes de la Bible: Etudes sur les réformateurs du XVIe siècle* [Paris, 1980], 11–29.)

————. "Les Sermons inédits de Calvin sur le Livre de Genèse." *RThPh* 97 (1965): 26–36.

————. "L'Exégèse de Genèse 1, 1–3 chez Luther et Calvin." In Centre d'études des religions du livre, *In principio: Interprétations des premiers versets de la Genèse,* 245–66. Paris, 1973. (This article is also found in Stauffer, *Interprètes de la Bible: Etudes sur les réformateurs du XVIe siècle* [Paris, 1980], 59–85.)

————. "Zwingli et Calvin, critiques de la confession de Schleitheim." In *The Origins and Characteristics of Anabaptism,* edited by Marc Lienhard, 126–47. The Hague, 1977. (This article is also found in Richard Stauffer, *Interprètes de la Bible: Etudes sur les réformateurs du XVIe siècle* [Paris, 1980], 103–28.)

Strasser, Otto E. "Calvin: Leben und Schriften." *RGG* 1 (1957).

Strohl, H. "Bucer et Calvin." *BSHPF* 87 (1938): 354–60.

————. "La Théorie et la pratique des quatre ministères à Strasbourg avant l'arrivée de Calvin." *BSHPF* 84 (1935): 123–44.

Stückelberger, Hans Martin. "Calvin und Castellio." *Zwingliana* 7 (1939): 91–128.

Stupperich, Robert. "Calvin und die Konfession des Paul Volz." *RHPhR* 44 (1964): 279–89.

Subilia, Ch. *La Dispute de Lausanne.* Lausanne, 1885.

Swanepoel, J. "Calvin as Letter-Writer." In *Our Reformational Tradition: A Rich Heritage and Lasting Vocation,* 279–99. Potchefstroom, 1984.

Tylenda, Joseph N. "Calvin's First Reformed Sermon? Nicholas Cop's Discourse—1 November 1533." *WThJ* 38 (1975–76): 300–318.

————. "The Calvin-Westphal Exchange: The Genesis of Calvin's Treatises against Westphal." *CTJ* 9 (1974): 182–209.

————. "Christ the Mediator: Calvin versus Stancaro." *CTJ* 8 (1973): 5–16.

————. "The Controversy on Christ the Mediator: Calvin's Second Reply to Stancaro." *CTJ* 8 (1973): 131–57.

————. "The Warning That Went Unheeded: John Calvin on Giorgio Biandrata." *CTJ* 12 (1977): 24–62.

van der Linde, S. "Calvijn en Coornhert." *ThR* 2 (1959): 176–87.

van der Merwe, N. T. "Calvin, Augustine and Platonism: A Few Aspects of Calvin's Philosophical Background." In *Calvinus Reformator: His Contribution to Theology, Church and Society*, 69–84. Potchefstroom, 1982.

van Ginkel, Albertus. *De ouderling.* Amsterdam, 1975.

van 't Spijker, Willem. *De ambten bij Martin Bucer.* Kampen, 1970.

———. "The Influence of Bucer on Calvin as Becomes Evident from the *Institutes.*" In *John Calvin's Institutes: His Opus Magnum*, 106–32. Potchefstroom, 1986.

———. "The Influence of Luther on Calvin according to the *Institutes.*" In *John Calvin's Institutes: His Opus Magnum*, 83–105. Potchefstroom, 1986.

———. *Luther en Calvijn: De invloed van Luther op Calvijn blijkens de Institutie.* Kampen, 1985.

———. "Prädestination bei Bucer und Calvin: Ihre gegenseitige Beeinflussung und Abhängigkeit." In *Calvinus theologus*, edited by Wilhelm H. Neuser, 85–111. Neukirchen, 1976.

van 't Veer, M. B. *Catechese en catechetische stof bij Calvijn.* Kampen, 1941.

Verboom, Willem. *De catechese van de Reformatie en de Nadere Reformatie.* Amsterdam, 1986.

Walchenbach, John Robert. *The Influence of David and the Psalms on the Life and Thought of John Calvin.* Pittsburgh, 1969.

———. *John Calvin as Biblical Commentator: An Investigation into Calvin's Use of John Chrysostom as an Exegetical Tutor.* Pittsburgh, 1974.

Warfield, B. B. "On the Literary History of Calvin's 'Institutes.'" *Presbyterian and Reformed Review* 10 (1899): 193–219.

Waskey, Andrew J. L., Jr. "John Calvin's Theory of Political Obligation: An Examination of the Doctrine of Civil Obedience and Its Limits from the *New Testament Commentaries.*" Ph.D. diss., University of Southern Mississippi, 1978.

Wendel, François. *Calvin: The Origins and Development of His Religious Thought.* Translated by Philip Mairet. New York, 1963; reprint, Durham, N.C., 1987.

———. *Calvin et l'humanisme.* Paris, 1976.

———. *L'Eglise de Strasbourg, sa constitution et son organisation.* Paris, 1942.

Wernle, Paul. *Calvin und Basel bis zum Tode des Myconius, 1535–1552.* Tübingen, 1909.

Wilkie, Robert G., and Verhey, Allen. "Calvin's Treatise 'Against the Libertines.'" *CTJ* 15 (1980): 190–219.

Wolf, H. H. "Die Bedeutung der Musik bei Calvin." *MGKK* 41 (1936).

Chronological Index of Calvin's Writings

For the editions of Calvin's sermons see pp. 110–17. This index mentions only the edition of the *Quatre sermons . . .* (1552).

* Works of which Calvin is a coauthor
† Calvin's editions of the works of others along with his commentary on them
§ Translations by someone else

General Index

Aarau, 66
Absoluta de Christi Domini et catholicae ecclesiae sacramentis tractatio (Bullinger), 185–86
Abuses, 99; abolition of, 217
Academy of Geneva, 53–56, 79, 145
Acts of the Apostles, 46
Ad Francisci Balduini apostatae Ecebolii convicia . . . (Beza), 208
Ad leges de famosis libellis et de calumniatoribus commentarius (Baudouin), 208
Adrets, François Des, 77
Adversus cuiusdam sacramentarii falsam criminationem iusta defensio (Westphal), 192
Advertissement sur les jugemens d'astrologie . . . (Saint-Gelais), 141
Affaire de placards, 24, 172, 196
Agricola, Johannes, 162
Albret, Jeanne d', 71, 76, 77, 106, 207
Albucius, Aurelius, 83
Alciati, Andrea, 22, 83–84
Alcuinus, 199
Alençon, 19, 172
Alliance, Swiss, 59–60
Amboise: Conspiracy of, 70, 71; Peace of, 77–78
Ambrose, 157
Ameaux, Pierre, 45–46
Amerbach, Bonifacius, 25
Anabaptists, 29, 101, 165–69, 199; evangelicals confused with, 196
Andelot, François d', 68–69
Anglois, Jacques L', 73
Angrogne, Val d', 73
Antapologia (Duchemin), 22, 83–84

Antidoto (Gentilis), 180
Antitrinitarians, 178–81, 212. *See also* Trinity, denial of the
Apologia (Alciati), 83
Archiv für Reformationsgeschichte, 219
Arianism, charge of, 172
Artichauds, 36
Articulants, 36
Assertio septem sacramentorum (Henry VIII), 207
Astrology, 141
Aubert (syndic), 50
Augsburg, 162; Confession, 75, 78, 154, 156, 192; Interim, 162–63
Augustijn, C., 154 n. 11
Augustine, 20, 85, 101, 118, 130, 141, 157, 158, 177, 193, 216
Aurelius Albucius, 83
Autin, Albert, 139 n. 30

Babelotzky, Gerd, 20 n. 8
Backus, Irena, 91, 125 n. 4, 134 n. 25, 153 n. 10, 156 n. 15, 157
Badius, Conrad, 155
Baduel, Claude, 113
Baehler, E., 172 n. 10
Bainton, Roland H., 173 n. 12, 177 n. 22
Bakhuizen van den Brink, J. N., 143 nn. 35–36, 160 n. 21
Balke, Willem, 105 n. 33, 134 n. 24, 167 nn. 4–5, 169 n. 6, 181 n. 38, 198 n. 5
Baptism, 130, 218; emergency, 163, 215, 216; infant, 163, 174, 176; in the Roman Catholic Church, 211; by women, 163, 216
Barrois, Georges, 221

Bullinger, Heinrich, 25, 45, 50, 57, 59, 60, 66, 67, 70 n. 48, 71, 74, 76, 77, 78, 91, 95, 104, 108, 118, 139, 159, 163, 176, 184–93, 210, 218
Burckhardt, Francis, 105
Bure, Idelette de, 32
Bürki, Bruno, 126 n. 8
Büsser, F., 210 n. 7

Cadier, Jean, 152 n. 8, 201 n. 13
Calais, 69
Calvin, Idelette, 32
Calvin, Jacques, 32
Calvin-Bibliographie 1901–1959 (Niesel), 219
Calvin Bibliography 1960–1970 (Tylenda and de Klerk), 219
Calvini Opera, 115, 219, 220, 221
Capito, Wolfgang, 25, 29, 30, 39, 92, 154, 166, 183
Caraccioli, Antonio, 75
Caroli, Pierre, 19, 31, 171–73
Carthage, Fourth Council of, 216
Cartier, A., 205 n. 2
Cassander, George, 207
Castellio, Sebastian, 40, 50–51, 53, 65, 92, 114 n. 48, 159 n. 19, 176–78
Cateau-Cambrésis, 53, 69
Catechism, 124, 132–33
Cauvin, Anne, 18 n. 1
Cauvin, Antoine, 18, 27, 79
Cauvin, Charles, 18, 22
Cauvin, François, 18
Cauvin, Gérard, 17–18, 21, 22
Cauvin, Marie, 18, 27
Cauvin, Richard, 19
Cecil, William, 104
Celestial flesh, 168, 181
Ceneau, Robert, 196
Censure between ministers, 61–62
Cerdo, 169
Cervenka, Mattias, 32
Chambéry, 73
Chambord, Treaty of, 67
Chambre ardente, 66
Champereau, Aimé, 37, 62
Chanforans, 90
Chant de victoire (Calvin-Badius), 155
Chaponneau, Jean, 61–62

Charles V (Holy Roman Empire), 19, 27, 34, 40, 48, 67, 155, 160–63, 173, 185, 196, 204
Charles IX (France), 71, 74, 75, 76, 79, 131
Chartier, Guillaume, 74
Châteaubriant, Edict of, 67
Châtelain, H., 134 n. 25
Chauvet, Raymond, 58
Chee, Paul Gerhard, 210 n. 5
Chenevière, Marc-Edouard, 42 n. 27
Chevallier, Antoine-Raoul, 55
Chimelli, Claire, 91, 125 n. 4, 134 n. 25, 153 n. 10, 156 n. 15, 157 n. 16
Christian III (Denmark), 99
Christianismi restitutio (Servetus), 174, 176
Christ in the Lord's Supper, presence of, 34, 75, 135, 151, 184, 186
Christology, 181
Chrysostom, 26, 90, 177
Church order, 41, 143, 144–47; and excommunication, 43–44
Cinquante pseaumes en françois (Marot), 131
Citoyens, 42
Civic rights, 42, 49, 59
Civil legislation, Calvin's involvement in, 42
Clairac, 24
Claix, 23, 195
Cochlaeus, Johannes, 157, 196
Cole, Henry P., 158 n. 18
Coligny, Charlotte de, 69
Coligny, Gaspard de, 68, 69, 70 n. 48, 71, 72, 73, 74, 75, 76, 77, 78
Coligny (island), 74
Colladon, Nicolas, 24, 68, 79, 105, 107, 108, 112, 125, 177 n. 24
Collectanea sententiarum D. Aurelii Augustini de coena Domini (Westphal), 101
Collège de La Marche, 19
Collège de La Rive, 35, 53
Collège de Navarre, 23
Collège des Capettes, 18
Collège Fortet, 23
Collège Montaigu, 20, 21
Collège Royal, 22, 54
Combourgeoisie, 27
Commentaries, Calvin's, 93–107
Commentary, criteria for, 94
Condé, Louis de, 71, 75, 76, 77, 78
Confessio Augustana, 75, 78, 154, 156, 192